Iris
Die

GTA

Grande Traversata delle Alpi

In 65 days through the Piedmont
all the way to the Mediterranean

ROTHER • MUNICH

ROTHER Walking Guides

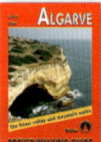 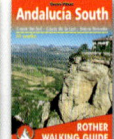    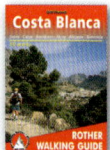

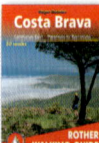   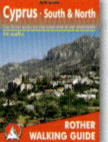 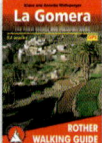 

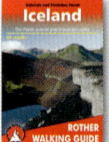   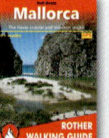 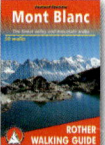 

   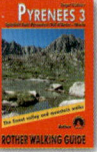 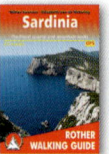 

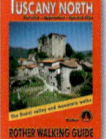 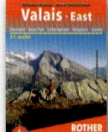 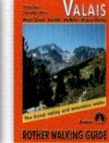   

Italian – English – French Glossary

Italiano	English	Français
aqua potabile	potable water	eau potable
altezza, quota	altitude	altitude
bergeria	sheepfold	bergerie
bivacco	bivouac	bivouac
bocchetta	notch	brèche
caduta	rockfall	chute de pierres
camoscio	chamois	chamois
canale	gully	couloir
cima, vetta, sommità	summit	cime, sommet
colle, passo	pass	col, pas
colletto	saddle	collet
cammino	trail	chemin
cresta	ridge	crête
custode	hut warden	gardien
detriti	scree	éboulis
difficoltà	difficulty, grade	difficulté
discesa	descent	descente
falesia	rock face	falaise
funivia	cable car	funiculaire
ghiacciaio	glacier	glacier
gias	alpine pasturage	alpage
gola	gorge	gorge
grange, grangia	alpine farmstead	grange
guglia	needle	Aiguille
itinerario	route	itinéraire
marmotta	marmot	marmotte
mucca, vacca	cow	vache
nebbia	fog	brouillard
neve	snow	neige
ometto	cairn	cairn
pastore	shepherd	berger
pendio	slope	pente
pericolo	danger	danger
pioggia	rain	pluie
rifugio custodito	hut with warden	refuge gardé
salita	ascent	ascension, montée
sella	saddle	baisse
sentiero	path, footpath	sentier
segnato	waymarked	balisé
stambecco	ibex	bouquetin
testa	peak	tête
torrente, rio	stream	ruisseau
tornante	zigzag	lacet
traversata	traverse	traversée
valle, val	valley	vallée
zaino	backpack	sac à dos

Cover photo:
Chiappera in the Maira Valley (Stage 46).

Frontispiece (photo on page 1):
Lago di Castello, Pontechianale (Stage 44).

Photo on pages 6/7:
Western Alps with the Valaisian 4000m peaks,
as seen from the Rifugio Garelli (Stage 59).

Photo on pages 32/33:
Summit chapel Rocciamelone, view of Monviso (Stage V33).

All 147 photos are by the authors.

Cartography:
79 walking maps with a scale of 1:75,000, drawn by
www.rolle-kartografie.de
2 overview maps with a scale of 1:1,000,000 and 1:3,500,000
© Freytag & Berndt, Vienna

Translation: Tom Krupp

The descriptions of all of the walks given in this guide are conscientiously made according to the best knowledge of the authors. The use of this guide is at one's own risk. As far as legally permitted, no responsibility will be accepted for possible accidents, damage or injury of any kind.

1st edition 2013
© Bergverlag Rother GmbH, Munich
ISBN 978-3-7633-4839-8

We heartily welcome any suggestions for amendment to this walking guide!
BERGVERLAG ROTHER · Munich
Keltenring 17 · D-82041 Oberhaching · Germany · tel. (0049) (89) 608669-0
Internet www.rother.de · E-mail leserzuschrift@rother.de

Preface

The »Wild West« of the Alps: if you think that the Alps have been completely tamed through tourism, you will get an entirely different view while walking the Grande Traversata delle Alpi (usually abbreviated as GTA). The trail leads to discovering a side of the Alps that seems to have been forgotten. Marvellous scenery, free from the usual hordes of walkers and from the monstrosities produced by tourism, such as kitsch pseudo-rustic huts, chalet-style resort complexes, motorways and luxury without end. Instead, you will experience a relatively remote, pristine landscape, in whose folds peasant culture, although constantly threatened with extinction, has continued its existence. Ancient settlements, arched bridges, old mills, alpine dairies and mules bringing homemade cheeses, packed on their backs, into the valley ... Regional diversity is a first-hand experience, since, and this is what makes the GTA so special, you will be spending most nights in villages and not in mountain huts. Here are the lovely Walser villages, where, with a little luck, you might hear the old Germanic dialects being spoken. Here are the Waldensian »Temples«, which are not only differentiated from other churches by the word they use for their place of worship. A long-suffering folk whose footsteps along the trail of the »Glorious Return« we will be retracing. Here are striking pilgrimage sites exuding a spiritual flair, which is best to savour in the evening after the hordes of pilgrims have left for the day. Occitan smugglers' villages, royal hunting lodges, nostalgic spas and, in between, the ancient, often stone-cobbled mule tracks connecting them; trader, salt and smuggling routes, royal hunting trails, military tracks – trails teeming with history are the threads which make up the GTA. The GTA is a truly ideal model for us because it manages to retain the still existent historical elements through modest, alternative tourism. Another feature of the GTA is that in this part of the Alps, the distance between the highest peaks and the plain is very short, allowing for marvellous panoramic views: you are face-to-face with the 4000-metre Valaisian summits and, at the same time, not so very high above the Po Valley plain. The route is a culinary journey at the same time, very much in the spirit of the Slow Food movement, which actually began in the Piedmont at the end of the 80s, promoting conscious savouring, fresh local ingredients, humane animal husbandry and traditional cuisine. The local people have also made a strong impression on us: their hospitality, their culinary art and their openness to talk about their lives. We hope that our enthusiasm for the many delights we find in trekking is made evident within these pages, so that the »Wild West« of the Alps must not face a future as an uninhabited wasteland.

Since trails and infrastructure are constantly undergoing change, the authors heartily welcome any helpful comments or tips, even of a personal nature, which are submitted to us by our readers.

Grenzach / Grindelwald, autumn 2012   Iris Kürschner / Dieter Haas

Contents

Preface 3

Overview map 8

GTA – the trail and its history 10
    Highlights of the GTA 11
    Overview of the Stages 13

Tourist information 16
    Symbols 16
    GPS tracks 17
    Equipment suggestions 18

Trekking the GTA 20

Information and addresses 28

Through the Lepontine Alps –
Walser trails and Devero e Alpe Veglia Nature Park 34
  1 Alpe di Cruina – Capanna Corno Gries 36
  2 Capanna Corno Gries – Rifugio Margaroli 38
  3 Rifugio Margaroli – Alpe Devero 42
  4 Alpe Devero – Alpe Veglia 44
  5 Alpe Veglia – Gondo 47

The Simplon region and the unchartered hinterland of
Domodossola – from the Gondo Gorge into the Val Anzasca . . 50
  6 Gondo – Zwischbergen 52
  7 Zwischbergen – Rifugio Gattascosa 54
  8 Rifugio Gattascosa – Rifugio Alpe Laghetto 56
  9 Rifugio Alpe Laghetto – Alpe Cheggio 58
  10 Alpe Cheggio – Alpe della Colma 60
  11a Alpe della Colma – Molini di Calasca 62

Walser country –
tracking the past in the nature park Alta Valsesia 64
  11b Molini di Calasca – Alpe del Lago 66
  12 Alpe del Lago – Campello Monti 68
  V12 Forno – Campello Monti 70
  13 Campello Monti – Rimella/Chiesa 72
  14 Rimella/Chiesa – Alpe Baranca 76
  15 Alpe Baranca – Carcoforo 78
  16 Carcoforo – Rima 80

| 17a | Rima – Alagna | 82 |

**From Monte Rosa to the gateway of the Aosta valley –
Valsesia, Biellese, Canavese** ... 84

17b	Alagna – Sant' Antonio di Val Vogna	86
18	Sant' Antonio di Val Vogna – Rifugio Rivetti	87
19	Rifugio Rivetti – Santuario San Giovanni	90
20	Santuario San Giovanni – Oropa	94
21	Oropa – Trovinasse	97
22a	Trovinasse – Quincinetto	100

**The Canavese and the wild side of the
Gran Paradiso National Park** ... 102

22b	Quincinetto – Le Capanne	104
23	Le Capanne – Fondo	106
24	Fondo – Piamprato	110
25	Piamprato/Ronco – Talosio	112
26	Talosio – San Lorenzo	114
27	San Lorenzo – Noasca	116
28	Noasca – Ceresole Reale	118

**Through the Lanzo valleys –
Turin's former summer holiday retreat** ... 122

29	Ceresole Reale – Pialpetta	124
30	Pialpetta – Balme	126
31	Balme – Usseglio	129
32	Usseglio – Rifugio Vulpot	132
33	Rifugio Vulpot – Il Trucco	134
V33	Rocciamelone	136
34a	Il Trucco – Susa	138

**Occitania and the birthplace of the Waldensians –
from the Susa Valley into the Po Valley** ... 140

34b	Susa – Meana di Susa	142
35	Meana di Susa – Alpe Toglie	144
36	Alpe Toglie – Usseaux	146
V35	Salbertrand – Rifugio Arlaud	150
V36	Rifugio Arlaud – Usseaux	152
37	Usseaux – Balsiglia/Didiero	154
38	Didiero – Ghigo di Prali	158
39	Ghigo di Prali – Villanova	160
40	Villanova – Rifugio Barbara Lowrie	164
41	Rifugio Barbara Lowrie – Pian Melzè	166

5

**The Monviso country –
from the Po Valley into the Varaita Valley** 168
- 42 Pian Melzè – Rifugio Alpetto 170
- 43 Rifugio Alpetto – Rifugio Bagnour 173
- 44 Rifugio Bagnour – Chiesa/Chiazale 176

**The Dolomites of Cuneo –
the valley heads of Varaita, Maira and Stura** 178
- 45 Chiazale – Campo Base 180
- 46 Campo Base – Chialvetta 183
- 47 Chialvetta – Pontebernardo 186
- 48 Pontebernardo – Sambuco 188
- V45 Chiesa/Chiazale – San Martino 190
- V46 San Martino – Celle di Macra 193
- V47 Celle di Macra – Santuario San Magno 196
- V48 Santuario San Magno – Sambuco 199

**Through the Western Maritime Alps – Smugglers Nest,
hot springs and Europe's highest lying monastery** 202
- V48a Pontebernardo – Ferriere 204
- V48b Ferriere – Rifugio Migliorero 205
- 49 Sambuco – Rifugio Migliorero 208
- 50 Rifugio Migliorero – Strepeis 210
- 51 Strepeis – Sant' Anna di Vinadio 212

| 52 | Sant' Anna di Vinadio – Rifugio Malinvern | 214 |
| 53 | Rifugio Malinvern – Terme di Valdieri | 216 |

Spellbound by the Argentera Massif – the Alpi Marittime Nature Park 218

54	Terme di Valdieri – Rifugio Genova-Figari	220
55	Rifugio Genova-Figari – San Giacomo	222
56	San Giacomo – Trinità	224
57	Trinità – Palanfrè	228
58	Palanfrè – Limonetto/San Lorenzo	230

The Ligurian Alps – from the Tenda Pass through the »Piccole Dolomiti« and to the Med 232

59	Limonetto/San Lorenzo – Rifugio Garelli	234
60	Rifugio Garelli – Upega	238
61	Upega – Monesi di Triora	242
62	Monesi di Triora – Colla Melosa	244
63	Colla Melosa – Gola di Gouta	246
64	Gola di Gouta – Rifugio Alta Via	248
65	Rifugio Alta Via – Ventimiglia	250

Index 252

Italian – English – French Glossary 255

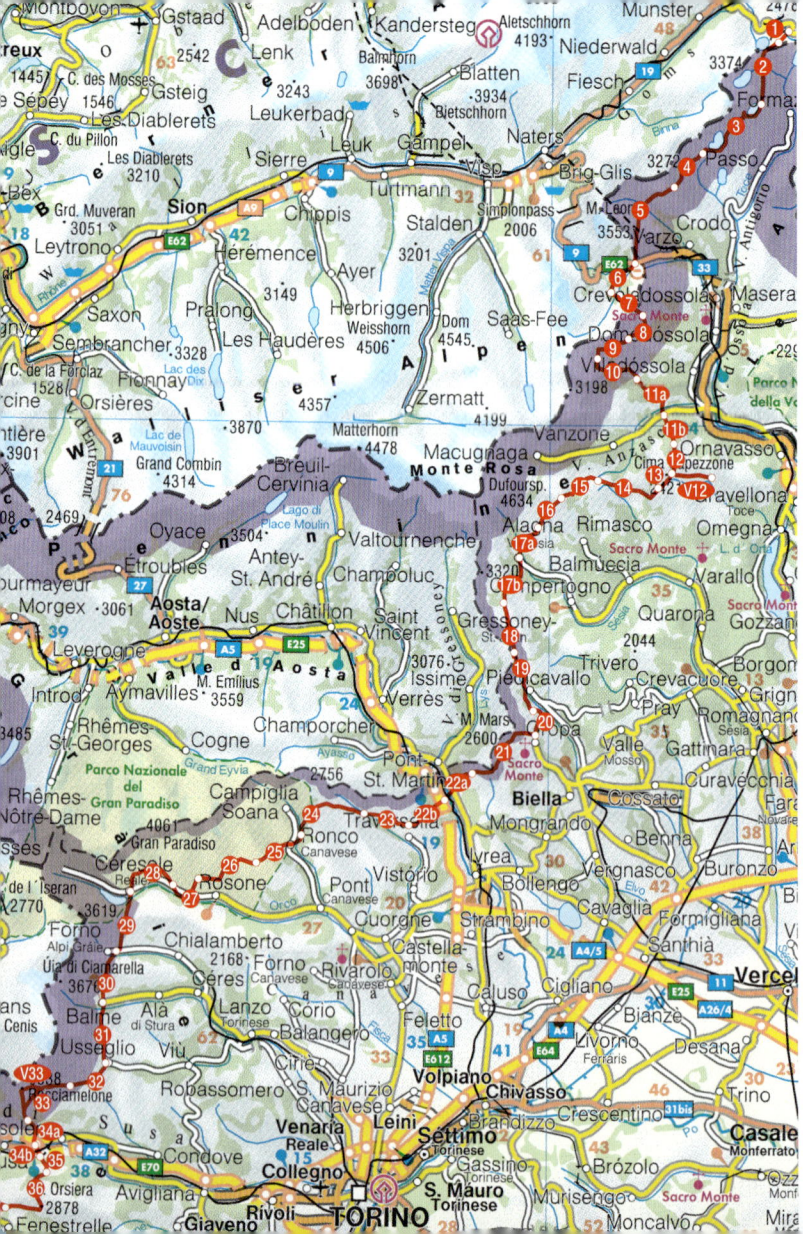

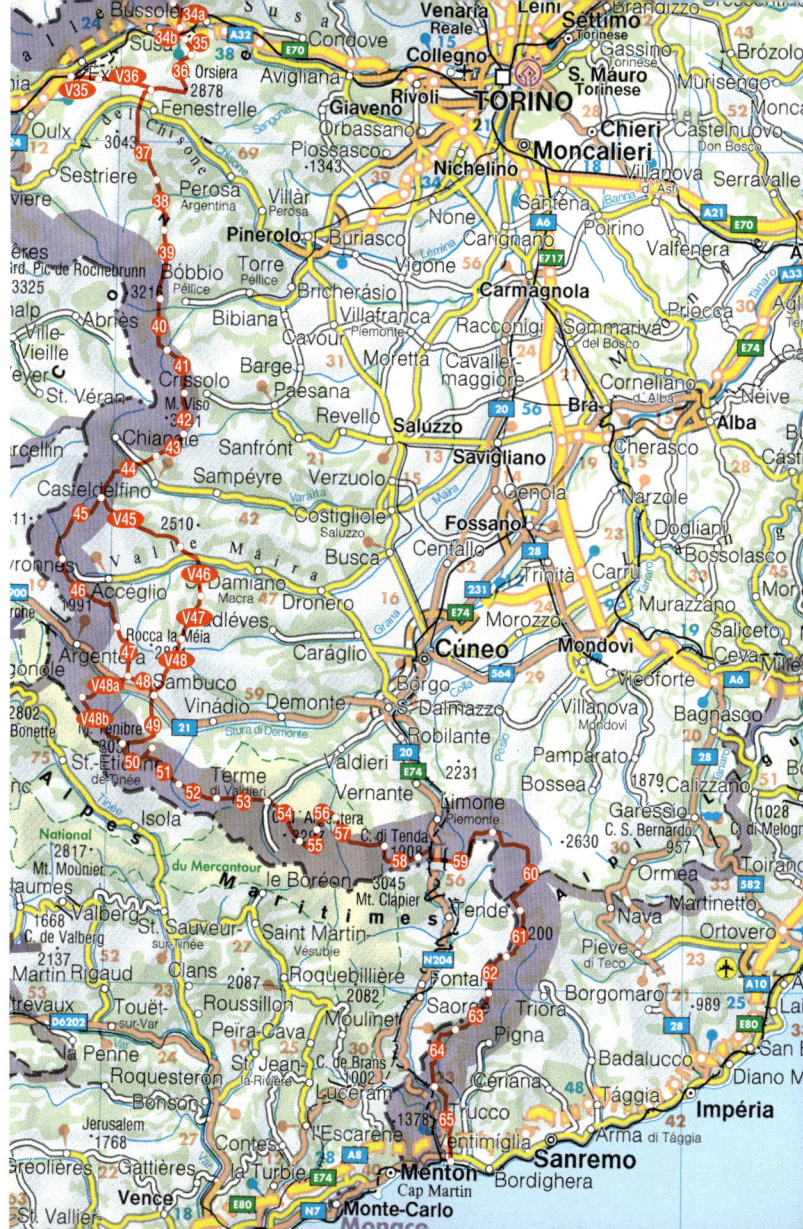

GTA – the trail and its history

Research

Because of our work on two Rother Walking Guides, Piedmont North and Piedmont South, we were already familiar with most stretches of the GTA. However, we were attracted to the idea of doing the trek in one long tour. From July until the end of September 2010, we travelled from the Swiss border all the way to the Med. In so doing, we were able to develop incredible physical fitness, but unfortunately, our receptiveness began to flag with time.

Therefore, we do not recommend doing the complete route in one go. Ideally, the route should be completed in separate, two to four week periods of trekking. Due to our heavy camera equipment, we necessarily had even more weight to carry on our backs than usual. How happy we were to find that luggage transportation services were at our disposal! Starting in summer 2011, this type of service actually became available, facilitating the problem, because we could convince the Summit Club (www.dav-summit-club.de) to add the GTA to their trekking programme. – Also we would like to thank the Cuneo and Torino Turismo offices for their support. They have agreed to restore all of the trail sections reported by us as ill-maintained, and in the future, these will be cleared and improved. During our journey by foot, we kept a diary on Facebook, with many beautiful photographs and written entries. This webpage will remain in publication: www.facebook.com/GTA.trek

Why the GTA?

The GTA makes it possible to experience the Alps in an entirely new way. »Trekking along the ancient traders' and farmers' trails, you will become acquainted with the Alpine world from the perspective of the people who put them to use. This opens up an entirely different perspective to the one you get through tourism«, points out the renowned German Alpine researcher, Werner Bätzing. A professor of cultural geography, he has explored the Alps for more than two decades and has shown a strong commitment to the GTA. An abridged English version of his definitive work on the Alps is published as: Werner Bätzing/Paul Messerli: »The Alps – an ecosystem in transition«, which appears in: »The State of the World's Mountains – a Global Report« (edited by Peter Stone), Zed Books, London/New Jersey 1992, pages 45–91.

Highlights of the GTA

Alpe Veglia
A high mountain valley, not accessible by road, in the breathtaking setting of the Monte Leone Range. The bigwig is the glaciated Monte Leone itself, whose reflection is very beautiful when mirrored in Lago Bianco; an excursion well-worth taking just before you reach the Alpe Veglia (Stage 4).

Val Vogna
A picturesque valley, dotted with Walser hamlets, where time seems to stand still. (Stages 17/18).

Punta Tre Vescovi
Watching the sun set here is a brilliant experience and quite feasible, since the Rifugio Rivetti is situated a mere 350 metres below the summit – naturally, you can ascend here directly from the Colle della Mologna Grande one day before. Unfortunately, experience has proven that afternoons are usually cloudy or hazy (Stage 18).

Oropa
A monastery that is so monumental, it impresses virtually everybody. The atmosphere here is a mixture of deep spirituality and touristic hype. Watching the goings-on from an observer's viewpoint can be quite entertaining. Pilgrim accommodation ranges from splendid to Spartan (Stage 20).

Rocciamelone
Climbing to the highest-lying pilgrimage site in Europe is simply a »must«, but only when you are assured of a clear day (Stage V33).

Monviso
From pass to pass, the »King of Rock« comes closer and closer: a fascinating pyramid-shaped peak that catches and holds the eye. When you stand at the foot of the mountain, you will be overwhelmed by its massiveness as well as the tarn-dotted rocky wasteland surrounding the summit, which is no less impressive (Stages 42/43).

The Dolomites of Cuneo
Striking *karst* peaks surround the valley heads of the Varaita di Bellino and the Maira Valley as well as their secondary valleys. A special feast for the eye is the high plain of the Gardetta, sporting a sea of Edelweiss (Stages 45–47).

Argentera
At the foot of the highest summit in the Maritime Alps, where Vittorio Emanuele II, Italy's first king, enjoyed spending his summers, is a combination of nature in the raw and pleasure troves: perfectly laid trails, a spa with hot springs ... (Stage 53).

Marguareis Massif
The »Piccole Dolomiti« – a fascinating *karst* landscape with distant views of the Mediterranean and all the way to the Monte Rosa (Stages 59/60).

Monte Toraggio
The *Alpini* trails, skirting around the mountain flanks, are delightfully daring routes, providing exciting vantage points (Stage 63).

Without his involvement, the GTA would perhaps have remained unknown beyond the borders of Italy. Even before the trail was »discovered«, he had already tracked sections of the route. That was in 1978.

In the French section of the western range of the Alps, the GR 5 route has caused a sensation. The first long-distance trekking trail passing through the entire French Alps was conceived to counteract the exodus of the inhabitants and, thanks to the wanderlust of the French, the project proved successful. A new source of income was created for the local inhabitants. The news spread to another organisation of mountain lovers from the Turin area, and especially to those from the Chisone and Germanasca Valleys, where the urbanisation of the lowlands and the progressive depopulation of the Alpine valleys had reached a crucial stage. The idea was developed for a counterpart to the GR 5, a *Grande Traversata delle Alpi*, traversing the western Alps of the Piedmont, through the »forgotten« Alpine valleys, as they were widely known, because the population decline was so drastic that, in some cases, entire settlements had become ghost towns.

In this spirit, the ancient trails that had been used for trade and toil between the valley heads were cleared and then marked and, in the villages, if inns were no longer available, accommodations for trekkers en route were established in vacant schools or community buildings and given the name »*Posto tappa*«. Up until 1985, fifty-five stages had been created. Unfortunately, the Italians are not generally attracted to walking and, after the initial euphoria was over, enthusiasm evaporated rather quickly again. Nowadays, the German-speaking trekking tourists, especially, appreciate the value of this route.

The GTA has been designed to bypass the few touristic-developed areas lying en route and therefore requires no new or additional infrastructure. This means that the Stages end mostly in the villages in the valleys, where the demands of the trekker produces income for the restored inns, restaurants, corner shops or dairies run by the locals, who reap the benefits directly and without the interference of outside investors. By the way, if you suffer with »mountain hut fever«, you don't have to worry here. Most of the accommodation is provided by small, family-run hotels, including farmstead inns, so-called »*Agriturismo*«, and, from time to time, monasteries, offering not only »snorer-filled dormitories«, but also double rooms.

What a stretch ...

In the meantime, the GTA has been extended. Neither the starting point (with the first Stage being too long) nor the destination of the original route – with 55 Stages from Molini di Calasca in the Anzasca Valley all the way to Viozene in the Tanaro Valley – present a convenient place to begin or to break off. While GTA waymarking is continued in the north, in the south, walkers are accustomed to following the route from the Tanaro Valley via the *Alta Via dei Monti Liguri* (AVML) to reach the Med. The most ideal starting point today begins at the northernmost corner of the Piedmont, which penetrates deeply into Switzerland; by using the public transport network of the Swiss Confederacy, this is easy to reach.

Depending on the personal goal being set, the GTA presents a real challenge to the long-distance walker. While one walker may decide to take the trek in one go, the other may choose to start off with a manageable initial stretch and then continue onward a year later at the point where he left off. After all, you must negotiate a distance of about 1000 kilometres with about

65,000 metres of ascent and descent, which works out, at an average walking pace of 5 to 6 hours per day, to a trek requiring 65 Stages.

The GTA leads from the furthermost corner of the Piedmont, which meets the Swiss border at Val Formazza, and passes through the entire range of the Western Alps. En route, you will wander from the Pennine Alps via the Graian, Cottian and Maritime Alps to the Ligurian Alps. The pass crossings, to be negotiated each and every day, reach heights between 2000 and 3000 metres above sea level. The highest point of the GTA is the Colle di Bellino (2804 m, the pass crossing between the Varaita and the Maira valleys). The lowest point, not counting, of course, the destination at the Med, is Quincinetto (295 m) in the valley of the Dora Baltea. Countless excursions taking in summits over 3000 metres (the highest is the Rocciamelone at 3538 m) are available en route and delight the eye with sweeping 360° views. This is even more beautiful when, at your feet, the mist and fog banks of the Po Valley plain are adrift and you are transported so high above life's daily routine that you feel as free as a bird.

Overview of the Stages

Stage		Grade	Ascent/descent	Length	Walking time
Lepontine Alps – Walser trails and the Devero-Veglia Nature Park					
1	Alpe di Cruina – Cap. Corno Gries	E	310/0 m	2.2 km	1.00 hr.
2	Cap. Corno Gries – Rif. Margaroli	M	1010/1150 m	17.0 km	5.30 hrs.
3	Rifugio Margaroli – Alpe Devero	M	500/1060 m	15.0 km	5.00 hrs.
4	Alpe Devero – Alpe Veglia	D	1000/870 m	13.7 km	5.45 hrs.
5	Alpe Veglia – Gondo	D	840/1740 m	17.9 km	7.30 hrs.
The Simplon region and Domodossola – from the Gondo Gorge into the Val Anzasca					
6	Gondo – Zwischbergen	E	570/70 m	6.2 km	2.30 hrs.
7	Zwischbergen – Rifugio Gattascosa	M	990/70 m	7.7 km	4.00 hrs.
8	Rif. Gattascosa – Rif. Alpe Laghetto	E	590/540 m	10.8 km	5.00 hrs.
9	Rif. Alpe Laghetto – Alpe Cheggio	D	690/1230 m	11.1 km	6.00 hrs.
10	Alpe Cheggio – Alpe della Colma	E	1010/940 m	14.0 km	5.30 hrs.
11a	Alpe della Colma – Molini di Calasca	E	30/1100 m	7.2 km	2.30 hrs.
Walser country – Alta Valsesia Nature Park					
11b	Molini di Calasca – Alpe del Lago	M	1180/140 m	8.9 km	4.00 hrs.
12	Alpe del Lago – Campello Monti	M	750/990 m	9.6 km	4.00 hrs.
V12	Forno – Campello Monti	E	450/40 m	5.2 km	2.00 hrs.
13	Campello Monti – Rimella/Chiesa	E	650/760 m	9.1 km	3.15 hrs.
14	Rimella/Chiesa – Alpe Baranca	M	970/580 m	11.6 km	4.30 hrs.
15	Alpe Baranca – Carcoforo	M	660/940 m	9.2 km	4.45 hrs.
16	Carcoforo – Rima	D	1050/940 m	10.8 km	6.00 hrs.
17a	Rima – Alagna	M	910/1120 mm	11.1 km	5.30 hrs.

Stage	Grade	Ascent/descent	Length	Walking time
From Monte Rosa to the gateway of the Aosta Valley – Valsesia, Biellese, Canavese				
17b Alagna – Sant' Antonio di Val Vogna	E	260/80 m	7.0 km	2.00 hrs.
18 Sant' Antonio – Rifugio Rivetti	D	1310/540 m	16.1 km	7.30 hrs.
19 Rif. Rivetti – Santuario San Giovanni	M	640/1770 m	16.0 km	6.45 hrs.
20 Santuario San Giovanni – Oropa	E	240/110 m	12.3 km	3.15 hrs.
21 Oropa – Trovinasse	D	860/1280 m	14.9 km	6.30 hrs.
22a Trovinasse – Quincinetto	M	30/1180 m	7.8 km	3.00 hrs.
Canavese and the Gran Paradiso National Park				
22b Quincinetto – Le Capanne	M	1110/0 m	5.8 km	4.00 hrs.
23 Le Capanne – Fondo	D	850/1170 m	13.8 km	6.00 hrs.
24 Fondo – Piamprato	D	1350/870 m	13.5 km	6.30 hrs.
25 Piamprato/Ronco – Talosio	M	1180/900 m	14.0 km	6.15 hrs.
26 Talosio – San Lorenzo	D	1370/1550 m	15.4 km	7.30 hrs.
27 San Lorenzo – Noasca	M	810/790 m	13.4 km	5.30 hrs.
28 Noasca – Ceresole Reale	E	980/550 m	11.1 km	4.30 hrs.
Through the Lanzo valleys				
29 Ceresole Reale – Pialpetta	M	1170/1610 m	15.0 km	6.30 hrs.
30 Pialpetta – Balme	M	1670/1230 m	17.5 km	8.00 hrs.
31 Balme – Usseglio	D	1120/1350 m	11.8 km	6.30 hrs.
32 Usseglio – Rifugio Vulpot	E	580/30 m	10.9 km	3.00 hrs.
33 Rifugio Vulpot – Il Trucco	M	820/930 m	15.5 km	5.00 hrs.
V33 Rocciamelone	D	1900/2000 m	21.0 km	2 days
34a Il Trucco – Susa	M	10/1220 m	8.1 km	3.00 hrs.
Occitania and the birthplace of the Waldensians – from the Susa Valley into the Po Valley				
34b Susa – Meana di Susa	E	120/20 m	2.6 km	0.45 hrs.
35 Meana di Susa – Alpe Toglie	M	1070/130 m	10.6 km	4.30 hrs.
36 Alpe Toglie – Usseaux	M	1340/1430 m	17.1 km	7.30 hrs.
V35 Salbertrand – Rifugio Arlaud	E	770/30 m	4.3 km	2.00 hrs.
V36 Rifugio Arlaud – Usseaux	M	800/1130 m	19.2 km	6.00 hrs.
37 Usseaux – Balsiglia/Didiero	M	1380/1450 m	20.6 km	7.30 hrs.
38 Didiero – Ghigo di Prali	E	730/520 m	12.6 km	4.30 hrs.
39 Ghigo di Prali – Villanova	M	330/1520 m	18.7 km	4.45 hrs.
40 Villanova – Rif. Barbara Lowrie	M	1210/680 m	13.7 km	5.00 hrs.
41 Rif. Barbara Lowrie – Pian Melzè	M	810/810 m	8.7 km	4.00 hrs.
Through Monviso country – from the Po Valley into the Varaita Valley				
42 Pian Melzè – Rifugio Alpetto	M	1000/480 m	11.9 km	4.30 hrs.
43 Rifugio Alpetto – Rifugio Bagnour	M	610/860 m	11.0 km	4.30 hrs.
44 Rifugio Bagnour – Chiesa/Chiazale	M	860/1170 m	16.0 km	5.30 hrs.

Stage	Grade	Ascent/descent	Length	Walking time
The Dolomites of Cuneo – the valley heads of the Varaita, Maira and Stura valleys				
45 Chiazale – Campo Base	M	1190/1240 m	18.7 km	6.30 hrs.
46 Campo Base – Chialvetta	M	810/970 m	15.8 km	5.30 hrs.
47 Chialvetta – Pontebernardo	M	1160/1340 m	19.2 km	6.15 hrs.
48 Pontebernardo – Sambuco	E	350/480 m	9.5 km	3.00 hrs.
V45 Chiesa/Chiazale – San Martino	M	1040/1140 m	18.0 km	6.00 hrs.
V46 San Martino – Celle di Macra	M	780/890 m	18.0 km	5.00 hrs.
V47 Celle di Macra – Sant. San Magno	M	960/470 m	16.3 km	5.45 hrs.
V48 Santuario San Magno – Sambuco	M	720/1300 m	18.5 km	6.00 hrs.
Through the Western Maritime Alps – Smugglers Nest, hot springs and a monastery				
V48a Pontebernardo – Ferriere	M	940/360 m	11.5 km	3.45 hrs.
V48b Ferriere – Rifugio Migliorero	M	1550/1340 m	16.5 km	7.00 hrs.
49 Sambuco – Rifugio Migliorero	M	1730/810 m	15.1 km	6.30 hrs.
50 Rifugio Migliorero – Strepeis	M	400/1220 m	10.6 km	4.00 hrs.
51 Strepeis – Sant' Anna di Vinadio	M	1180/430 m	11.2 km	5.30 hrs.
52 Sant' Anna – Rifugio Malinvern	M	810/1000 m	14.7 km	5.30 hrs.
53 Rif. Malinvern – Terme di Valdieri	M	780/1250 m	15.7 km	5.30 hrs.
Spellbound by the Argentera Massif – the Alpi Marittime Nature Park				
54 Terme di Valdieri – Rif. Genova-Figari	M	1290/640 m	16.8 km	6.00 hrs.
55 Rif. Genova-Figari – San Giacomo	M	490/1290 m	13.3 km	4.30 hrs.
56 San Giacomo – Trinità	E	380/500 m	14.2 km	4.00 hrs.
57 Trinità – Palanfrè	M	1120/840 m	11.3 km	5.00 hrs.
58 Palanfrè – Limonetto/San Lorenzo	M	940/810 m	11.4 km	4.30 hrs.
The Ligurian Alps – from the Tenda Pass to the Mediterranean				
59 San Lorenzo – Rifugio Garelli	M	1450/990 m	23.1 km	8.00 hrs.
60 Rifugio Garelli – Upega	D/M	970/1640 m	17.5 km	7.00 hrs.
61 Upega – Monesi di Triora	E	490/410 m	9.6 km	2.30 hrs.
62 Monesi di Triora – Colla Melosa	M	1350/1180 m	23.3 km	7.00 hrs.
63 Colla Melosa – Gola di Gouta	M	550/890 m	17.0 km	5.30 hrs.
64 Gola di Gouta – Rifugio Alta Via	E	180/860 m	17.6 km	4.30 hrs.
65 Rifugio Alta Via – Ventimiglia	E	240/770 m	13.1 km	4.00 hrs.

E – easy, M – moderate, D – difficult, demanding.
These classifications are always based on the most difficult stretch of a Stage, which could well be only a short one; sometimes we also recommend alternative routes. More detailed information is included in the »Grade« key point for the individual Stages.

Tourist information

Use of the guide
Only a very few will trek the entire GTA in one go. Because of this, we have separated the route into logical Stages – mostly using weekly timeframes – and have pinpointed starting points and destinations easy to reach with public transport. Some Stages exceeding this time limit have been sub-divided and given the suffixes »a« und »b«.

Each of these weekly Stages begins with a characterising preface. Following this is a detailed Stage description whereby the most important information (for the Stage itself and also for the infrastructure which surrounds it) is presented as a series of key points. The Stage descriptions are simple and concise, especially when trails are distinct and appropriate waymarkers are present. Coloured walking maps show the course of the route. The height profile gives you, at a glance, the metres of altitude that must be negotiated, the walking times and the length. For a clearer overall picture, all of the important points in the height profiles appear in bold print in the Stage description. In addition, the text, height profiles and maps all include waypoint numbers from the GPS tracks.

In the index, there is a listing of the important settlements, starting points, stage designations and destinations found along the GTA. The overview map presents an image covering the complete route.

We have taken the liberty to comment on the individual accommodation. If none are made, the food was not so uplifting; this can, of course, always change. Any reader comments on this subject would be gratefully received.

Abbreviations: to save space, we have used some abbreviations: B = beds, R = rooms, DR = double room, HB/AV = half-board rate for non-members/for Alpine Club members (*soci/non soci*), GTA-HB = inexpensive half-board special offer for GTA trekkers with a simpler menu, CAI = Club

Symbols

Symbol	Description	Symbol	Description
▲▙	settlement offering refreshment	†	summit, peak
▲	staffed hut, country inn	)(	pass, saddle
⌷	lodging	⸸	church, chapel, monastery
⌂	hut without warden or services, shelter	◭	viewpoint
		˥ ˦	turn-off
🚌	bus stop	●	mountain spring, fountain
	cable car station, - transport	⛲	waterfall
	chairlift station, chairlift transport		bathing spot

GPS tracks

For this walking guide, GPS tracks are available for download without charge from the Rother website (www.rother.de). For downloading, you need the following password: wfGTAgb01fgh5D.

All of the GPS data was recorded *in situ* by the authors. The authors and publishers have conscientiously reviewed the relevant GPS data to the best of their knowledge. However, errors and deviations may have occurred and the physical properties of the area may have changed between times. GPS data is certainly a great help for planning and navigation, but still requires meticulous preparation and a certain degree of orientation skill as well as expertise in judging the (geographical) situation at hand. You should never depend solely on GPS devices or data for orientation.

Alpino Italiano. If the accommodation does not carry the note, CAI, then it is in private hands.

Getting ready

It is important to have good physical fitness, so that trekking is truly enjoyable as well. If you don't already have a routine of physical exercise, you should start one at least several weeks before your planned tour. This could include two to three times a week of jogging, cycling, swimming or any other

The Pizzo Camino ridge, Anzasca Valley, in the background, Weissmies (Stage 12).

endurance sport. And, ideally, at the weekend, you should plan to do some shorter walking tours and then gradually increase them to longer ones. Here, you not only get a glimpse of your abilities, such as your sure-footedness, your endurance of vertigo and your generally physical fitness, but at the same time, you can also determine whether your backpack sits comfortably and if your walking shoes rub, causing blisters.

Long-distance walking requires good pre-planning. Study the maps and familiarise yourself with the terrain. Consider in advance the number of hours of walking you can handle without overtaxing yourself. Make a correct assessment of your physical fitness and constitution.

Equipment

It is often amazing to see what gets unpacked from some rucksacks. Family-sized packs of cereal, biscuits, toothpaste, aftershave, cologne, sometimes even a hair-dryer appears. When observing minimalists among the long-distance walkers, it comes as no surprise to see that they have even shortened the grip of their toothbrushes.

The ideal »humping kit« begins with the purchase of a backpack. It must be robust and sit comfortably and still be lightweight. Fully packed, the total carrying weight should be limited to between 10 and 11 kilograms and not a gram more. A capacity of 40 litres should be sufficient. We highly recommend a backpack with side pockets for a water flask, quick snacks, map,

Equipment suggestions

- sturdy walking shoes, walking poles
- light footware for evenings
- water repellent/breathable undergarments
- durable, comfortable trousers (the best bet is with zip-off legs)
- extra garments, alternatively, a set of clothing for evenings
- bathing gear
- wind and rainproof jacket
- warm fleece jumper
- rain gear
- lightweight gloves
- head covering
- toiletries
- hut sleeping bag (ideal is a silk sleeping bag, which weighs practically nothing and can be stored in a little bag)
- head torch
- telescopic walking poles

- maps and navigation materials, a GTA guide
- pocket knife
- mini-sewing kit
- first aid pack (i.e. disinfectant, antibiotic powder or ointment, tiger balm, aspirin)
- adhesive plasters for blisters
- earplugs (for sleeping better while in dormitory accommodations)
- water bottle and/or thermos
- suntan lotion
- sunglasses
- provisions/energy bars
- rubbish bag
- ID, passport, Alpine Club card, money
- mobile phone (with alarm clock function)
- additional personal effect like eyeglasses, photographic equipment ...

sunscreen etc., as well as one with an integrated rainproof cover. As far as the contents are concerned, it makes practically no difference at all if you are trekking for four or for twenty days along the GTA. Basic items like weatherproof wear and an extra change of clothing are always necessary – also see our list »Suggested Equipment«. The necessary elimination of family-sized packaging is really no problem since the GTA passes through villages where you can replenish your provisions. Also, you can save a lot of weight when putting together your toiletry kit: avoid large-sized tubes and creams and a weighty wash bag.

The other most important factor for walking is footgear. Never break in new walking shoes during a trek because tortuous blisters are almost a sure thing. Sturdy, ankle-high walking shoes with gripping soles, well broken-in (ideally as comfy as house slippers) and completely free from rubbing and pinching zones are best. Special stockings for walking provide a better »climate« for your feet, which is ideal for preventing blisters. For leather shoes, stockings with a high percentage of wool fibre are good, for Gore Tex shoes, stockings made from »high-tech fabric« have proven the most suitable.

After walking the GTA, some walking shoes begin to sprout.

Telescopic trekking poles facilitate steep ascents and descents and are a valuable assistance in keeping balance while crossing over fields of old glacier snow. When purchasing these poles, you should look for the so-called anti-shock feature, so that your wrists and arms will be protected when taking a pounding.

The outdoor apparel line of clothing has much improved in recent years. Bright colours and figure-hugging designs make for a chic outfit. Materials are durable, quick-drying, wind and/or water repellent but still breathable, and above all, in most cases, they have become more lightweight. Countless tests have shown that high-quality products are actually a better buy than the cheaper products whose functionality usually dissipates more quickly. It is best to clothe yourself using the »layered clothing principle«, whereby you can, depending on the weather, take off or put on layers of clothing as need be. This saves weight but is nevertheless effective for any weather.

Trekking the GTA

Grade
Technically, the GTA is simple; there are no glacier crossings or rock climbing sections, however, it does lead through alpine terrain. First and foremost, physical fitness is demanded since about 1000 metres of altitude must be negotiated almost daily. A large part of the route leads along ancient pack mule hauler's trails (so-called »mulattiere«), sometimes these are narrow, sometimes broad and sometimes cleverly cobbled, and, further southwards, more often along military tracks. The remainder of the route is a mixture of mountain paths, access roads and tarmac roads, most of which are infrequently used. In the terrain around the passes, sometimes you must cross over boulder fields and scree. Therefore, as a general rule, sure-footedness is required. The route is marked the entire way in red/white/red waymarking, sometimes also including the GTA logo. From time to time, at lower altitudes and depending on the undergrowth, the waymarkers may be grown over. Even in the higher altitudes, you may have to search for waymarkers, for example, while crossing broad meadows where possible points for waymarking are not at hand. If visual conditions are good, this should be no problem, but during foggy conditions, it is possible that you might stray from the route. As soon as you notice that no further waymarking for the GTA has appeared, you should turn back along the way you came until you pick up the correct waymarkers once again. Exposed or cross-country stretches are relatively seldom, usually only quite short and, under good conditions, can be negotiated without problem. All tricky spots are described in detail in the respective Stage description. During inclement weather or winter-like onsets, the challenges involved are naturally increased, especially at the pass crossings. It's true that no glacier crossings must be made en route, but, especially after a snowy winter, there may be fields of old snow to negotiate, often at pass crossings, even as late as July; under these conditions, telescopic trekking poles prove very helpful.

Dangers
For well-equipped, sure-footed and fit mountain walkers, the GTA should present no problems. The majority of accidents are rooted in human error, such as overconfidence, improper choice of equipment or lack of foresight for possible problematic situations. Particular attention must be paid during thunderstorms, especially in summer, since the stifling heat of the Po Valley plain creates hazy conditions. What, in the morning, may be aglow in golden sunlight, can be quickly enveloped in cloud cover from the hot, moist air that originates in the Mediterranean, on the one hand, and the sudden warming of the mountain terrain, on the other, and is often the cause of severe thunderstorms, especially in the afternoon. The areas along the route of the GTA

most affected by this are the Biella region and the regions around the Pellice and the Po valleys at Monviso. The other valleys are usually protected from the encroachment of haze originating in the Po Valley plain by the ridges that lie in between or by the long courses that they follow. The threat of thunderstorms in the afternoon is, however, always to be taken seriously. In general, it is advisable to start walking the Stage early in the morning, especially since the scenery in the clear morning light is at the highpoint of its beauty.

Best times of the year
The ideal time for trekking the GTA is between July and September. According to statistics, the driest month for the Piedmont region is July. The Italian holiday season falls between the end of July and the end of August. In particular, on the dates around the *Ferragosto*, August 15, it seems that everyone in Italy is on holiday; this doesn't necessarily affect trekkers along the GTA, since Italians do not have a tradition of mountain walking. It's true that they do drive to the mountains, but usually only to enjoy a picnic not far from their parked cars and perhaps to take a short stroll. Nevertheless, we recommend reserving early for accommodation in the villages, especially in those days around 15th of August. An advantage for the GTA trekker to be en route during the *Ferragosto*: at this time, you can experience Italian festivities at first hand; it is also not rare to find a religious procession taking place.

Weather
The most accurate weather forecasts for the Italian Alps (only in Italian) can be found at www.nimbus.it. Other useful websites: www.ilmeteo.it, www.3bmeteo.it, www.regione.piemonte.it/meteo. A number of mountain huts are provided with a webcam, so that you can take a look at the current weather conditions in real time: www.regione.piemonte.it/montagna/areemontane/webcam_rif.htm.

Orientation aids
During periods of fog and poor visibility, GPS devices with an altimeter and a built-in compass can prove very valuable. The altimeter also functions as a barometer and registers changes in the weather. If the barometric pressure drops (the altimeter displays an altitude higher than reality), you can expect the weather to deteriorate; if the barometric pressure rises (the altitude drops lower than reality), you can expect better weather. Since the correct altitude reading depends on barometric pressure, the altimeter must be adjusted as often as possible at places where the correct altitude is posted (at a hut, a peak ...).

Walking times
The walking times noted are based on averages and do not take breaks into consideration. Naturally, every walker has his own pace and it would be inappropriate to try to "beat" the times given, especially if this is not within the

borders of one's actual physical fitness. Thus, do not be tempted to start off too enthusiastically. It is important to maintain a slow, rhythmic pace with shorter strides and keeping normal breathing, so that you can store up extra energy without wasting it, in case unforeseen situations come up, such as inclement weather, a mistake in orientation requiring backtracking or an emergency. If you must keep stopping to catch your breath, you are walking too fast. Taking shorter strides, by the way, improves your sure-footedness. Normally, mountain walkers can travel four kilometres of trail per hour with about 350 metres of ascent and about 600 metres in descent. Experience has shown that larger groups walk slower, so that four kilometres may only include 300 metres of ascent and 500 metres in descent. With a walking time of 5 hrs., for example, you should allow an additional 2 hrs. for taking breaks.

Rest breaks
Regular rest stops are important for your performance, especially for drinking. You should not only drink to quench your thirst! Only a small amount of fluid loss occurs through sweating, the majority is lost through the mucous membranes while breathing. The higher you climb in the mountains, the drier the air is and even more fluid is lost through the respiratory tract. Drinking frequently keeps up your performance (not beer or wine, but ideally, only water!).

Refreshment and drinking water
As a standard rule, we recommend taking along a day's provisions for each GTA Stage, since places offering refreshment between the starting points and destinations are very rare. Moreover, in the mountains, something unforeseen can always happen, whether because a rain shower has forced you to seek shelter for a long stretch of time, or whether, for one reason or another, the route has proved to take longer than was expected. Either you can arrange the night before that the accommodation provide you with a lunch packet or you can procure some provisions in a local shop (remarks about shopping opportunities are provided in the individual Stage descriptions). Quite often, you can find alpine farmstead huts on the way where cheese can be purchased. Before each day's departure, you should be sure to fill your water bottles. En route, you can find fountains in the lower altitudes and, in the higher, you can find clear mountain streams and springs for the necessary top-up. When you are around cattle pastures, you should avoid drinking or stocking up on the waters there.

Piedmontian cuisine
A journey through the Piedmont is also always a culinary tour because food is a very important issue for Italians. This is certainly the reason why the traditional way of enjoying a meal and also why home-cooked foods have been so much better preserved than in other countries. Thus, it is no wonder

that plans made by the American fast-food conglomerate, at the end of the 80s, to open the first McDonalds restaurant in Rome met with so much outrage. The journalist, Carlo Petrini, and countless supporters of traditional cuisine, set down a manifesto for the Principles of Gastronomy in Bra (Piedmont): enjoyment with understanding, the use of fresh, regional ingredients, humane animal husbandry and traditional dishes. From this manifesto, the Slow Food Movement has developed (www.slowfood.it). Thus, in the Piedmont, apart from the environs of the bigger cities, you will rarely find fast-food outlets or snack bars, and mealtimes are still established and ritualised as they have been in the past. This is even truer in the remote GTA Stage destinations: dinner is served almost everywhere punctually at 7:30 in the evening.

If you take a look at the rich selection offered in the courses displayed in the menus, you will certainly wonder how the Italians can keep so slim. Is it their temperament that eats up calories or is it because of the meagre breakfast they take, usually dry toast and espresso? Or is there, perhaps, some truth to be found in the philosophy of Slow Food? Be that as it may, with each Stage of the GTA, the evening meal, rich in calories, will most certainly be well used since the challenging terrain of the rugged mountains and valleys downright demands it.

Hotel Arrucador, San Lorenzo (Stage 58).

Agriturismo Belvedere, Trovinasse (21).

Agriturismo Aquila Bianca (Stage 24).

Rifugio Alpe del Lago (Stage 11). *Posto tappa Pzit Rei in Usseaux (36).*

A full menu is composed of four courses: starting with *antipasti* (hot and cold appetisers), then the first main course (*primo piatto*), which is almost always a pasta dish (sometimes risotto) or minestrone. Usually this is served in such quantity that most diners are already full to bursting. So, be forewarned, because usually a second main course follows (*secondo piatto*), normally a meat dish with garnish. You should also leave a little room for the dessert (cheese, fruit or something sweet). Naturally, a good wine belongs to a good meal. Most of the wines served in the Piedmont come from the Langhe region. Barolo and Barbaresco wines, made from the Nebbiolo grape, are the royal fruits of the vine. As house wine, a dry, full-bodied Barbera or Dolcetto is often served. Most accommodations offer an inexpensive »GTA menu«, but if you can order »à la carte«, it is usually worth your while to try regional specialities. A whole spectrum of culinary discoveries has originated in the Piedmont and many have even become world-renowned. You only have to consider Nutella (the Ferrero Company in Alba first marketed the nut-nougat cream under this name in 1964), or Mon Chéri, made with the Piedmont cherry, or grissini, the crispy breadsticks that were first made in 1668 at the order of the court physician for the ailing Vittorio Amedeo II, Duke of Savoy.

Naturally, walking makes you thirsty. Instead of quaffing a couple of beers brewed by a big international company, it pays to ask if a local bevvy can be had, for example, Menabrea from Biella or Beba from Villar Perosa.

Accommodation

As a rule, you will be spending the night along the GTA in so-called *Posti tappa*, »Stage Stations«. But indeed, the route also touches upon settlements which offer a wide choice of accommodation and, in some sections of the trek, you will also use a mountain hut as a Stage destination.

- Albergo/Locanda: Lower-priced inns and boarding houses offering home-cooked meals, typical for the region.

- Bed & Breakfast: Room with breakfast, www.bed-and-breakfast-in-italy.com, www.bbitalia.it.
- Posto tappa: A simple walker's accommodation, usually in a dormitory room, sometimes set up in schools or community buildings. Often there is supplementary accommodation in an albergo, where you may choose to spend the night in a double room instead.
- Agriturismo: Accommodation in a rural area, often in a farmstead, with meals prepared from self-produced farm products: www.agriturist.it, www.agriturismo.com, www.agriturismo.it.
- Rifugio: A rustic mountain hut, normally only accessible on foot, often managed by the Italian Alpine Club (www.cai.it). Most huts offer the luxury of a shower, but sometimes there is a charge. Also internet via satellite has become standard in the meantime. Few trekkers will be carrying their laptops along, but for the most up-to-date weather forecast, the internet has proven to be a boon when spending the night in a hut. CAI accommodations almost always provide a winter shelter which is always open.
- Bivacco: Self-catering shelters which are always open; usually situated in the high mountain areas. Naturally, during the peak season, there is always the risk that the few available bunks are already occupied. The beds are equipped with blankets and pillows, but cooking facilities are very rare.

Hygiene

All of the accommodations along the GTA, including the huts, are equipped with a shower. The only exceptions are the self-catering huts Alpe del Lago and Pian del Lago (Stage 11).

Costs

So that you can know roughly what costs you can expect, the prices for accommodation have been noted, but of course, at the publication of this guide, these are no longer fully up-to-date.

Walking with dogs

Dog owners will be pleased to know that Italians love dogs. In the majority of accommodation, a well-behaved, four-legged chum is a welcome guest. An exception is the CAI huts. Here, dogs are forbidden inside, sometimes they are restricted to the vestibule, sometimes a kennel is available for use. Dogs are not allowed in the Parco delle Alpi Marittime, so you have to omit Stages 53–59 from the itinerary.

Merlin, the Sherpa dog.

Walking maps

Even though the maps included in this guide should suffice for orientation, we recommend bringing along additional walking maps. The route of the GTA is covered by the IGC (Istituto Geografico Centrale) series of maps. If you are used to the precision of the Swiss walking maps (LKS), you will probably have to get used to the IGC maps. Not every route is drawn correctly, and furthermore, some are drawn in that no longer exist. But since these are the only walking maps drawn at a scale of 1:50,000, they are the most comprehensive and most practical, especially for the GTA, whose course is more or less correctly entered. If you prefer even more exactness, you could turn to the French IGN maps, »Alpes sans Frontières«, in a scale of 1:25,000, which are, however, very expensive and include the central Alpine ridge between France and Italy. It has been announced, unfortunately, that these maps will no longer be printed.

Escursionista (www.escursionista.it), whose maps strive for the precision and clarity of Swiss quality, are working to cover the entire mountain region of the Piedmont, but this takes a lot of time (at least a year is needed to produce one map). So far, only maps covering the Gran Paradiso Region and the Maira Valley are available.

List of maps

- IGC 1:50,000, No. 11 Domodossola e Val Formazza (Stages 1–9)
- IGC 1:50,000, No. 10 Monte Rosa, Alagna e Macugnaga (10–17)
- IGC 1:50,000, No. 9 Ivrea Biella e Bassa Valle d'Aosta (18–24)
- IGC 1:50,000, No. 3 Parco Nationale del Gran Paradiso (25–28)
- IGC 1:50,000, No. 2 Valli di Lanzo e Moncenisio (29–34)
- IGC 1:50,000, No. 1 Valli di Susa, Chisone e Germanasca (35–38/39)
- IGC 1:50,000, No. 6 Monviso (39–44/45)
- IGC 1:50,000, No. 7 Valli Maira, Grana Stura (45–52)
- IGC 1:50,000, No. 8 Alpi Marittime e Liguri (53–62)
- IGC 1:50,000, No. 14 San Remo, Imperia, Monte Carlo (62–65)

For one of the stretches particularly poorly presented in the IGC map, we recommend:

- MU Edizioni, 1:20,000, Alpi Canavese 02 (21–23).
- And for the final map: Kompass, 1:50,000, No. 640, Nizza, Monaco, San Remo (63–65).

Environmental protection

»Leave nothing but your footprints, take nothing except photographs and memories!« This is a principle to live by on every hike and one to keep alive, as well. Anyone who loves the mountains and the unique natural oases found there will naturally want to preserve this pristine and unspoiled landscape. But among these mountain-lovers, there are those who have overlooked that certain behaviour can easily damage the sensitive natural balances at work. The conservation of natural landscape is dependent on the conscientiousness of each and every individual. While walking, many show their carelessness by forgetting, time and again, to take their refuse away with them. Why? There is no refuse removal service in the mountains! Everyone (!!!) should make sure that the rubbish heap up there doesn't grow even bigger. The leavings that are already lying around should not necessarily inspire you to do the same. On the contrary! Why not make a habit of not only packing back to the valley your own waste, but also the litter that the consumer world has already left behind? Litter weighs almost nothing at all and the self-satisfaction stemming from a clean conscience can increase your posi-

Stone Art: a whole heap of cairns have been left by walkers at the Passo San Chiaffredo (Stage 43).

tivity towards life in general. So, always remember to take along an empty litter bag in your backpack!

There is most certainly a good reason to walk only on the marked trails. By doing so, one is allowing the timid mountain animals the sanctity of their habitat, for they need to save all of their energy in their fight for survival and should not be forced to waste it because they must flee from curiosity seekers. It is very easy to be tempted to use zigzag paths as shortcuts. Many walkers are not aware of the fact that this promotes erosion. Much too often, such short-cut paths create gullies, through which, mudflows can occur, even falling into the valleys.

Environmental protection begins with your arrival. You are already doing the environment a big favour when you choose to reach your starting point via public transport. Driving a car produces carbon dioxide, a gas that promotes global warming which leads inevitably to climate change. It has also begun to increase in the fragile mountain ecosystem. Every person who leaves his car at home not only saves on expensive petrol, but is also freed from traffic stress. Sitting comfortably on a train, getting mentally prepared for the trekking tour, and then afterwards, returning home again from any chosen spot without having to return to a car doubles the rest and relaxation to be won.

Information and addresses

Getting there
Bus & rail: Prices for tickets are considerably less expensive than in Great Britain. For long distance trekking in general, there are great advantages to using public transport, including an additional relaxation factor. The best rail connections (www.trenitalia.com) are found in the larger cities and from there, a bus service to the Alpine valleys is available (links to schedules are noted in the individual Stages). The main hubs are Torino (Turin), Pinerolo and Cuneo.

Most schedules use the following abbreviations: »fer«(iale) = working days, »fest«(ivo) = Sundays and holidays, »sc«(olastica) = school days.

Important! In Italy, tickets must be cancelled by the automatic ticket puncher located on the platforms before boarding the train, otherwise you may have to pay a heavy fine. At smaller stations, there may not be a ticket office, so you might have to buy tickets in a nearby bar or kiosk. If nothing is available, you have to buy a ticket from the conductor on the train and there shouldn't be an extra charge.

In Airolo: jumping on the bus to the Nufenenpass.

Plane: Good flight connections from major airports in Great Britain to Milan, Turin and Cuneo.

Information
General
■ Italian State Tourist Board, 1, Princes Street, London W1B 2AY, tel. +44 20 7408 1254, www.enit.it, info.london@enit.it. Open to the public: Mo–Fr 9 a.m.–5 p.m.

Regional
■ Turismo Torino e Provincia, tel. +39 011/53 51 81, www.turismotorino.org
■ Azienda Turistica Locale del Cuneese (ATL), tel. +39 0171/69 02 17, www.cuneoholiday.com

Getting there by rail.

Internet
You will search in vain for internet cafés along the GTA. The only possibility is to ask at the accommodation at the Stage destination if you can use their private internet connection. In 2007, as part of an experimental project, all of the mountain huts in the Piedmont were provided with WiFi. Since 2011, this service is subject to charge and perhaps some huts will choose to do without it instead.

Useful internet sites
- www.klingenfuss.org/gta_engl.htm: a treasure trove of information for the GTA, with valuable updates, links, etc. provided by Jörg Klingenfuss. Only partially in English.
- www.facebook.com/GTA.trek: photo reportage of the GTA by the authors of this guide (German).
- www.tradizioneterreoccitane.com: information concerning the Alpine valleys of Cuneo (Italian).
- www.chambradoc.it: worthwhile information concerning Occitan (Italian but some English text).
- www.piemontefeel.it: information concerning the region as a whole (Italian/English).

A shepherd with his goats in the Gesso Valley (Stage 56).

Natural and national parks
The GTA crosses through, or touches on, a number of nature parks as well as a national park.
- Parco Naturale Veglia Devero, Villa Gentinetta, Viale Pieri 27, I-28868 Varzo, tel. +39 0324/725 72, www.parcovegliadevero.it
- Parco Naturale Alta Valle Antrona, same address as above, www.parks.it/parco.alta.valle.antrona
- Parco Naturale Alta Valsesia, C.so Roma 35, I-13019 Varallo, tel. +39 0163/546 80, www.parcoaltavalsesia.it
- Parco Nazionale Gran Paradiso, Segreteria turistica, Via della Rocca 47, I-10123 Torino, tel. +39 011/860 62 33 or 860 62 11, www.pngp.it or www.parks.it/parco.nazionale.gran.paradiso
- Parco Naturale Orsiera-Rocciavrè e Riserva di Chianocco e Foresto, Via San Rocco 2, Frazione Foresto, I-10053 Bussoleno, tel. +39 0122/470 64, www.parco-orsiera.it or www.parks.it/parco.orsiera.rocciavre
- Parco Naturale del Gran Bosco di Salbertrand, Via Fransuà Fontan 1, I-10050 Salbertrand, tel. +39 0122/85 47 20, www.parks.it/parco.gran.bosco.salbertrand
- Parco Naturale delle Alpi Marittime, Piazza Regina Elena 30, I-12010 Valdieri, tel. +39 0171/973 97, www.parks.it/parco.alpi.marittime or www.parcoalpimarittime.it

- Parco Naturale del Marguareis (Alta Valle Pesio e Tanaro), Via Sant' Anna, 34, I-12013 Chiusa di Pesio, tel. +39 0171/73 40 21, www.parks.it/parco.valle.pesio
- Parco Naturale delle Alpi Liguri, Piazza Roma, I-18100 Imperia, tel. +39 0183/70 43 41, www.parks.it/parco.alpi.liguri

Emergency phone numbers
Throughout Italy: police, tel. 112; emergency help in case of accident, tel. 118.

Language
If you do not speak Italian well, we recommend taking a little dictionary along with you. Unlike in the southern Alpine valleys (Province of Cuneo), French will not be much help while in the northern Piedmont (and especially not in the regions of Domodossola, Valsesia and Biella). Exceptions are the areas bordering on France and which belong to the Occitan or Franco-Provençal linguistic regions, such as parts of the Canavese, the valley heads of the Lanzo valleys, the Val Germanasca and the Val Pellice. Some of the younger locals can speak English quite well.

Domodossola (Stage 8, Alternative).

Through the Lepontine Alps – Walser trails and Devero e Alpe Veglia Nature Park

The northernmost point of the Piedmont and the eternal ice of the Gries Glacier, which once, long ago, spread over the Gries Pass, all the way to the Mediterranean Sea – where better to begin the trek along the GTA, a journey by foot marked by inexhaustible variety?!

Open up a whole library of exciting stories stored in Piedmont's northernmost corner, which pokes its way geographically deep into Switzerland. Stories of *Walser* and pack mule haulers who traded their goods via the rugged Swiss passes – of *Strahlern* (Swiss for crystal and mineral collectors) who discovered brilliant seams of crystal, and of partisans who took advantage of the difficult terrain to establish their hideouts – stories that spark the imagination. Some of these were written down as novels and are the perfect reading material while roaming this unique landscape.

According to the annals, it was the autumn of 1944 when partisans proclaimed the autonomous Republic of Ossola which only lasted for 40 days before fascists and Nazis struck back with retaliation. Everyone who was able fled to Switzerland. The partisan leader, Gino Vermicelli, wrote a first-hand description of these events in his novel, »Viva Babeuf« (unfortunately, only available in Italian or as a German translation titled »Die unsichtbaren Dörfer«).

Especially in post-war times, smuggling flourished; a lucrative undertaking since the Swiss had money, but not enough food. The murder of customs officers peppered the headlines again and again. The media even called it the »Wild West on the southern border«.

The Lepontine Alps: that sounds exotic. This epithet, which is used more on Italian side than on the Swiss, designates the ridges acting as borders between the Splügen and the Simplon Pass (in modern usage, the *Ticino Alps* and the *Adula Alps*) and was derived from Lepontii, a group of people who occupied the area In the Middle Ages, and whose capital was Domodossola. The western part, between the Simplon and the Nufenen Pass, is considered a part of the Monte Leone Range.

It takes five days to cross the westernmost region of the Lepontine Alps – an area that is characterised by unusual mineral wealth, which in turn, supports a wide variety of alpine flora – a landscape throbbing in dazzling hues, teeming with moors, lakes and colourful flowers – and rocky landscapes, aglow in white, red and green. The high terrain and alpine valley basins of Devero and Veglia, high above the spring-fed Toce Valley, are under special protection as a nature park.

Lago di Devero (Stage 3).

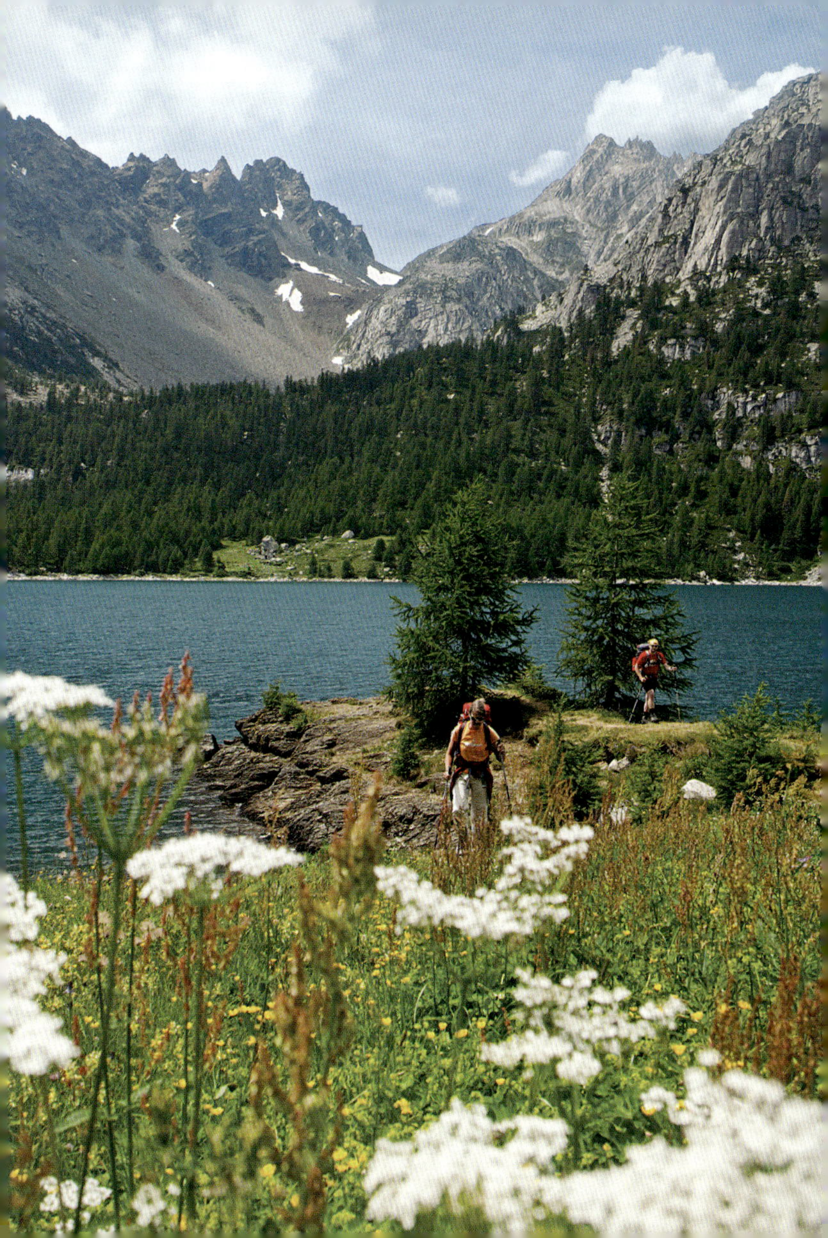

1. Alpe di Cruina – Capanna Corno Gries

1.00 hr.
↑310 ↓0

The ideal starting point

»Out of the dark tunnel into a new light and another world«, wrote Carl Spitteler in his travel guide published in 1897, »Der Gotthard«. Winner of the Nobel Prize for Literature, he captures everything that has always captivated travellers from the north: in Airolo, the first palm trees appear, a whiff of southern climes permeates the air and a different mentality underlines daily life. From here, even after a long journey, the short crossing to the first base camp in the farthest corner of Ticino can be easily made.

Starting point: Alpe di Cruina, post bus stop at the eastern side of the Nufenen Pass, 2033 m.
Destination: Cap. Corno Gries, 2338 m.
Length: 2.2 km.
Grade: Short ascent to a hut along a well-trodden, well-marked path.
Refreshment: Nothing en route.
Accommodation: Capanna Corno Gries: 2338 m, CAS, June–Sept., 50 B, comfortable beds with duvets; good meals, delicious cakes, HB/AV 67/59 CHF, Jutta Jerono, tel. +41 (0) 91/869 11 29, www.capanneti.ch.
Shopping and Services: Nothing available.
Public transport: Multiple daily service to the Alpe di Cruina from the railway station at Airolo and Ulrichen (timetable: www.sbb.ch).
Information: Leventina Turismo, CH-6780 Airolo, tel. +41 (0) 91/ 869 15 33, www.leventinaturismo.ch.
Alternative: Of course, you could also start off from the Nufenen Pass road on the Valais side, that is, from the bus stop at the turn-off for the Gries Pass, 2303 m. It takes 1 hr. to get to the Gries Pass.

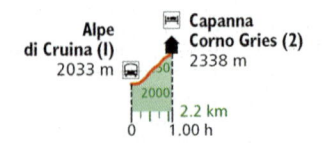

From the bus stop, **Alpe di Cruina (1)**, go through the underpass and then turn left, following the yellow signposts, to cross the Ticino (at this point, only a spring-fed creek). At first on the level then ascending more steeply, climb up the right flank of the Val Corno to the alpine hut of the same name. At the end, cross to the other side of the river bed to the **Capanna Corno Gries (2)**.

Capanna Corno Gries.

2 Capanna Corno Gries – Rifugio Margaroli

5.30 hrs.
↑1010 ↓1150

Overture in ice

After only a good hour of walking, you are already at the northernmost point of the Piedmont, having enjoyed an impressive view of the Gries lake and the Gries Glacier flowing down from the Blinnenhorn. The trail over the Gries Pass was one of the most vital trading routes between the Swiss interior, the Bernese Oberland and Italy. At the top of the export list: the aromatic hard cheese, Sbrinz, which traded for a good price at the markets in Milan. Naturally, wine flowed in the other direction, with a rich taste endowed by the sunny climate. The opening of the Gotthard railway in 1882 put an end to this bustling business. Here and there one still stumbles upon the remains of the ancient stone-paved trail, an historic trail, which at the end of the 12th century, provided a way for the first families of emigrants coming from Upper Valais to settle further on in the Val Formazza (»Pomatt« in Walser German). Thus began Walser settlement.

Starting point: Capanna Corno Gries, 2338 m.
Destination: Rifugio Margaroli, 2196 m.
Length: 17 km.
Grade: Well-marked; a short, steep descent from Gries Pass; the ascent to the Passo Nefelgiù is a tough one; on the north side, there can still be a lot of snow, even as late as mid-July, but at midday, you can usually walk this stretch without any problems.
Refreshment: Nothing en route.
Accommodation: Rifugio Margaroli: 2196 m, CAI, mid-June – end of Sept., 46 B, HB/AV 49/39 €, Tiziano Pianzola & Barbara Vedova, tel. +39 0324/631 55 or +39 327/019 74 44, www.rifugiomargaroli.it. – **Rifugio Miryam:** 2050 m, open year-round, 50 B, tel. +39 0324/631 54, www.rifugiomiryam.org. – **Rifugio Città di Busto:** 2482 m, CAI, from beg. June–end of Sept, 50 B, rustic, HB/AV 41/36 €, the hut warden, Marco Valsesia, tel. +39 0324/630 92 or +39 347/556 68 08, www.rifugiocittadibusto.it. – **Albergo Pernice Bianca:** Alpe Stafel, 1700 m, privately-owned, DR 56 €, gourmet tip, tel. +39 0324/632 00, www.pernicebianca.it.
Einkauf: Nothing available.
Public transport: None.

Information: Ufficio Turistico, Frazione Ponte, I-38863 Formazza, tel. +39 0324/630 59, www.valformazza.it.
Alternatives: 1. To become better acquainted with the world of glaciers, plan an extra overnight in the Rifugio Città di Busto: from Gries Pass, follow the signs to the right, keeping at the same height, then a steeper ascent through the eastern flank of the Bättelmatthorns until you reach a high plateau (to the right here, an excursion will take you in 1 hr. to the summit with a superb 360° view and a very impressive sheer drop to the Gries Glacier). Afterwards, a tricky descent through gullies and slippery slopes of scree demands being sure-footed and vertigo-free (1.30 hrs., the next day, onwards to the Rifugio Margaroli about 4 hrs.).
2. In the Val Formazza: until reaching the Toce waterfall, expect pristine pureness, but thereafter, the Walser settlements are criss-crossed with high tension cables.
3. Alternative, especially if there is a lot of snow on the north side of the Passo Nefelgiù: Capanna Corno Gries – Gries Pass – Riale – Albergo Pernice Bianco at the Alpe Stafel, 3.30 hrs. – Frua – Bocchetta del Gallo – Rifugio Margaroli, 3 hrs.

From the **Capanna Corno Gries (1)** head up the valley to the **Passo del Corno (3)**, 2500 m, situated above a glacial lake; it is not rare to find ice flows on the surface. At the two junctions that follow one after another, turn left at each one to reach the **Gries Pass (4)**, 2479 m, with a lovely downwards view of the reservoir and also taking in the glacial landscapes.

> *Since the conversion of the **Griessee** to a reservoir in 1966, the lake's waters no longer flow to the Rhone. The operating authority, Maggia Hydroelectric Power Plants, has altered the course of nature and has diverted the energy-producing waters via the Maggia Valley to Lago Maggiore. On the other side of the Gries Pass, the power plants have struck again, and in the Val d'Ossola alone, nine lakes have been turned into reservoirs. Because of this, the Pomatt enjoyed a period of high employment, but now, through increased rationalisation and the changed landscape where electric pylons and cables weave a high-tech spider web over the villages, the inhabitants have been left empty-handed. The route crossing through the Walser villages sometimes follows the main road and there are also more ascents to negotiate, which is why we cling to the alpe terrain to reach the GTA at the Rifugio Margaroli. The Gries Pass drops steeply towards Italy. Richard Wagner, during his journey to Italy on 18 July, 1852, had to struggle over icy terrain. At the little chapel on the pass, a plaque has been erected in the composer's honour. Every year, the first Sunday in August, a Walser event takes place here: the »Griespassfest«, commemorating the annual pilgrimage of the Pomatt inhabitants to Einsiedeln Abbey.*

Val Corno, view of the Blinnenhorn.

Zigzag trails lead through the steep slope to reach the bright green valley floor of the **Alpe Bettelmatt (6)** which gives its name to the special cheese produced in this area. After you meet a track road and just before crossing the stream, the trail forks off; this is a more direct route to the Lago di Morasco, 1826 m. In 1940, an entire village was submerged by the waters of the reservoir: Moraschg, the highest-lying settlement of the Pomatt villages.

Lago Vannino.

A new church was built on the hill above Cherbäch (Riale), the nearest cluster of houses, to replace the church lost to the flood. The new church is in view when we cross over the reservoir wall. Beyond the wall, turn right onto the path that short-cuts the *alpe* road towards Nefelgiù; the path is sometimes overgrown with alder thicket. If weather is wet, it is better to take the track road that ends at the **Alpe Nefelgiù (7)**, 2049 m. Don't take the path there since it becomes somewhat more difficult further up when crossing a stream. The marked trail leads just behind the *alpe* huts along the right bank of the stream, crosses through a gorge-like narrows and, at the end, over blocky boulders, scree and old snow reaches the **Passo Nefelgiù (8)**, 2583 m. Enjoying a view of Lago Vannino and Lago Sruer, continue steeply (a short, precipitous stretch through a gully is somewhat toilsome) along the right-hand flank of the valley to reach the lower lake and the **Rifugio Margaroli (9)**.

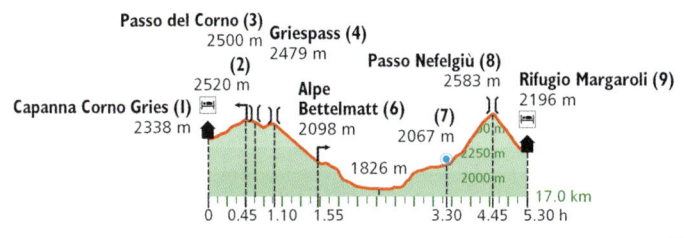

3   *Rifugio Margaroli – Alpe Devero*

5.00 hrs.
↑ 500 ↓ 1060

Almost Canada

Crampiolo.

This route is identical to the first leg of the Walser trail and leads along lakes and idyllic high terrain. At the highest point of the tour, the Scatta Minoia, a view opens up of the borderline ridge which glows in the most beautiful colours, presaging the immense mineral wealth to be found. In the Binntal beyond, a valley which is listed as one of the ten most important mineral regions of the world, the coveted crystals are mined. Around the lakolands of the Lago di Devero, vast pine forests blanket the landscape and conjure up the wilds of Canada. After a dip in the lake, the picturesque hamlet of Crampiolo tempts us to a refreshment stop.

Starting point: Rif. Margaroli, 2196 m.
Destination: Alpe Devero, 1634 m.
Length: 15 km.
Grade: Well-marked route. Steep sections alternate with more level ones. Boulder fields, snow on the last leg over the pass. Descent from the Scatta Minoia at first through a couple of rocky sections.
Refreshment: In Crampiolo.
Accommodation: Bivacco Ettore Conti: 2599 m, always open, 9 B, not very clean. – **Crampiolo:** 1773 m, Agriturismo, from beg. June–end Sept. as well as at weekends, 7 B, HB from 52 €, Adolfo e Fiorella Olzeri, tel. +39 0324/621 40 or +39 347/817 94 94, www.agriturismoalpecrampiolo.it. Albergo La Baita, from beg. June–beg. Oct., 32 B, HB from 42 €, Clorina Francioni, tel. +39 0324/61 91 90. Locanda Punta Fizzi, open year-round, Elvira Scaciga, tel. +39 0324/61 91 08. – **Alpe Devero:** 1634 m, good selection starting from simple hut (Rifugio Castiglioni, CAI, 35 B, open almost year-round, HB/AV 38/33 €, tel. +39 0324/61 91 26 or +39 333/342 49 04) all the way to luxurious inns. We recommend the Antica Locanda Alpino, beg. June–beg. Oct., lovely interior, very good meals, HB 47 €, Alessandro Francioli, tel. +39 0324/61 91 13 or +39 348/331 03 39. Additional accommodation: www.alpedevero.it.
Shopping/Services: Alpe Devero: shops, campsite. Baceno: pharmacy, cash dispenser, post office.
Public transport: Baceno, www.alpedevero.it/prontobus.htm.

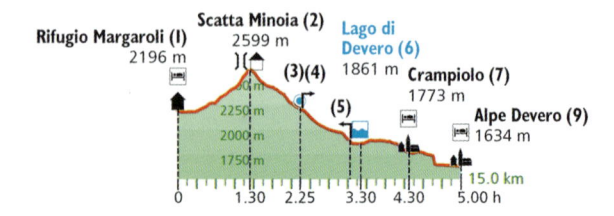

42

From the **Rifugio Margaroli (1)** descend to the right to Lago Vannino, crossing several small streams then traverse the slope west of the lake to the Alpe Curzalma, 2279 m, an idyllic spot with a turquoise coloured stream. Cross over the floating barrel bridge and head southwards, then westerly through an ever rockier terrain in the **Scatta Minoia (2)**, 2599 m, with the Bivacco Ettore Conti. Beyond this, the trail zigzags through a couple of short, rocky heights then follows the stream to the Alpe Forno Inferiore, 2213 m, where you meet up with a track road. Descend along this for a while and then turn off onto the walking trail again, through an idyllic little valley, to reach **Lago di Devero (6)**. Continue along the eastern shore to the *alpe* settlement **Crampiolo (7)**, 1773 m, Bettelmatt cheese, only produced here, can be bought in the *Agriturismo*. Just past the Locanda Punta Fizzi, turn right onto a »Sentiero Natura«. Pass a garden of Edelweiss and herbs, then through a splendid larch forest where the trail dips down to the **Alpe Devero (9)**. To the right, before continuing through the vast floodplain, the Rifugio Castiglioni lies hidden away in a prehistoric rockslip landscape. Further accommodation is available in the main settlement of Ai Ponti on the opposite side.

4 Alpe Devero – Alpe Veglia

5.45 hrs.
↑1000 ↓870

A real showpiece – enchanting mountain moors and bleak rock faces

We recommend an early start since this magnificent landscape is a temptation to dawdle. In the high mountain valley of the Alpe Buscagna alone, you could stay for hours. Here, a turquoise stream meanders through colour-splashed alpine meadows; an excursion to Lago Nero or to Lago del Bianco, is well worthwhile. At the outset, two passes are waiting for us; on the Scatta d'Orogna we will be charmed by the edelweiss, and from the Passo di Valtendra, enjoy a view of the high valley basin of the Alpe Veglia.

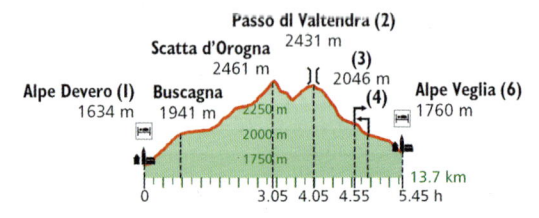

Starting point: Alpe Devero, 1634 m.
Destination: Alpe Veglia, 1760 m.
Length: 13.7 km.
Grade: Well-marked; distinct path; a somewhat precipitous craggy terrain between the Scatta d'Orogna and the Passo di Valtendra, one stretch of which is protected by chains.
Refreshment: Nothing en route.
Accommodation: Alpe Veglia: 1760 m, Rifugio Città di Arona, beg. June–end Sept., 65 B, HB/AV 35/32 €, tel. +39 0322/480 80, www.rifugiocaiveglia.it. Albergo Lepontino, beg. June–end Sept., 40 B, HB 54 €, tel. +39 0324/725 77 or 331/265 06 03. Albergo della Fonte, May–Oct., 42 B, HB 59 €, tel. +39 0324/725 76 or +39 338/621 22 14, www.alpeveglia.it.
Shopping/Services: Shop, campsite in Isola, a village district of Alpe Veglia.
Public transport: Bus service to Varzo from San Domenico (1 hour's walk away; see map/Stage 5): www.valdivedro.it/prontobus-varzo.

In the hamlet of **Piedimonte**, pick up the trail to Alpe Buscagna. After a steep stretch, the trail becomes quite pleasant as it crosses through a lovely high mountain valley. An excursion to Lago Nero, 1974 m, is worthwhile (20 mins., there and back). Head southwest at the valley's end; then the trail steepens to the **Scatta d'Orogna**, 2461 m. From the pass, the trail dips down into a craggy basin with a lake and then passes boldly under a ravaged rock face (one ledge is protected with chains) and through a steep slope onto the **Passo di Valtendra (2)**, 2431 m. Here, enjoy a lovely view of the Wasenhorn, the Furggubäumhorn and the Bortelhorn and also of the Pian Sass Mor, towards which we descend steeply, passing between crags at the outset. If you still have the strength, take an alternative route via the Lago del Bianco, 2157 m, the region's most beautiful lake (an additional 45 mins.). Otherwise, from the **Pian Sass Mor**, 2070 m, continue descending to pass the Alpe Stalaregno and then reach an enchanting alpine moor. Now continue through an unspoiled larch wood to reach the **Alpe Veglia (6)**.

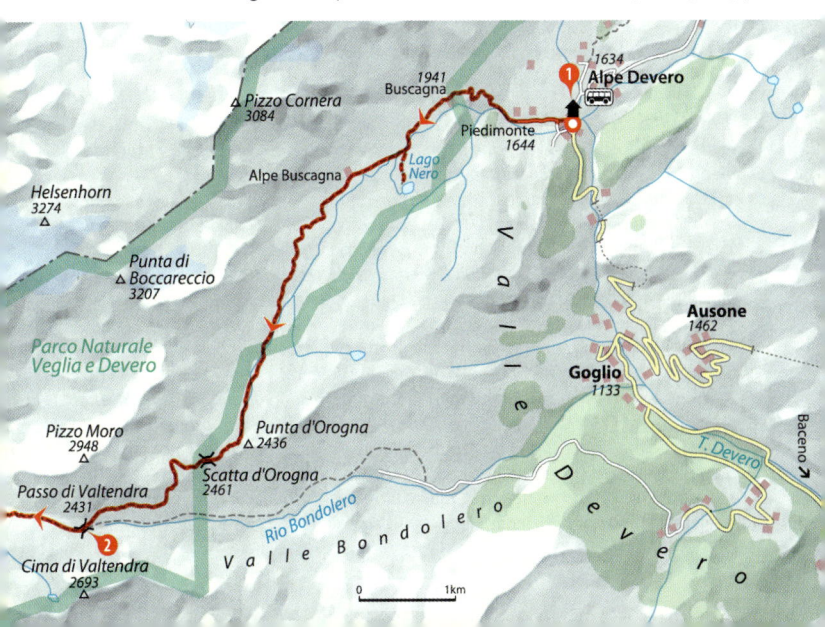

Alpe Buscagna, the trail between Alpe Devero and Alpe Veglia.

Monte Leone in the morning light, as seen from the Alpe Veglia.

Alpe Veglia: *the striking valley basin, over which the majestic glaciated peak of Monte Leone looks down from the heavens, almost became a victim of a water reservoir project. Fierce resistance from the inhabitants and the possible danger threatening the Simplon Tunnel situated below, put an end to the idea. The protected status was made official in 1978 through the establishment of the »Parco Naturale dell'Alpe Veglia«. Piedmont's first nature park set a precedent; since then, many more have been established. In 1990, the Alpe Devero was added as a nature reserve and, five years after that, was fused into the Alpe Veglia to create a single nature park.*

The touristic development of the Alpe Veglia began in 1875 when two soldiers, walking along the stream bed of the Rio Mottiscia, discovered an iron-rich mountain spring. For a number of years, the delicious mineral water was sold commercially and won a silver medal during the state fair held in Torino in 1884. In that same year, the first hotel was opened; the Albergo Monte Leone profited from the fame of the medicinal spring. An earthquake in 1981 caused the spring to run dry. After being restored, the flow had been so reduced that a commercial profit was no longer possible. If you want to fill your canteen with this acqua frizzante, at the bridge before Isola, a path leads along the stream to the enclosed spring (20 mins.).

7.30 hrs.		
↑840 ↓1740	**Alpe Veglia – Gondo**	5

A little romp in Switzerland: daring alpe and smuggler's trails

According to the IGC map No. 11, the GTA dead-ends in San Domenico, instead, the waymarked route continues, crossing over the Passo delle Possette and via Trasquera to Varzo. We recommend, however, an about-turn over the Swiss border and onwards to the smuggler and gold-digger's nest, Gondo. High above the Gondo Gorge, continue along the secret paths of the contrabbandieri and the poachers. They had no time for a leisurely pause to enjoy the lovely view, taking in the mountain chains of the national park Val Grande, behind which, Lago Maggiore lies hidden, whilst not far to the west, you can see the icy citadels of the 4000 mtr peaks – Weissmies, Laggin and Fletschhorn.

Starting point: Alpe Veglia, 1760 m.
Destination: Gondo, 855 m.
Length: 17.9 km.
Grade: Well-marked route with distinct paths. The Sentiero dei Scinc, reserved for sure-footed and vertigo-free walkers, can be skirted around; past the Passo dei Gialit, a pleasant high mountain trail. The direct descent into the Gondo Gorge is steep and precipitous, tricky when wet.
Refreshment: Nothing en route.
Accommodation: Gondo: 855 m, Stockalperturm, historic inn with a Gold Museum, open year-round, 42 B, DR 75 CHF p.p., dormitory, 50 CHF, Antonio Mendes, tel. +41 (0) 27/979 25 50, www.stockalperturm.ch. – Trasquera: Agriturismo La Fraccia, 1300 m, June–end Sept., 4 DR, HB from 40 €, Angela Comazzi, tel. +39 0320/148 92 13, www.fracciaagriturismo.it. Albergo La Sotta, ca. 1240 m, open year-round, 27 B, HB 45 €, Roberto Vergottini, tel. +39 0324/79 33 14.
Shopping/Services: Shop in the petrol station; post office in Gondo.
Public transport: Bus service Brig – Domodossola. Dial-a-ride service Gondo-Zwischbergen, PubliCar, tel.+41 (0) 79/713 70 02.
Information: www.valdivedro.it.
Tip: Guided tour of the gold mines: Rolf Gruber, tel. +41 (0) 79/469 54 36, www.goldmine-gondo.ch.
Alternative: Over the Passo delle Possette, 2179 m, to the railway station in Varzo: 3.30 hrs. Or the easier way from the Ponte Campo, 1310 m, along the right bank via the valley trail and past the Alpe Fraccia to reach the Trasquera road to meet up again with the GTA which leads via *Mulattiera* di Brocc to Varzo, 3.30 hrs.

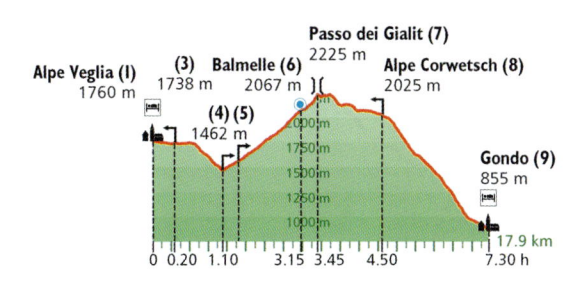

Below the inns of **Alpe Veglia (1)**, pick up the trail at the eastern edge of the valley floor. At the point where the rock barrier at the southern end of the *alpe* basin opens up to the gorge, the trail meets up with the track road. Descend steeply along this through the remarkable gorge. Past a chapel, the Sentiero dei Scinc forks off to the right. This route saves you a couple of metres of height, but leads precipitously along outcroppings of rock (especially tricky sections are secured) to reach the Alpe Valle. If you prefer to avoid this stretch, continue descending a short way along the road and turn off at

Alpe le Balmelle.

P. 1462 (4) onto the track to **Alpe Valle**, 1792 m. From here, our trail for the next 2 hrs. follows the same route as the Alta Via della Valle Divedro. Continue up the valley to the high plateaus of **Balmelle (6)** with its trim and tidy alpine huts. Now keep to the right-hand slope above the Alpe Pianezzoni to reach the **Passo dei Gialit (7)**, 2225 m (the crossing just a little west of the Passo delle Possette is nameless on the IGC map). Starting now, a fantastic panoramic view opens up along the high mountain trail above Camoscella, Vallescia (where the Alta Via della Valle Divedro turns away from our route) and Alpjerung. Since 2002, an association has preserved the **Alpe Corwetsch (8)** by authentically reconstructing the tumbledown buildings and then using these to provide accommodation (www.corwetsch.ch).

Before crossing the stream in front of the Alpe Corwetsch, a direct descent to Gondo turns off to the left. The ancient smugglers' and custom officers' trail heads, at first, to two dilapidated huts and then steepens as it leads below rock faces, passes the abandoned *alpes* Presa-Cima and Bruciata into the Gondo Gorge and then meets the road. Continue along the Stockalper trail to **Gondo (9)**. An old saying goes that in Gondo, you have to lie on your back in order to see the sky ...

49

The Simplon region and the unchartered hinterland of Domodossola – from the Gondo Gorge into the Val Anzasca

Kaspar Jodok Stockalper (1609–1691) was much admired and much despised, leading to his ultimate fall in 1678 – brought about by envy and by those that he harmed: the captain of commerce from Brig turned everything he touched into money, took no end of bribes, created monopolies in his own interests, »used and abused« mercenaries and appropriated the gold mines near Gondo. To improve his several businesses in the 17th century, he constructed the pack mule haulers' trail over the Simplon Pass; today, the trail has undergone a revival as the »Stockalper trail«. Gondo's visual impact is stamped by the stately *sust*, which Stockalper had constructed there as an administration building, lodging and warehouse. For centuries, the solid stone walls of the building seemed indestructible, until in 2000, a land slip carried away half the village along with the western section of the Stockalper tower. Thanks to the Glückskette (a Swiss fundraising organisation), so many donations were collected that the village landmark has been resurrected and has even been improved as a result, since the long-disused tower was converted to a hotel and a gold museum and is now an overnight accommodation par excellence.

Starting in 1660, Stockalper instigated a large-scale exploitation of the mines at the valley head of the Zwischbergental, which were steadily in operation since Roman times. The absolute heyday of the gold rush was reached at the end of the 19th century. Stockalper's mule track had been long since converted to a road (a project instigated by Napoleon from 1801–1805); the previously established routes skirting around the Gondo Gorge were made passable through gallery tunnels. French companies scrambled for the gold mines. In 1894, the Parisian joint-stock company, »Société des Mines d'Or de Gondo«, took over the concession and brought the gold mining operation to its peak. The existing mineshafts were extended and stamping mills, foundries and residential buildings were erected. In addition, a cable car and a private electric power plant were put into operation. At the time, this was considered a real pioneering innovation. Daily production reached about 6 tons (gold content was about 40 grams per ton); 33 kilograms of gold was won between 1874 and 1896. There was direct stage coach service between Paris and Gondo, a newspaper and a luxury hotel; furthermore, Gondo was the first Valaisian settlement to be provided with electricity. The media spoke of a »New California in the Pennine Alps«. While up to 500 workers laboured in the mines, lavish parties were in full swing in Gondo village.

But just as fast as the corks popped out of the champagne bottles, there quickly followed the crash which hit on May 17, 1897. The gold content of the ore had plummeted and the operation became suddenly unprofitable; future probing of the mines came up with the same sad results. From the »Gold Rush Town« only ruins remain and a couple of »Gold Vreneli« – one of the coins is the property of the municipality of Gondo who purchased the shiny souvenir in 1999 for about 45,000 Swiss francs.

In six days, the course of the GTA leads through the little-known eastern valleys of the Pennine Alps. Lakes and marvellous panoramic trails alternate with long-abandoned *alpe* terrain and daring mountain paths. The route touches on the newly established (2010) nature park, Alta Valle Antrona, and ends this stage of the trail at the gates of the Monte Rosa.

Alpe Waira; Lukas Escher making cheese (Stage 7).

6 Gondo – Zwischbergen

2.30 hrs.
↑570 ↓70

Gold from Gondo

This is an entertaining stretch which runs past the tumbledown ore processing works for the gold mines. You can get a much better glimpse if you join in on a guided tour of the mines. Along the stream »Grosses Wasser«, with its delightful rock pools, the route leads through a nature reserve protecting a beech forest to ascend into the remote Zwischbergental. An exodus began here in the 70s; from the 12 full-time farmers that once lived here, only one is left.

Starting point: Gondo, 855 m.
Destination: Zwischbergen, 1359 m.
Length: 6.2 km.
Grade: Well-marked, distinct trail; easy river walking.
Refreshment: Nothing en route.
Accommodation: Restaurant Zwischbergen (Pension Bord): 1359 m, mid-May–end of October, 15 B, 3 DR in a chalet, HB 75 CHF, chalet 80 CHF, Lukas Escher, tel. +41 (0) 27/979 13 79 or +41 (0) 78/826 14 61. After spending the night, the next day, you might be able to watch Lukas Escher making cheese at the Alp Waira.
Shopping/Services: In Gondo.
Public transport: Dial-a-ride service Gondo – Zwischbergen, PubliCar, tel. +41 (0) 79/ 713 70 02.
Tip: Guided tour of the gold mines: Rolf Gruber, tel. +41 (0) 79/469 54 36, www.goldmine-gondo.ch.

Zwischbergen Valley.

From the hotel in **Gondo (1)**, cross the main street. Take the narrow road to descend to the river and, at the playground, turn off onto the ancient mule track leading into the Zwischbergental. Short-cutting the bends, climb steeply to the mouth of the valley and then along the road. At **Hof (2)**, 1052 m, where the ruins of the smelting works are located, pick up the trail again and head upstream. On the way, you will spot tantalising rock pools; it's a pity that the signs warn of flood waters – the stream, *Grosses Wasser,* is dammed for hydroelectric energy further upstream. The community profits from water tariffs and the inhabitants enjoy some of the lowest tax rates in the entire canton of Valais. Nevertheless, when people depend mostly on over-the-border trading and nothing more than rocks and the forces of nature rule daily life, it is difficult to convince the locals to stay where they are. At the settlement of **Pianeza** cross over to the other bank via a wooden bridge. Now ascend to the road higher up and pass a tunnel. As soon as you pass the reservoir of Sera, do not continue climbing up the road, but instead, keep straight ahead until you reach a trail board and then turn right onto the path which leads to the hamlet of **Bord (Zwischbergen) (5)**.

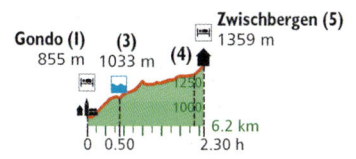

Stockalperturm in Gondo.

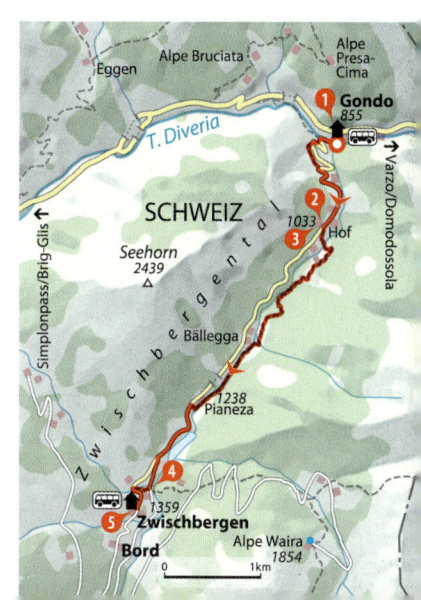

7 — Zwischbergen – Rifugio Gattascosa

4.00 hrs.
↑ 990 ↓ 70

Via pluvial lakes into the Val Bognanco

Josef Squaratti, who lived just above the Pension Bord, wrote about the lively life of a smuggler in his book »Mein Zwischbergen« (published only in German). Coffee, chocolate and cigarettes coming from Switzerland could fetch double the price in Italy. Whoever got caught had to reckon with a fine or even imprisonment. »Sometimes they came in droves; 10, 20 or more men at one time. Sometimes even a group of women would be involved (...). In winter, especially, the profession was extremely dangerous. With a heavy load of 30 kg per smuggler, they had to cross over huge amounts of snow in the valleys and also over mountain passes, sometimes at a great risk to life and limb. My mother often told one story of how, on 29 October, 1914, nine smugglers were killed in an avalanche, all of them from San Lorenzo and each one a family man.« In their footsteps, we will ascend to Gattascosa. Since the leg is so short, we can pay a visit to the Alpe Waira, and, if arranged in advance, we can watch Lukas Escher make cheese.

Starting point: Zwischbergen, 1359 m.
Destination: Rifugio Gattascosa, 1991 m.
Length: 7.7 km.
Grade: Well-marked trail but not always distinct; numerous steep stretches.
Refreshment: Nothing en route.
Accommodation: Rif. Gattascosa: 1991 m, June–Sept., at the weekends open year-round, 21 B, HB 40 €, tel. +39 328/315 16 69 (or +39 347/709 42 11).
Shopping: You can buy cheese at the Alpe Waira.
Public transport: Dial-a-ride Gondo – Zwischbergen, see Stage 6.
Alternative: The shortest route leads over the Passo di Monscera, 2105 m, but the landscape isn't as striking, 3 hrs.

Tschawiner See (Lake Tschawiner), Zwischbergental.

From your **lodgings (1)**, head back a short way to the trail board at the stream and then continue towards Passo di Monscera and Tschawiner Lake. En route, you will touch on the access road to the Alpe Waira time and again. After a long stretch along this track and before a bridge, 1700 m, meet up again with the trail, and at the following trail junction, turn right to reach the **Alpe Waira (2)**, 1854 m. From the farmyard at the huts, head south to meet a path crossing over to ruins and then climb south-westwards, through open larch woods and blueberry bushes, along the plateau with the little Waira lake. An escarpment stands between us and **Lake Tschawiner (3)**, 2174 m. Once there, continue along the left shore. At the half-way point, turn left to cross over a rise into a cirque where the next idyllic tarn is lying. The red/white markings lead eastwards to the **Bocchetta di Gattascosa (4)**, 2158 m, where we find ourselves in Italy once again. On the other side of the gap, a snowfield can be found, often lasting much of the summer through. When descending through the snow, keep left along the path and through a little valley to soon arrive at the **Rifugio Gattascosa (5)**.

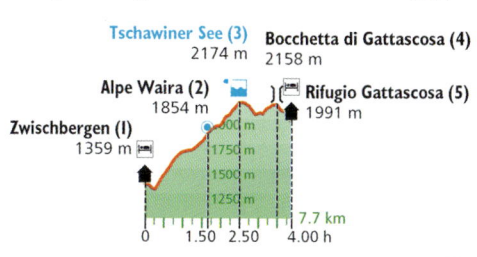

| 8 | **Rifugio Gattascosa –
Rifugio Alpe Laghetto** | 5.00 hrs.
↑590 ↓540 |

The »piano nobile« of the Val Bognanco

Above idyllic alpine terraces, descend to the chapel of San Bernardo where a mountain hut will welcome you to a cappuccino break. Afterwards, enjoy a pleasant stroll along the panoramic trail high above Domodossola. Below our feet, wooded slopes drop down to the valley floor of the Val Bognanco, where in 1863, mineral springs were discovered, and during the Belle Époque, a very popular spa was established. Despite the close proximity to Domodossola, this valley is virtually shunned by tourism.

Starting point: Rifugio Gattascosa, 1991 m.
Destination: Rif. Alpe Laghetto, 2039 m.
Length: 10.8 km.
Grade: Well-marked, distinct trail. A steep stretch at the end.
Refreshment: In San Bernardo.
Accommodation: Rifugio San Bernardo: 1628 m, June–Sept., 16 B, HB 37 €, Maura e Adriano, tel. +39 334/139 79 05. – **Rifugio Alpe Laghetto (Rif. Arsago Serpio):** 2039 m, CAI, mid-July–end Aug., June/Sept. at the weekends, 27 B, HB/AV 45/35 €, various hut wardens, tel. +39 347/032 02 98, +39 333/640 72 22, www.caiarsago.org. – **Bivacco Marigonda:** 1823 m, always open, very well equipped self-catering hut, 12 B with blankets, kitchen, bath, fountain.
Domodossola: Da Sciolla, tel. +39 0324/24 26 33 (in the pedestrian zone).
Shopping/Services: Nothing available.
Public transport: Bus service between San Lorenzo – Bognanco – Domodossola.
Information: Pro Loco Val Bognanco, tel. +39 0324/23 41 27, www.valbognanco.com; www.altavallebognanco.it.
Alternative: From San Bernardo to the Terme di Bognanco in Fonti (www.bognanco.it), 669 m (1.45 hrs.), and along a lovely *mulattiera*, via Monte Ossolano to Domodossola (3.15 hrs.). A good starting point when walked in the other direction (excellent rail connections, picturesque old town).

Bivacco Marigonda, Val Bognanco.

Slightly below the **Rifugio Gattascosa (1)**, turn right over the stream and reach the idyllically situated Lago Ragozza, 1958 m, which lies to your right as you pass by. Now descend, somewhat steeper, through the open larch wood, then cross an open moorland plain, through a dense forest where you follow a *suone* (watercourse) for a good way. Later, the path becomes a forestry track and then reaches a parking area and the **Rifugio San Bernardo (2)**, 1628 m. Descend between the garden and the toilet to reach the **chapel (3)** dedicated to the patron saint of mountaineers. Inside is a painting of Saint Bernhard at the old *sust* (mule haulers warehouse) below the Simplon Pass. Around 1050, the saint founded the hospice, run by Augustinian Canons, on the Great St. Bernard Pass.

At the chapel, turn right onto the road, keep to the right of the next house and, once past, descend slightly through the wood. About 40 mins. later, ignore the fork to the left that leads to Graniga. Another 30 mins. later, enjoy a marvellous, high mountain trail with lovely views; continue by turning left at the next fork in the trail. Pass the tumbledown huts of the **Alpe Oriaccia**, 1561 m, to reach a hillock with a cross. Here, you can either choose to take the direct route to the right and head to the **Rifugio Alpe Laghetto (5)**, 2039 m (the altitude noted in the IGC map is incorrect), or turn right to head to the Alpe Vallaro, from where only a few minutes are needed to reach the Bivacco Marigonda.

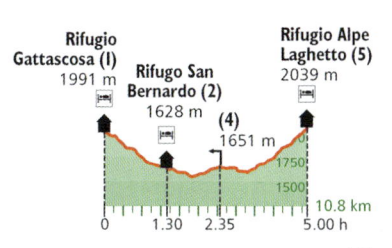

9 — Rifugio Alpe Laghetto – Alpe Cheggio

6.00 hrs.
↑ 690 ↓ 1230

Unspoilt valley heads and the nature park Alta Valle Antrona

This is an adventurous Stage requiring some sense of direction. At the Passo della Preia, you enter the most recently established nature park in the Piedmont; hopefully the responsible authorities will soon make the effort to make the spectacular trail via the turquoise-coloured Lago Alpe dei Cavalli more accessible.

Starting point: Rifugio Alpe Laghetto, 2039 m.
Destination: Alpe Cheggio, 1500 m.
Length: 11.1 km.
Grade: Very poorly marked; some stretches of the trail are barely discernible. Orientation problems crop up in the area around the Alpe Campo, at the outset, and the Alpe Teste Inferiore, towards the end of this leg. Crossing the steep grassy slope to Alpe Preia is a little tricky.

Refreshment: Nothing en route.
Accommodation: Alpe Cheggio: 1500 m, Albergo Alpino, mid-June–beg. Sept, open year-round at the weekends, 24 B (9 rooms), HB 40 €, tel. +39 0324/57 59 75 or 338/278 53 27. Rifugio Città di Novara, June 20–Aug. 20, as well as at the weekends, 24 B, HB/AV 38/35 €, Mariano Scotto, tel. +39 0324/57 59 77.
Shopping/Services: Nothing available.
Public transport: None.
Information: www.valleantrona.com.

From the alpine moor below the hut, head west in a short, steep ascent to the **Passo di Campo (3)**, 2169 m. On the other side, a high mountain trail leads to the Laghi di Campo. However, you must head down the valley; in a south-westerly direction to the alpine huts of Campo. The path disappears

Lago Alpe dei Cavalli.

from time to time, but shortly before reaching **Campo (4)**, 1892 m, becomes more distinct. Afterwards, path-finding is, again, demanded since the way-markings are sometimes badly faded or no longer visible. Keep heading southwest, on the level, to reach a stream, and when you reach the other side, turn right to ascend over the slope to a hilltop. Afterwards, a tricky crossing leads over a precipitous grassy slope. A broad trail, recently laid, has made this stretch much easier. Before you reach the alder thicket, climb a few metres higher onto the high plateau of the Alpe Preia, 2043 m. Back on a well-marked and better maintained trail, continue southwest to reach the **Passo della Preia (6)**, 2327 m. Now, descend steeply (sadly, the trail-marking team didn't choose to mark the old *mulattiera*) to the **Alpe della Preia (7)**, 2083 m. Descend southwards to the stream and towards the Alpe Teste Superiore, but before reaching the plateau, you must take the path to the right. The descent is steep, sometimes overgrown, then heads to the **Alpe Teste Inferiore (8)**. Once there, meet up with yet another orientation problem; the only clearly marked trail is the one to the right which leads to the Alpe Gabbio. We must, however, turn left and keep left over the meadow if we want to find the spectacular high mountain trail (admittedly, this trail is badly neglected). Far below, the Lago Alpe dei Cavalli is sparkling, and later, a lovely view opens up of the **Alpe Cheggio (9)**, which we reach along a trail (now again distinct) that zigzags down to it.

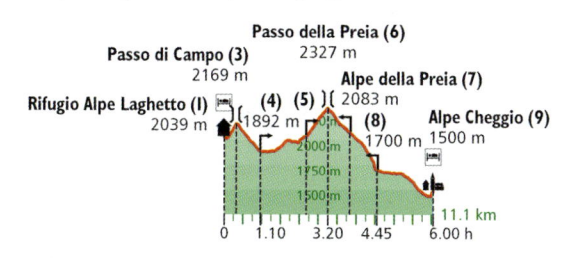

59

10 — Alpe Cheggio – Alpe della Colma

5.30 hrs.
↑1010 ↓940

Through the Valle Antrona

A romantic mulattiera leads in zigzags to Antronapiana – a village to village stroll through the valley until a steep ascent takes your breath away and leaves you in a sweat. The reward is waiting on a panoramic high ridge where you will be warmly greeted and delightfully hosted.

Starting point: Alpe Cheggio, 1500 m.
Destination: Alpe della Colma, 1570 m.
Length: 14 km.
Grade: Well-marked trails; mulattiere; some stretches along tarmac secondary roads; steep, vigorous ascent at the end.
Refreshment: A Pizzeria in San Pietro.
Accommodation: Rifugio Alpe Colma: 1570 m, mid-June–mid-Sept, 12 B, HB 36 €, very good food, stone-oven baked bread and pizza, Olindo & Patrizia Gurgone, tel. +39 339/751 16 53.
Shopping/Services: Antronapiana: shop, cash dispenser, post office, pharmacy.
Public transport: You can shorten the stretch by taking the bus to Domodossola, but get off at Prato, alternatively, one bus stop past Prato (you save 2 hrs.); timetable: www.comazzibus.com.
Information: www.valleantrona.com.

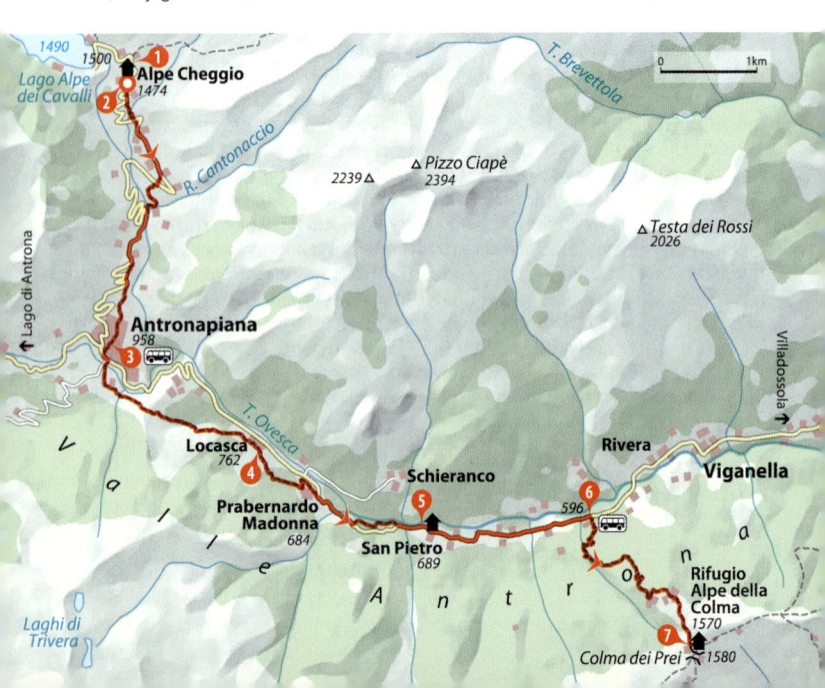

San Pietro, Antrona Valley.

From the **Alpe Cheggio (1)**, take the access road to the first bend where you turn right onto the *mulattiera* which repeatedly meets up again with the road. In **Antronapiana (3)**, 958 m, descend to the river and cross the bridge towards the campsite; turn left towards Locasca, and pass the cemetery. Before the unpaved road bends to the right, keep straight ahead. The *mulattiera* meets up with a tarmac road, but immediately afterwards, continues to the right. At the end, another stretch of road leads to **Locasca (4)**, 762 m. At the church, meet up with another trail board, bearing incorrect walking times. Past the playground, turn right onto a meadow trail, then again via a road. At the village fountain in **Prabernardo**, 684 m, take a passageway to a shrine dedicated to the Virgin Mary, then descend to the left to the main street. Just past the church, turn left onto a path which leads through bushy undergrowth to a road, then turn right through a wood and meet another road. In **San Pietro (5)**, you can have lunch in a pizzeria. After skirting around via the former main street, meet up with the current one and continue along it. Past a football pitch, meet up with a house with a dog pen. Here, turn right onto the steep *mulattiera* and cross through the woods to reach the **Alpe della Colma (7)**.

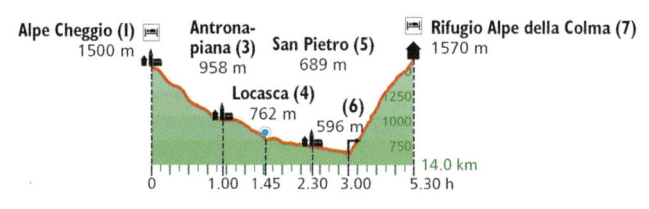

| Alpe Cheggio (1) 1500 m | Antronapiana (3) 958 m | San Pietro (5) 689 m | Rifugio Alpe della Colma (7) 1570 m |

Locasca (4) 762 m
(6) 596 m

14.0 km
5.30 h

11a Alpe della Colma – Molini di Calasca

2.30 hrs.
↑30 ↓1100

Where have all the farmers gone?

A perfectly constructed trail through the steep slope, artfully built dry stone walls, terraces and tumbledown alpine settlements, long since overgrown by forest, the mulattiera into the Anzasca Valley illustrates what happens to the landscape when cultivation comes to a halt. The eleventh stage of the GTA is divided here into 11a and 11b (see Note).

Starting point: Alpe della Colma, 1570 m.
Destination: Molini di Calasca, 500 m.
Length: 7.2 km (to the Alpe del Lago: about 16 km).
Grade: Well-marked *mulattiera*, sometimes steep, almost always through forests.
Refreshment: Nothing en route.
Accommodation: Locanda del Tiglio: 500 m, open year-round, 8 DR, HB 40 €, tel. +39 0324/ 811 22.
Shopping/Services: Unfortunately, the Locanda del Tiglio no longer sells groceries; cash dispenser in Pontegrande, 3 km away.

Public transport: Frequent daily bus service Macugnaga – Domodossola with a stop in Molini di Calasca (timetable: www.comazzibus.com).
Note: The crossing from the Anzasca Valley into the Strona Valley includes an overnight in a self-catering hut (Rifugio Alpe del Lago; see 11b/12) – not everyone's cup of tea. Alternative: if you feel fit enough to take on the whole leg from Molini di Calasca to Campello Monti in one go (8 hrs.), you can indulge yourself with a leisurely morning at the Alpe della Colma, and afterwards, descend into the

Rifugio Alpe della Colma.

valley, so that on the next day at the crack of dawn, you can start off from the Locanda del Tiglio. If thunderstorms threaten or if the weather is bad, this alternative is not recommended. You can avoid the leg by taking a bus, enjoy a stroll through the charming Omegna on the Orta lake and then continue the trek again in Forno (V12).

Alternative: If you wish to end the trek in the Anzasca Valley, you can follow the panoramic high ridge eastwards, starting at the Alpe della Colma, and then from Pizzo Castello, 1607 m, descend directly to Cimamulera. From there, it's only another 3 km along the road to the railway station at Piedimulera (about 4 hrs.).

From the **rifugio (1)**, ascend some metres then, on the level, cross the meadowland ridge to the ruins. The trail leads through a field of ferns into a wood. Descend in zigzags to reach a clearing with a house. At the trail junction, you can take your choice, since the two trails meet up again with each other at the **Alpe la Barca**, 1045 m. Further down, we meet up with the car park Coletta. Now take a track road until you reach the car park **(3)** below **Olino**. From there, turn right into the forest. Now cross through the terraced slope to reach **Vigino**. Walk through the village then down to the valley road. Turn left to the large Via Alpina trail board where the GTA continues and also where the bus stop for **Molini di Calasca (4)** and the **Locanda del Tiglio (5)** are located.

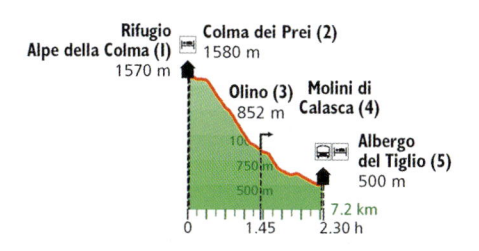

Walser country –
tracking the past in the nature park Alta Valsesia

A lot of speculation has been made concerning the Walser, the »highest« mountain settlers in the Alps – farming families from the German speaking part of Valais. They began to emigrate at the high point of the Middle Ages to Graubünden, Liechtenstein, Vorarlberg and Piedmont. In various waves of emigration, entire clans undertook the arduous journey over the high passes in search of new homelands in the most remote mountainous regions. But why did they emigrate at all? One possible motivation may have been their fierce desire for freedom. The dynasties and feudal lords of the time had a strong interest in the management of new arable land, so that they could consolidate their territory and cultivate land once used only for pasturage, thereby turning a higher profit. For this reason, the Walser were encouraged to resettle. In return, the new colonists were granted more rights and freedoms.

Since the end of the 19th century, the Walser have suffered terrible harassment. With the birth of the Italian state in 1861, the Italian language was furthered and the German-speaking enclave no longer recognized as such. The two World Wars closed the borders to Switzerland and broke off the lively exchange, via the passes, with relatives and friends on the Valais side. The spread of industrialization caused an agricultural crisis, which resulted in an ever-increasing exodus. Even the advent of tourism gnaws at Walser tradition. In recent years, a higher value has been given to traditional ways, and since 1983, the »Titschu« is again recognized as a valid minority language in Italy – even German language courses are available – but still many Walser traditions can hardly be revived. Nevertheless, at least in part, the legacy of the Walser people remains in that their tidy farmhouses are converted, quite often, into holiday homes and, here and there, small museums have been created to preserve everyday objects of the past.

Starting from Campello Monti, the GTA follows the Great Walser Trail along five of its stages. In the course of this trail, the stretch also leads along the edge of, and, one section, through the Parco Naturale Alta Valsesia, which reaches an altitude of 4559 metres above sea level at its highest point, the Punta Gnifetti (Signal Peak) of the Monte Rosa, and is, therefore, the highest-lying nature park in the Alps.

Descending from Belvedere in the Mastallone Valley, Ronco catches the eye (Stage 14).

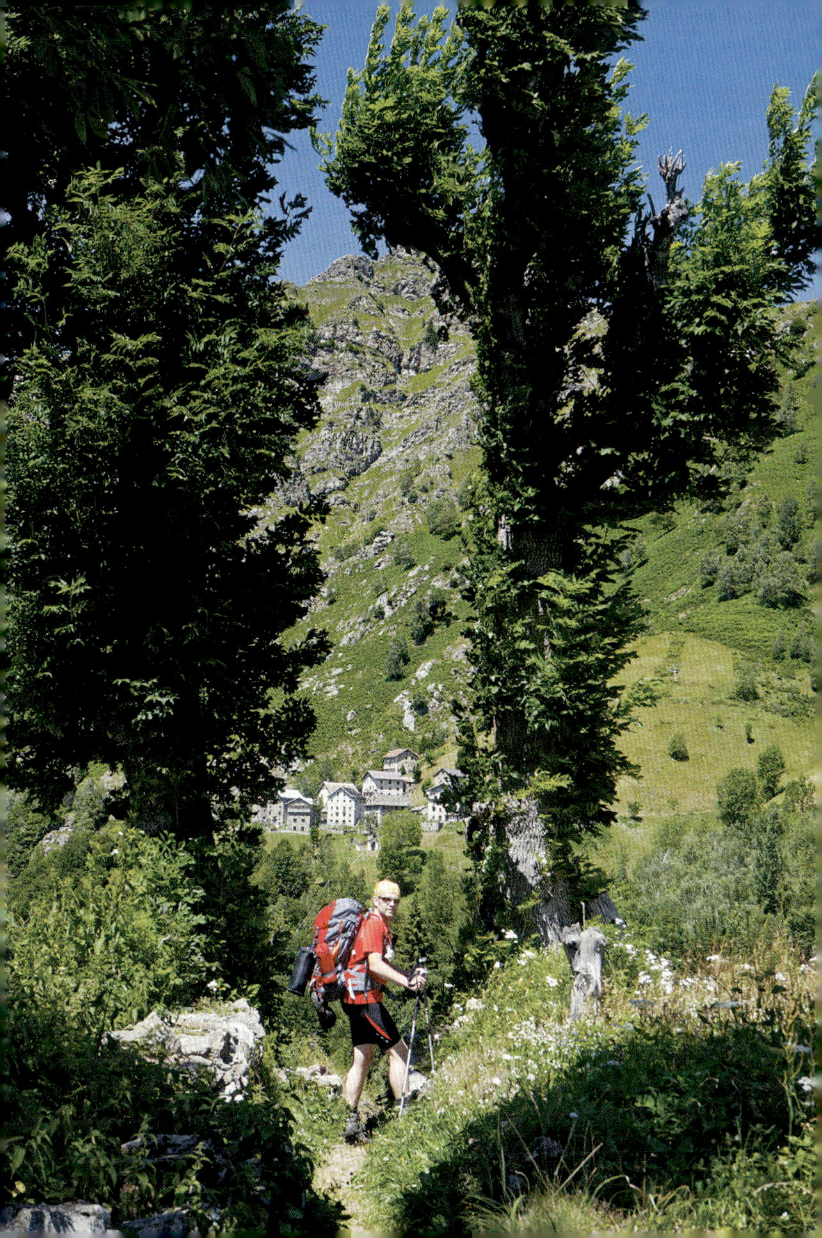

11b *Molini di Calasca – Alpe del Lago*

4.00 hrs.
↑1180 ↓140

Through chestnut forest to panoramic heights

A sanctuary in a deep valley notch – a forest walk that goes on and on – in autumn, collect some chestnuts, and above the timberline, let your soul take flight. In the Rifugio, step into the shoes of an »Älpler«.

Starting point: Albergo del Tiglio/Molini di Calasca, 500 m.
Destination: Alpe del Lago, 1545 m.
Length: 8.9 km.
Grade: Well-marked route along an almost always distinct trail. At the half-way point, a somewhat tough ascent. Until reaching the Alpe Camino, the route leads through forest then continues along a pleasant high mountain trail.
Refreshment: Nothing en route.

Accommodation: Rifugio Alpe del Lago: 1545 m, self-catering hut, always open, 9 B, blankets, gas stove, dishes, wood-burning oven, fountain. – **Bivacco Pian del Lago:** 1743 m, 6 B (no blankets), gas stove, wood-burning oven, fountain.
Shopping: In the Albergo del Tiglio.
Public transport: From Molini di Calasca, bus service to Domodossola, Milano, Omegna (timetable www.comazzibus.com).

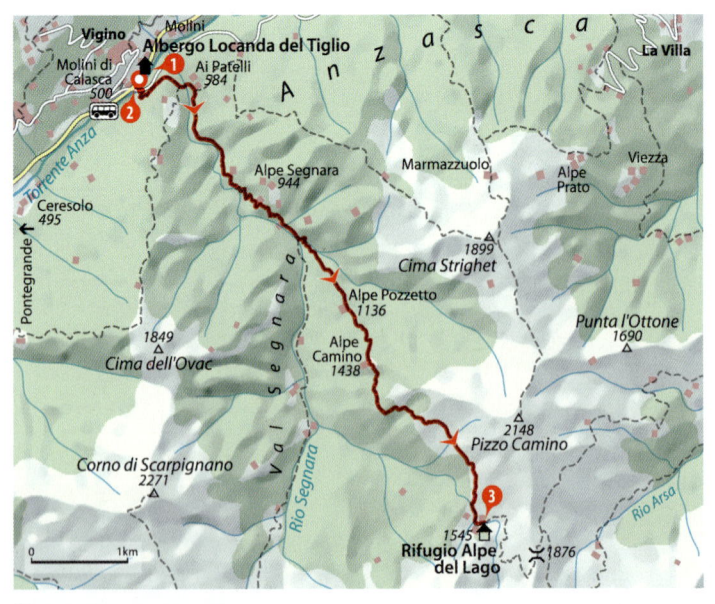

Val Segnara, Anzasca Valley, the ascent to the Rifugio Alpe del Lago.

A large Via-Alpina trail board on the main street of **Molini (2)**, only a few steps away from the Albergo del Tiglio, marks the turn-off. In the maw of the valley, you can already spot the pilgrimage church of Madonna della Gurva, to which you make a short descent. On the other side of the Torrente Anza, a path climbs up to a narrow road; turn left here. Past a bridge, turn right into the **Val Segnara**, following a lovely *mulattiera* upstream through chestnut woods. Reach another bridge about 1.20 hrs. from the starting point and at the trail junction, turn left. Now continue, quite a bit steeper, passing the Alpe Pozzetto to reach the **Alpe Camino**, 1438 m, where the woods open up. Follow the contour line along an exposed, indistinct path (tricky sections are secured by a cable) enjoying lovely views to reach the **Alpe del Lago (3)**.

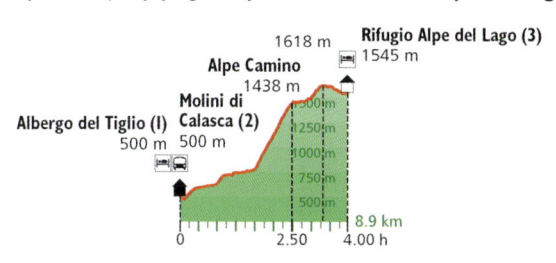

12 *Alpe del Lago – Campello Monti*

4.00 hrs.
↑ 750 ↓ 990

One of the very finest panoramic routes

Campello Monti.

The splendour of the Valaisan 4000 metre peaks is more apparent as you climb higher up. The first passage takes in the Monte Rosa. The second passage expands the view from the Ossola Valley all the way to Monte Leone and the Po River plain. At the third one, the marvellous alpine basin of Campello Monti lies at our feet

Starting point: Alpe del Lago, 1545 m.
Destination: Campello Monti, 1305 m.
Length: 9.6 km.
Grade: Well-marked, except for the last descent along a rather indistinct trail.
Refreshment: Nothing en route.
Accommodation: Bivacco Alpe Pian Lago: see Stage 11b. – **Campello Monti:** 1305 m, Posto tappa Campello Monti in the old schoolhouse, mid-June–mid-Sept., 14 B, pick up the key from the Milesio family in the Via Paolo Zamponi 6, only evenings and mornings, during the day, at the Alpe Sass da Mür, tel. +39 338/478 57 83. Dinner in the restaurant »Alla Vetta del Capezzone«, here, you could also enjoy a somewhat comfy overnight stay, but only 2 DR and a 4-bed room, May–Oct HB 40 €, Giovanni Volpone, tel. +39 0323/88 51 13.
Shopping: Nothing available.
Public transport: None.

From the **rifugio (1)**, cross over the bridge and follow the waymarkings eastward to ascend to a more distinct path. This leads in a southerly traverse to reach the next level terrain. In summer, the path may be somewhat overgrown. Cross through alpen rose undergrowth, somewhat

The view above the Alpe del Lago taking in the Pizzo d'Andolla and Weissmies.

above the basin, in a sweep towards the northeast along the southern ridge, which is sloping down from the Pizzo Camino; enjoy a fantastic view of the Monte Rosa, Rimpfischhorn, Strahlhorn, Alphubel, Täschhorn and Dom. The descent towards Val Arsa is a bit tricky, but only for a short stretch through a steep grassy slope, before traversing southwards to reach the **Alpe Pian Lago (3)** and the next bivouac. In an ascending traverse, heading eastward, keep along the extension of the ridge of the Punta dell'Usciolo. Now a slight descent south-westwards brings you to a depression and then you ascend to the Lago di Ravinella, only to continue to the **Colle dell'Usciolo (6)**, 2037 m. From here, descend in zigzags to reach **Campello Monti (7)**.

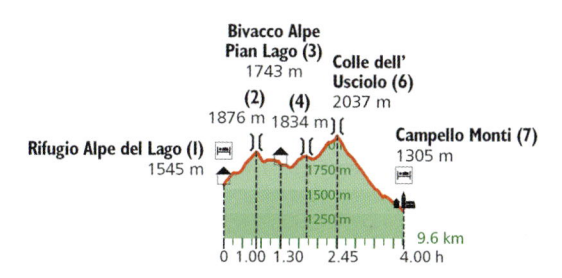

V12 Forno – Campello Monti

2.00 hrs.
↑450 ↓40

The »Pinocchio Valley«

The manufacture of wooden consumer goods and toys enjoys a long tradition. Most of the Italian wooden cooking spoons are produced in Forno. Because of this renown, the valley has been given the nicknames of Val di Cazzuj (Spoon Valley) and Valle di Pinocchio.

Starting point: Forno, 892 m, in the Strona Valley, 15 km from Omegna.
Destination: Campello Monti, 1305 m.
Length: 5.2 km.
Grade: Easy valley walk along a well-marked, distinct trail.
Refreshment: Nothing en route.
Accommodation: Forno: 892 m, Albergo del Leone, May–Oct., 8 R, tel. +39 0323/88 51 12, www.albergodelleone.it.
Shopping/Services: In Forno.
Public transport: From Omegna (Piazza Beltrami at the bus stop just opposite the Banca popolare di Novara), frequent bus service to Forno (www.trenitalia.it; www.comazzibus.com).
Tip: In Forno, the handicrafts museum run by Barba Guéra, a humorous fellow who taught wood carving for some years in the Black Forest, tel. +39 0323/88 51 33.
Information: Associazione Turistica, I-28887 Omegna, tel. +39 0323/619 30, www.proloco.omegna.vb.it.

Campello Monti.

The foot path to Campello Monti, with red/white and with ZO markings, forks away from the long bend below Forno and then follows the Strona upriver. At the half-way point, in the hamlet of **Piana di Forno**, touch on the road for a short way before the route turns off left to descend to the river.

After twice crossing over to the other bank, reach **Campello Monti** – a most charming village.

> *Campello Monti:* »*The last permanent resident of this village died in 1980 after reaching the age of 86. He was renowned as a real ›patriarch of the mountains‹, and Italian newspapers wrote admiring articles about him for a very long time. His name was Augusto Riolo. He bore a visage as ravaged as the steep and barren grassy slopes of his homeland, always topped by a few white stubbles of beard, and had rather tiny, squinting eyes brimming with humour, but also full of wonder at all that happened around him. A constant challenge existed between him and the mountains, and the entire valley participated in this duel between a mortal man and the callousness of nature. After every severe snowstorm, a helicopter set off for Campello to see if anything was amiss with him. He would wave joyfully to the pilots to let them know: I made it through one more time! Augusto, his dog, his cat, the goats and the chickens, a small community for whom the mountains were not made for the enjoyment of a summer holiday, but instead, as a place where one cemented close and decisive relationships in order to persevere and survive. Augusto Riolo, the ›hermit of Campello‹, is laid to rest now in the cemetery of a certain village, that since his departure, not a single soul has lived a whole year through*« *wrote Kurt Wanner in his walking guide* »*Unterwegs auf Walserpfaden*« (»*Walking the Walser Paths*«).
>
> *Surely, Augusto Riolo would have been pleased to see that the abandoned school-house has been restored again – but not for school children; instead, as an accommodation for GTA trekkers. Also, the Ristorante* »*Alla Vetta del Capezzone*« *has a couple of rooms to rent. Giovanni, the patron, worked for an entire decade in the wooden spoon factory in Forno.*

13   Campello Monti – Rimella/Chiesa

3.15 hrs.
↑ 650 ↓ 760

The pallbearers' path

We climb up to the Bocchetta di Campello. This must have been a bustling spot at one time since the valley head of the Val Strona used to belong to the pasturelands of Rimella, which is located in the neighbouring Mastallone Valley; this was the reason that Campello Monti was established. Today, the trail is quiet and only the resting place of the dead, which we will pass when we descend again, is a reminder of the close relationship between the two valleys. At a time when Campello Monti had neither a cemetery nor a church, the deceased had to be carried over the steep ramp to their final rest. At the so-called Posa dei Morti (Töturaste in Walser German), pallbearers could finally rest their loads, for the heavy corpses could then be turned over to the priest from Rimella. In winter, however, when snow would make the crossing impossible, the bodies had to be temporarily stored in their frozen condition. The dedication of Campellos' cemetery, in 1551, finally put an end to this custom.

Campello Monti.

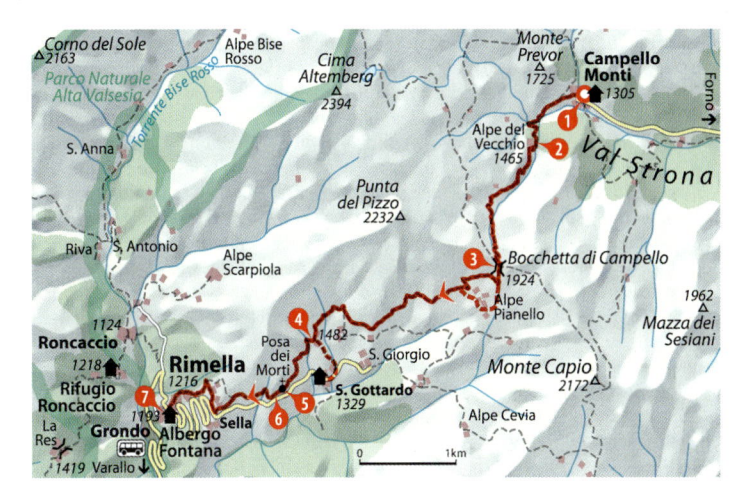

Starting point: Campello Monti, 1305 m.
Destination: Rimella/Chiesa, 1193 m.
Length: 9.1 km.
Grade: Well-marked, mostly distinct trail. An easy mountain walk.
Refreshment: Rifugio dei Walser (see Alternative).
Accommodation: Rifugio dei Walser: 1329 m, Easter–Oct., 14 B, delicious meals, tel. +39/338/9761975, www.rifugiowalser.it. – **Rimella/Chiesa:** 1193 m, Albergo Fontana, end May–end Sept., the restaurant is open year-round, the food (especially the *antipasti*) are legendary, bountiful breakfast, 12 R, HB 52 €, the Rosa family, tel. +39 0163/552 00.
Shopping: Alpe Pianello (cheese), village shop in the Albergo Fontana.
Public transport: Bus service Rimella/Chiesa –Varallo.
Information: www.rimella.de.
Alternative: From the Alpe Selle, descend towards San Gottardo to reach the Rif. dei Walser, 1329 m.

Above the church in **Campello Monti (1)**, turn left onto the mule track. A gentle ascent leads to a bridge and, on the other side, the route becomes steeper as it passes the **Alpe del Vecchio (2)**, 1465 m, via Alpe Scarpia, and then southwards to the **Bocchetta di Campello (3)**, 1924 m.

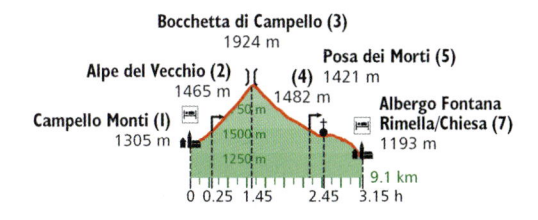

i *The **Bocchetta di Campello** (»Störnerfurku« in Walser German; the villagers of Campello call it the Bocchetta di Rimella), divides the Piedmont provinces of Novara and Vercelli and opens up a view of the Monte Rosa massif. Once, Samuel William King, a British priest, and his wife, Emma, were completely overwhelmed from the unexpected view which awaited them on a clear morning in 1855: »It was a spectacle never to be forgotten«. How, above the deeply chiselled furrows running into the Mastallone Valley, the majestic rock face of the Monte Rosa, with its manifold icy peaks, towered into a deep-blue sky »with a grace and grandeur indescribable«. Weeks had already gone by since they began their route with mules and porters through the southern valleys of the Monte Rosa, attracted by the exciting reports from Horace-Bénédict de Saussure, Ludwig von Welden and James David Forbes which told of an almost totally unknown territory. Perhaps they were the first visitors here that came without scientific ambitions, without barometers and thermometers. Curiosity and an adventurous spirit were their motivations, but a botanical interest as well. Thus, King was delighted when he discovered the rare clubmoss below the crest of the pass, something which he hadn't seen anywhere else in Piedmont, but was growing here in great abundance. The Älper used this fern-like plant by first crushing it in a wooden vessel and then filtering cow's milk through the mixture, as King reported in his published travelogue, »The Italian Valleys of the Pennine Alps«. He also comments on the hearty reception they received in the strange German »patois« once they were below in Rimella. This Walser German is rarely heard in this day and age, but the museum that the couple visited in Chiesa (the very first Walser museum, opened in 1836 by Giovanni Battista Filippa), still exists, as well as the Albergo, whose fare is swarmed about just as much now as it was then.*

From the pass, continue south-eastwards to a grassy knoll, and from there, sharp to the right, through the southern slope of the Punta del Pizzo. Or you could head to the Alpe Pianello, 1801 m, buy some cheese and then head to the right, through the meadowland slopes. The trail leads only a little above the Alpe Selle before it enters a patch of woods and then passes the **Posa dei Morti (5)**. At the trail junction soon after, turn right through woods and meadows, along the »Sentiero 2«, to reach Villa Superiore. In the village, the waymarkings are missing. You bear right while going through the passageways and then meet up with a street, which takes a bend, to lead to the main road. Turn right here onto the *Way of the Cross* and then descend steeply, passing the Villa Inferiore, to reach **Chiesa**, 1216 m. Somewhat below the church, you will find the **Albergo Fontana (7)**.

i ***Rimella** is not a village, but instead, a community which consists of numerous hamlets spread out along an extremely topographical landscape with great differences in altitude (the lowest lying is Grondo at 961 m above sea level, the highest* is Villa Superiore at 1333 m). In most descriptions of the area, when Rimella is mentioned, the central hamlet of **Chiesa** is meant. In the cemetery there, the name Termignone recalls the origin of the emigrants who, in the summer of 1256, started off from Visperterminen (at the time known as Terminum) in Valais to settle in Rimella. Around 1900, some of these emigrants returned again to Switzerland, others moved into the cities, only a few commuted and even fewer continued farming. From its peak in 1831 with 1381 inhabitants, the numbers dropped steadily. In 2012, a mere 136 individuals remain loyal to their community the whole year round.

San Gottardo, a hamlet of Rimella.

14 — Rimella/Chiesa – Alpe Baranca

4.30 hrs.
↑970 ↓580

What a relief

Hamlets so close and yet so far, »...because the way here is only through the deepest gorges and, despite the much shorter distances ›as the crow flies‹, the actual route can often take hours on end. Daily life is extremely hard: (...), when a woman does the washing up and a bowl is mistakenly thrown out with the water, then it rolls all the way to the stream and that would be the last she sees of it«, writes Albert Schott. As a German language teacher, he was extremely interested in lingual »islands«. He travelled through the region in the summer of 1839 and left behind the first research material on the Walser people.

Starting point: Chiesa, 1193 m.
Destination: Alpe Baranca, 1580 m.
Length: 11.6 km.
Grade: From time to time, insufficiently marked. The trail is sometimes rather indistinct. In the highest stretch of the ascent to La Res, there are a couple of precipitous spots guarded by a rope.
Refreshment: Rifugio Roncaccio.
Accommodation: Rif. Roncaccio: 1218 m, in Roncaccio superiore, mid-June–end Sept., 12 B, Gallo Leandro, tel. +39 345/718 73 04. – Santa Maria di Fobello: 1083 m, Posto tappa, open year-round, 40 B, HB 30 €, Andrea Bossi, tel. +39 348/030 07 67. – **Rifugio Alpe Baranca:** 1580 m, mid-June–end Sept., 15 B, HB 35 €, an incredibly hearty welcome, delicious *Älpler* food, bountiful breakfast, Sergio und Alda Falcione, tel. +39 347/865 93 85.
Shopping: Village shop in Chiesa; at the Alpe Baranc, you can buy cheese and sausage.
Public transport: None.
Information: www.rimella.de.

From **Rimella/Chiesa (1)**, descend along the main street. At a bend, the road to Pianello turns off. With a material cable hoist to your right, turn onto the path to reach the stream and, on the other side, continue on to **Roncaccio inferiore**,

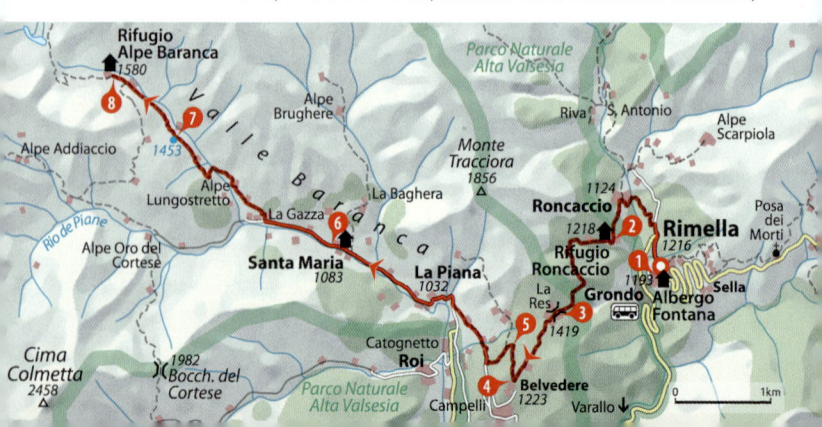

Alpe Baranca.

1124 m. At the church, the hamlet's highest lying building, keep heading up the mountain to Roncaccio superiore, 1179 m. The woods open up from time to time, to give views of the Rimella hamlets. Above Roncaccio superiore, traverse the steep wooded slope in a southerly direction. The path is narrow and slippery when wet; a tricky stretch is secured with a cable. At the end, cross over meadows to the houses of **La Res (3)**, 1419 m, perched on a panoramic saddle. A large trail board points out the altered route of the GTA, which no longer leads via Ronco (overgrown), but instead, via the hamlet of **Belvedere (4)** and Boco superiore. Past the chapel, descend in a south-westerly direction and, before Belvedere, turn right towards the San Antonio chapel. As soon as you enter the woods, a path leads to the left to a clearing with a house. Descend over the meadow to reach a parking place, then turn right along the lower trail to reach **Boco superiore**, 1089 m. The trail leads past the lower houses of the hamlet, then turns right before the last house. Now traverse through a wood to reach **La Piana**, 1032 m, and then along the road via **Santa Maria di Fobello (6)**, 1083 m, until the road ends at Campo. Now along a well-marked, broad trail, head upriver to the **Alpe Baranca (8)**.

15 Alpe Baranca – Carcoforo

4.45 hrs.
↑ 660 ↓ 940

A crossing with the loveliest view of Monte Rosa

Natural wonders all in a row: the Baranca waterfall and lake, higher up, the idyllic Alpe Selle, on the Colle d'Egua, a mind-boggling view of the Monte Rosa massif, perhaps a couple of donkeys taking a curious sniff at the walkers going by... and, last but not least, the picturesque village of Carcoforo with its archaic passageways.

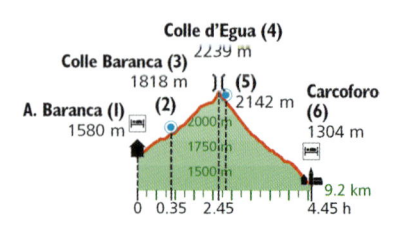

```
Colle d'Egua (4)
       2239 m
Colle Baranca (3)  )( (5)
  1818 m            2142 m    Carcoforo
A. Baranca (I) (2)              (6)
  1580 m          2000m        1304 m
                  1750m
                  1500m
                              9.2 km
0  0.35  2.45              4.45 h
```

Starting point: A. Baranca, 1580 m.
Destination: Carcoforo, 1304 m.
Length: 9.2 km.
Grade: Well-marked, distinct path. Steep stretches are followed by more level ones.
Refreshment: Rifugio Boffalora.
Accommodation: Rifugio Boffalora: 1635 m (somewhat above the trail), CAI, June/July/September/October at the wookondo, ond July–end Aug. daily, 40 B, tel. +39 0163/956 45. – **Agriturismo Alpe Brüc:** 1400 m, tel. +39 0163/956 00. – **Carcoforo:** 1304 m: Albergo Alpenrose, beg. June–end Sept., 8 R (24 B) in the hotel (HB 55 €), 18 B in a Posto tappa (HB 44 €), very good meals, bountiful breakfast buffet, Bianca Soci, tel. +39 0163/956 46 or 956 01.Ristorante Lo Scoiattolo, 2 R, a member of Slow Food, which means, top-quality meals, May–October, Pier Aldo Manetta, tel. +39 0163/956 12, www.ristorante-scoiattolo.tk.
Shopping/Service: Shop in Carcoforo.
Public transport: Bus service Carcoforo – Rima –Varallo.
Information: www.comunecarcoforo.it.

Along the cobbled mule track running only a little above the **Rifugio Alpe Baranca (1)**, reach a cleft in the rock face where the waters of the Lago di Baranca drain out, creating a waterfall which cascades into the valley. The lake is nestled in a pristine, romantic alpine basin, above which, you can already spot the *alpe* settlement of Selle. Continue onward above the outlet of the lake and along the meadowland ridge of the **Colle Baranca (3)**, 1818 m, where a few tumbledown huts are mixed in. The inscription on a façade reveals that there was even a hotel here at one time.

Alpe Selle, Lago di Baranca.

Enthusiastic tales told by British alpine pioneers and explorers, who used this crossing to descend into the Anzasca Valley, had ushered in a modest tourism back then. A ruin off to one side catches the eye. Does the ghost of Vincenzo Lancia (1881–1937) still lurk around here? The famous automobile designer and racing car driver, who was born further down in the mountain village of Fobello, once built a magnificent villa in this remote spot as a summer retreat.

Above the ruin, the path winds upward in a bend towards the southwest to reach the **Colle d'Egua (4)**, 2239 m, where what is perhaps the most beautiful view of the Monte Rosa is revealed.

From the crest of the pass, continue past the Alpe Sellette into the wide, high mountain valley of the Alpe Egua. Slightly above the trail, the **Rifugio Boffalora**, 1635 m, tempts the walker to take refreshment. In a gentle gradient, head out to a scenic overlook above the Val d'Egua, with a lovely view of the archaic cluster of houses at **Carcoforo (6)**, and then continue, climbing down a few zigzags into the village below.

---

*From left to right, the nine peaks of the **Monte Rosa massif** appear: Punta Giordani, Vincentpyramide, Schwarzhorn, Ludwighöhe, Parrotspitze, Signalkuppe, Zumsteinspitze, Dufourspitze, Nordend. Until 1822, all of these peaks were simply called the Monte Rosa (in the local dialect, »Rosa« is the word for glacier and not inspired by the gorgeous pink colouration that appears at sunrise). It was not until the Austrian General and topographer, Ludwig Freiherr von Welden, became irritated by the inadequate nomenclature, whereby he created additional names that have stuck to this very day, with the exception of the »Höchste Spitze« (»highest peak«), which was later renamed as the Dufourspitze. Von Welden's book, published in 1924, »Der Monte-Rosa«, became a classic. On August 25, 1822, he himself stood on the little rocky spur between the Schwarzhorn and the Parrotspitze and gave it his own first name.*

16 Carcoforo – Rima

6.00 hrs.
↑1050 ↓940

Tough going

The Colle del Termo is a tough nut to crack: an ascent that seems to last forever and a descent which, at the beginning, can make your hair stand on end. After carefully negotiating the first steep section, the way gets a little easier as the zigzagged path winds downwards into the Val Sermenza. Rima does not come into sight until the very end. What a pretty village!

Ristorante Grillo Brillo, Rima.

Starting point: Carcoforo, 1304 m.
Destination: Rima, 1416 m.
Length: 10.8 km.
Grade: Well-marked and, for the most part, a distinct trail.

Refreshment: Nothing en route.
Accommodation: Rima: 1416 m, Posto tappa, on the top floor of the Casa del Parco Naturale Alta Valsesia, beg. June–end Sept., 9 B (for larger groups, more room is available), HB 34 €, the key can be picked up in the restaurant Grillo Brillo near the Marisa Soci, good food, tel. +39 0163/ 950 01. Another 4 R are available in the neighbouring Hotel Tagliaferro, B&B 40 € p.p., tel. +39 0163/950 40. Additionally, a new Wellness hotel is being built. In San Giuseppe, 3 km away, the Albergo Nonay offers comfortable accommodation, HP 45 €, Tel. +39 0163/95161, www.alpenresortnonay.it. From Rima, Marco, the Albergo's *patron*, provides pick-up service for his guests and a shuttle back.
Shopping: Nothing available.
Public transport: Bus service to Carcoforo und Varallo.

From **Carcoforo (1)**, take the track road past a holiday home resort while heading into the valley. The stream is not crossed until the unpaved road comes to an end. Pass the huts of Selva Bruna while ascending steeply to **Alpe Trasinera Bella (3)**, 1925 m (mountain spring). At the first stone house, ascend past the Alpe del Termo and then onto the **Colle del Termo (4)**, 2351 m. Here turn left (ignore paths to the right), climbing down in steep bends. This stretch was tricky in the past but has been newly upgraded and widened. Reach the tree line and, in sweeping bends, continue to the Alpe Chiaffera, 1706 m (refreshment) and then on to **Rima (6)**.

> »The village was deserted, not a soul to be seen«. What surprised the traveller King, had a different reason than the one today. In the summer months, the womenfolk took over the farming to be done, and aside from the village priest, all of the adult males had gone away. Farming alone was not sufficient to keep a large Walser family above water. Because of this, the men went off every year to foreign lands: the Gressoneyan worked as shopkeepers, the Alagnan as stonemasons, plasterers and bricklayers. Some of them created true architectural masterpieces, such as the Lucern City Hall, the Spiesshof in Basel, the Stockalper Palast in Brig and the church at Raron. The Walser from **Rima** (founded in the 14th century by colonists from Alagna) were specialized in the production and processing of artificial marble and had made a name for themselves abroad. »Their clients included kings, princes, merchants and clergymen from all over Europe, even in Morocco their product was much admired. Each and every one contributed to the village's prosperity. When compared to the number of inhabitants, Rima was the richest settlement in Italy in the year 1908«, wrote the Walser researcher, Max Waibel. One individual who enjoyed special distinction was Piaru Axerio. The fortune that he brought home with him benefited the entire village. Rima was bestowed a road, its own water supply system and a hotel where Axerio received guests. »The magnificently decorated walls of the Bavarian royal castles at Herrenchiemsee and Neuschwannstein, created from stucco, deceptively similar to marble; these are chiefly the work of our friendly host.« Wilhelm Halbfass, who wrote an article on Rima and Rimella in 1894, was clearly impressed. – Freed from any financial worries, Axerio was able to devote himself to his artistic bent, but now as a poet in his own dialect. Since 1905, he has been laid to rest in Rima's cemetery. For generations, the Dellavedova family has also worked in the art of marble. If you take a stroll through Rima, you will inevitably stumble on the studio of the last progeny, Silvio Dellavedova, who turned 80 in 2011, but is still creating fantastic works of art. His children have no interest in family tradition and have long since resettled in the valley. As long as he is able, Silvio passes on his knowledge of the craft to art students coming from the cities. Be sure to ask for the key to the gipsoteca, where you can admire the true treasures of his art.

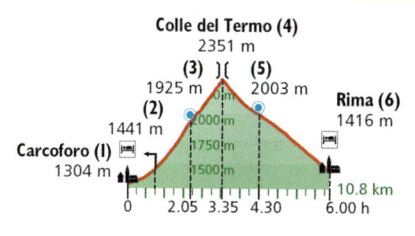

17a Rima – Alagna

5.30 hrs.
↑920 ↓1120

In the heart of Valsesia

A new day, a new pass to cross. The differences in altitude have become relatively routine now. »He walks like a Walser« was an expression in times gone by, used to describe the soft, rhythmic gait of this people who seemed to take the arduous mountain trails as lightly as a stroll. A rarity in the high western Italian Alps: just past the Colle del Mud, lunch will be served.

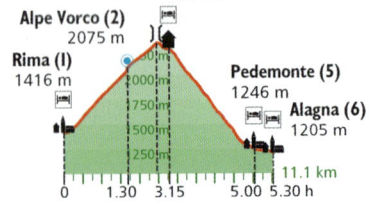

Colle del Mud (3) Rifugio Ferioli (4)
2324 m   2264 m
Alpe Vorco (2)
2075 m
Rima (1)   Pedemonte (5)
1416 m   1246 m
                            Alagna (6)
                            1205 m
                  11.1 km
0   1.30 3.15   5.00 5.30 h

Starting point: Rima, 1416 m.
Destination: Alagna, 1205 m.
Length: 11.1 km.
Grade: Well-marked, distinct path. A steep ascent and a steep descent.
Refreshment: Rifugio Ferioli, somewhat below the Colle del Mud as well as in Pedemonte.

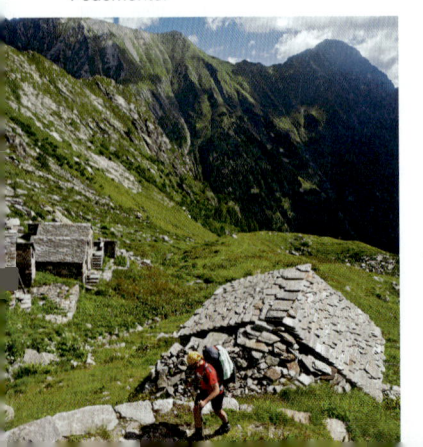

Accommodation: Rifugio Ferioli: 2264 m, CAI, end July–end Aug., July/Sept. at the weekends, 20 B, HB/AV 41/29 €, various hut wardens, tel. +39 0163/912 07 oder +39 334/563 11 05. – **Pedemonte:** 1246 m, Hotel Montagna di Luce in a typical Walser house, 8 R, HB from 60 €, tel. +39 0163/92 28 20, www.montagnadiluce.it. – **Alagna:** 1205 m, numerous choices, for example, B&B in a lovely Walser house, Casa Prati, Marisa Castagnola, tel. +39 0163/92 28 02, www.zimmercasaprati.com.
Tip: Casa dei Fiori, Frazione Bonda 6, tel. +39 0163/92 29 90.
Tip: An extra day in Pedemonte or Alagna is worthwhile, since a trekker who has walked the long stretch of this stage into the Val Vogna is not likely to take the time for the Walser Museum in Pedemonte or for other attractions in and around Alagna. Also very impressive is an excursion to the valley end where you stand directly below the gargantuan, sheer, southern faces of the Monte Rosa. There is a shuttle bus to the waterfall, Acqua Bianca.
Shopping/Services: Alagna: shops, cash dispenser, post office, pharmacy, internet café.
Public transport: Alagna: bus service to Milano (airport), Vercelli, Varallo (railway station): timetables at www.alagna.it.
Information: Tourist office on the Piazza Grober, I-13021 Alagna, tel. +39 0163/92 29 88, www.atlvalsesiavercelli.it.

Alpe Vorco.

From the upper passageways in **Rima (1)**, follow the waymarkers to descend to the stream. At the fork past the bridge, turn right to follow a zigzag course through the woods to the alpine huts of Valmontasca, 1819 m, above the treeline. Continue, not quite so steeply, to **Alpe Vorco (2)**, 2075 m (enclosed spring), and then head further through a barren, rocky terrain to the **Colle del Mud (3)**, 2324 m. Despite being so close to the Monte Rosa, the massif is still hidden behind the gigantic rock barrier of the Corno Mud. You could slog on to the top of the summit (traces of a path; cairns), with the promised reward of a unique view

Pedemonte bei Alagna.

stretching to the Strahlhorn and the Weissmies. But keep in mind; the walk ahead is still a long one for the trekker who wants to reach the Val Vogna. After about 10 mins. from the top of the pass, you reach the **Rifugio Ferioli (4)** (refreshment). With lovely downward views into the Val Sesia, descend steeply via the Alpe Mud to reach **Pedemonte (5)**, 1246 m, the oldest Walser settlement in the valley. This is a village made for lingering, especially since you can visit the informative Walser Museum there. Afterwards, you pick up the footpath to the settlement of Ponte, then continue along the road to **Alagna (6)**.

From Monte Rosa to the gateway of the Aosta valley – Valsesia, Biellese, Canavese

The Val Vogna presents a stark contrast to Alagna. Not a single road penetrates into this deep cleft valley. A car can be driven only as far as the first houses of Cà di Janzo (Cà is an abbreviated form for casa) at the valley mouth. Here, a mansion-like building catches the eye. Today, a home for the handicapped, in times gone by, it was the Albergo Alpina, where, in 1898, Margherita von Savoyen and her entourage were quartered during a walking holiday. She was, perhaps, Italy's most popular queen, who had not only lent her name to everybody's favourite pizza, but who had also fallen in love with mountain walking. She simply could not miss the chance of personally climbing her mountainous namesake, the Capanna Margherita, as she awaited her forthcoming inauguration in 1893. In the Val Vogna, she took such a liking to *puncetti*, the bobbin lacework that was such a lovely decoration for the local traditional costumes, that she introduced this fashion into her court. Mary Jane Corrigan, an Irishwoman, was also enchanted by this lacework during her own journey to the Val Vogna: »She became the sales representative for a small group of woman from the Piedmont. She rushed

Posto tappa Sant' Antonio di Val Vogna (Stage 17b).

Santuario di Oropa, the most important pilgrimage site in the entire Italian Alps (Stage 20).

from city to city, from country to country and from one trade show to the next, campaigning for the lace here, and for a fair price there, and soon earned the name ›Lady Puncetto‹ «, so wrote Eberhard Neubronner. This writer had dug out a whole treasure of other wonderful stories that had been buried away in the Val Vogna, stories you can find in his book, »Das Schwarze Tal« (The Black Valley). The once extremely bustling valley, lying on the »Antica Via Regia«, the historical trading route from Milan to Lyon, is today, »dull as ditch water«. Only a handful of mostly elderly people still live in the hamlets and cultivate the fields. Relics of the *tempi passati* are on display in the *Museo etnografico*, a restored Walser house from the 16th century, which is located in Rabernardo, further up from Sant' Antonio.

From Val Vogna, we now enter Biellese (the youngest and smallest province in the Piedmont), following pilgrimage trails and spending the night in monasteries. The hinterland of Biella is chock-full of churches and chapels, *Sacri Monti* and pilgrimage sites, including Oropa, one of the most important shrines in Italy. From no other point is the distance between the Alps and the Po Valley so short, ensuring sweeping views, heaping with contrast. At the final pass before the mouth of the Aosta Valley, you enter the Canavese, as the terrain surrounding Ivrea (boasting the headquarters of the Olivetti Company) is called. The name comes from hemp (cannabis) once cultivated here.

17b Alagna – Sant' Antonio di Val Vogna

2.00 hrs.
↑ 260 ↓ 80

Cultural ramble

After a stroll through the pretty passageways of Alagna, continue on the level along the Sesia until reaching Riva Valdobbia, where a painting of »The Last Judgement«, decorating the church, is so striking. Now a steep section, then continue past Walser houses with their typical overhanging wooden porches which were once used to dry hay.

Starting point: Alagna, 1205 m.
Destination: Rif. Sant' Antonio, 1381 m.
Length: 7 km.
Grade: Only occasionally marked. Several kilometres along tarmac. An easy walk.
Refreshment: There is a bar just next to the church at Riva Valdobbia.
Accommodation: Rifugio Sant' Antonio di Val Vogna: 1381 m, open year-round, 20 B, HB 35 €, Silvana und Silvano Ferraris, tel. +39 0163/919 18 or +39 347/336 89 50.
Shopping/Services: Alagna, Stage 17a.
Public transport: From Alagna, bus service to Milano (airport), Vercelli, Varallo (railway station): timetables at www.alagna.it.

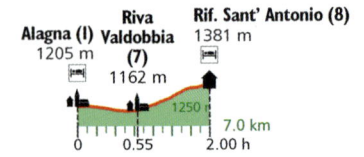

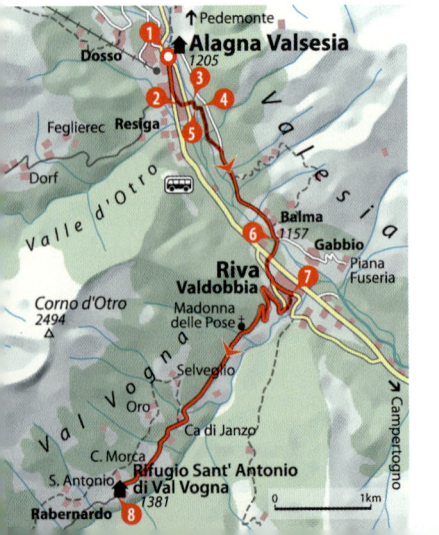

According to the IGC map, the GTA runs along the road; not a good choice. It is better, to cross over to the other bank of the Sesia in **Alagna (1)**, follow the unpaved road to Balma and then turn right along the road to reach **Riva Valdobbia (7)**. Past the church, ascend along the old *mulattiera*, which short-cuts the bends of the road into the Val Vogna. Unfortunately, we must soon follow the road again – a couple of hard kilometres until reaching **Sant' Antonio di Val Vogna (8)**, the *rifugio* is just next to the pretty church.

Photo above: »The Last Judgement« on the church at Riva Valdobbia.

7.30 hrs.
↑1310 ↓540

Sant' Antonio di Val Vogna – Rifugio Rivetti 18

Back and forth between Aosta and the Piedmont

This is a mammoth stretch; at the end, the exhausted trekker can put his legs up at the Rifugio Rivetti. But what a landscape! The Alpe Maccagno, with an enchanting lake, offers a midday repast hosted by the dairy farmers there. One level of height further on, the Lago Nero provides a bathing break. Three passes, connected by a high mountain trail, open up a panorama par excellence.

Starting point: Sant' Antonio, 1381 m.
Destination: Rifugio Rivetti, 2150 m.
Length: 16.1 km.
Grade: Well-marked, only insufficient above the Alpe Maccagno. Until the Passo del Maccagno is reached, the trail isn't very distinct; then it continues over the well-constructed Alta Via della Valle Aosta Nr. 1, a long, mountainous route taking in three passes. Key point is the precipitous descent through crags to the first pass. The other two passes are easy going.
Refreshment: Alpe Maccagno.
Accommodation: Rifugio Rivetti: 2150 m, CAI, , mid-June–mid-Sept., 44 B, HB/AV 45/35 €, creative meals, Sandro Zoia, tel. +39 015/247 61 41.
Shopping: Alpe Maccagno (cheese, sausage).
Public transport: None.

Alpe Maccagno.

Magical sunrise as seen from the Punta Tre Vescovi.

Unfortunately, the old *mulattiera* at the valley floor had to give way to a broader version, at least along the first stretch. Just before reaching **Peccia**, 1529 m, the track road comes to an end and you fork off to the right onto the footpath. To the rear of the hamlet, the little church San Grato appears. A plaque commemorates Giacomo Clerino. He was the first warden of the hospice, high above at the Colle Valdobbia (the pass crossing into the Gressoney valley), and had devoted himself to the care of his guests. On 13 February, 1870, he was killed by an avalanche while showing some trekkers the way to go on.

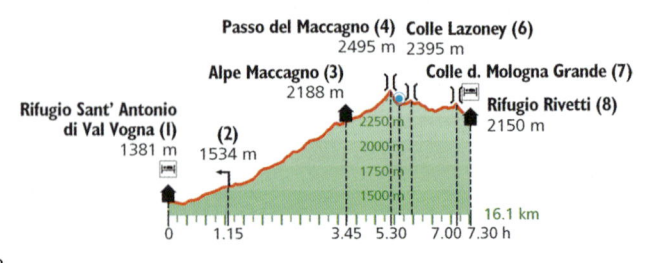

88

Immediately past the Napoleon Bridge, leave the historical traders' trail: turn left and cross over the Torrente Vogna. Then continue into the valley, keeping above the banks of the stream. Past *alpe* pastureland, reach the **Alpe Maccagno (3)**, 2188 m, where the dairy farmers, when asked, will serve you pasta, cheese, sausage and wine (10 €). The young man there, Germano Narchialli, is operating the *alpe* just as three generations of his family have done before him. Every day, about 20 kilos of Toma di Maccagno are produced here. To the right of the Maccagno lake, the route continues. The coloured waymarkers are no longer distinct. For orientation, keep an eye out for cairns, first heading south-eastwards, then southwards to Lago Nero, 2322 m. The route increases in steepness as it crosses through a barren, rocky terrain and onto the **Passo del Maccagno (4)**, 2495 m.

The descent is very precipitous. At a couple of rocky outcrops, you might have to use your hands for scrambling. Now crossing a meadowland plateau, an easy ascent brings you to the **Colle Lazoney (6)**, 2395 m. The traverse along a paved path through numerous boulder fields is located on Aostanian terrain as it reaches the **Colle della Mologna Grande (7)**, 2364 m. If the weather is clear, an excursion onto the Punta Tre Vescovi is tempting; this can be climbed in only 20 mins. starting from the pass. A very steep descent leads in about 30 mins. to the **Rifugio Rivetti (8)**.

19 Rifugio Rivetti – Santuario San Giovanni

6.45 hrs.
↑640 ↓1770

All the things you can build with stones – marvels of the Cervo Valley

The descent to Piedicavallo is a tough one, but delicious cappuccino and brioches are the rewards waiting at the bar there. It is tempting to stay where you are and wait for the bus to come that takes you to Rosazza in comfort. The GTA, however, turns its nose up at modern transport and instead, ascends, at first steeply, to the Selle di Rosazza, only to descend steeply back down again. The route to Rosazza couldn't be more complicated. Is it worth it? For a polenta in the Rifugio Madonna delle Neve, where you can enjoy a stupendous view overlooking the valley, the answer is »yes, it is!« With its unique stone-built buildings, Rosazza is definitely worth an attentive ramble.

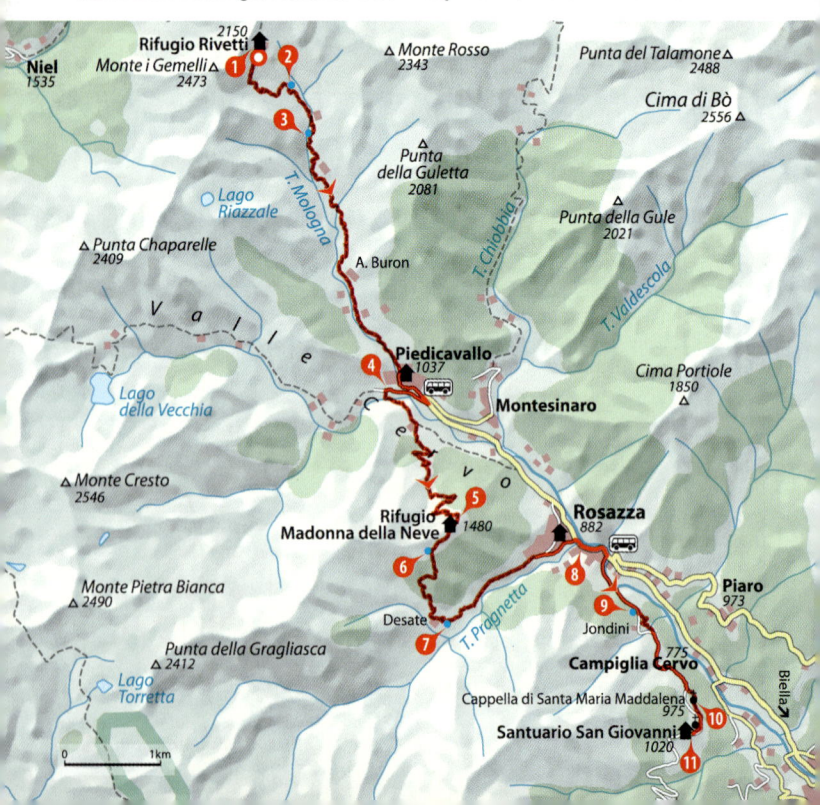

Santuario San Giovanni.

Starting point: Rif. Rivetti, 2150 m.
Destination: San Giovanni, 1020 m.
Length: 16 km.
Grade: Well-marked, distinct trail. A long descent that is hard on your knees.
Refreshment: In Piedicavallo, Rosazza and Madonna della Neve.
Accommodation: Piedicavallo: 1037 m, Albergo Rosa Bianca, open year-round, 20 B, tel. +39 015/60 91 00, www.rosa-bianca.com. – **Rifugio Madonna della Neve** (IGC map: »Rifugio la Sella«): 1480 m, May–Oct., 15 B, HB 33 €, Alberto Rosazza, tel. +39 015/609 70 00, www.rifugio-madonnadellaneve.it. – **Santuario San Giovanni:** 1020 m, open year-round, DR and Posto tappa, 50 B, HB 45 €, tel. +39 015/600 07.
Shopping/Services: Shop, cash dispenser, post office in Piedicavallo and Rosazza.
Public transport: From Piedicavallo and Rosazza, the bus line 16 service to the railway station in Biella (timetable: www.atapspa.it).
Tip: Guided tour of Rosazza/museum, F/I, Gianni Valz Blin, tel. +39 331/283 77 79.
Alternative: The trail along the stream to Rosazza saves about 1 hr. of time.

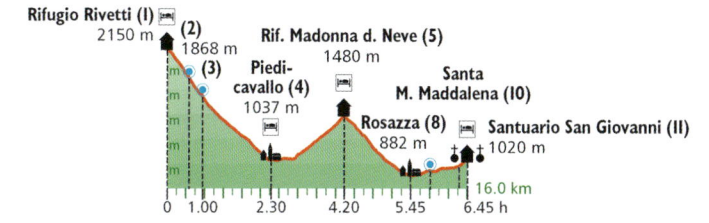

From the **rifugio (1)** a well-marked route leads down the valley to **Piedicavallo (4)**, 1037 m. Head to the stream at the sports complex and then cross over the Ponte della Coda. At first, turn left along the stream bank then turn right, ascending steeply, to reach **Madonna della Neve (5)**, 1480 m, and then descend again via the lovely hamlet **Desate (7)** to reach **Rosazza (8)**, 882 m.

> *Rosazza preserves the memory of a renowned architect, not only through its name. A native son, who was both a lawyer and a senator, Federico Rosazza (1813–1899), had invested his money in the construction of a number of public buildings. Inspired by his countless journeys exploring many different architectural styles, the village has developed a very unusual appearance. The church reflects the Lombard style. Other buildings are reminiscent of Scotland. Nestled between the old Walser houses, these present an interesting contrast. Gianni Valz Blins' ancestors were Walser who had settled in the upper Cervo Valley or »Bursch«, as they called it. Without the personal initiative of this 75 year-old architect, one would shamble through the village without a single clue. Instead, information boards have been erected to point out what's interesting, and, above all, his museum. In the »Casa Museo«, not only are the usual everyday utensils on display, but also time-yellowed photographs portray bold visages of men who had mastered the art of quarrying stone and who, in the winter months, went away to all corners of the earth to work as stone masons and bricklayers. Men from the Cervo Valley took part in the construction of the cathedral in Milan, the Certosa di Pavia, the Savoyian fortresses such as Fenestrelle and Exilles, the pass roads at Mont Cenis and Simplon ..., but also overseas, in New York, South America, Asia ... Some of the quarries located in the Cervo Valley, the »Valle di Pietra«, have been abandoned, it's true, but syenit is still quarried even today. This hard, granitic rock, named after the ancient Egyptian Syene where it was once mined (modern-day Aswan), is extremely rare in Europe. The yellowed photographs also portray the resilient womenfolk; while the men hammered away, they were the matrons of domestic life, of child-rearing and of farming. On top of that, they fashioned harvested hemp into clothing, bedclothes and »Scapin«, as the warm and comfy house slippers were called. Today, most of the inhabitants of the Cervo Valley are commuters – in the morning, driving away to their employers in the lowlands, and in the evening, returning to the valley.*

From Rosazza, take the main road down the valley. At the intersection, turn right onto the road which ascends to San Giovanni, then turn left into the hamlet of Jondini (also called Gliondini). Along a romantic *mulattiera*, reach the **Cappella di Santa Maria Maddalena (10)**. A peek inside, using your head torch to light up the pitch dark interior, is worthwhile.

Here, meet up with an ancient pilgrim's trail which runs parallel to the road heading to **San Giovanni (11)**.

Rosazza.

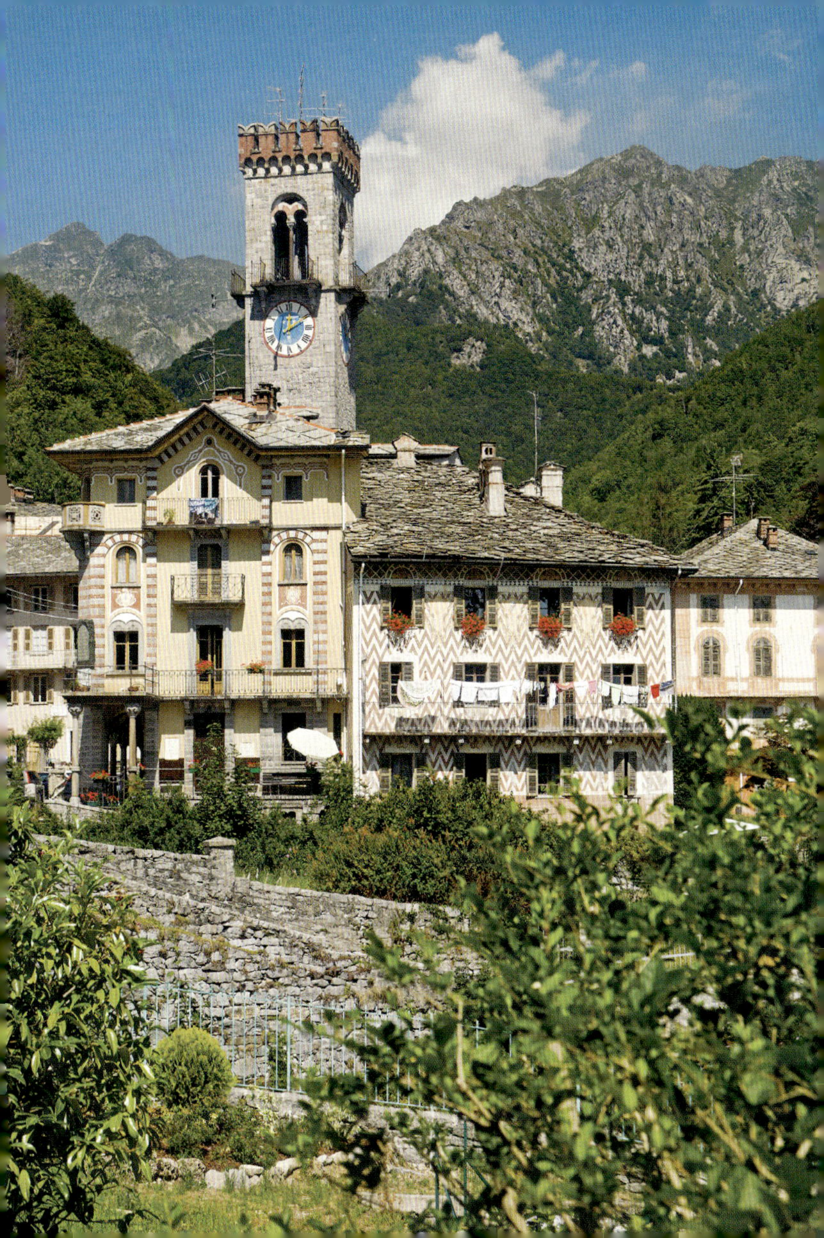

20 Santuario San Giovanni – Oropa

3.15 hrs.
↑240 ↓110

Mosey along to a monastery

The GTA ascends steeply to Locanda and Galleria di Rosazza, two interesting constructions (1897). The only disadvantage for the trekker: the road that had once been closed now is open to public use and, as the continuation of the »Strada Panoramica Zegna«, connects the Cervo Valley to Oropa. Because of this, we recommend continuing along the quiet and contemplative Tracciolino, that connects two monasteries without negotiating any great differences in height. The course of the route, which is also known as the Alta Via della Feda, is displayed on a information board directly at the arched gate of the hospice of San Giovanni.

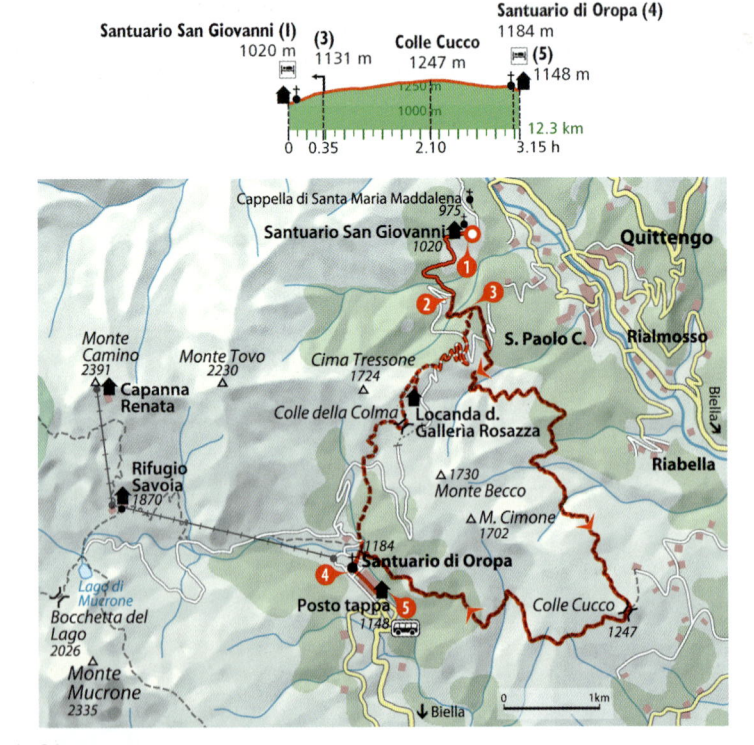

94

The view from Monte Camino of Biella and the Po Valley plain.

Starting point: Santuario San Giovani, 1020 m.
Destination: Oropa, 1148 m.
Length: 12.3 km.
Grade: Well-marked but sometimes the Tracciolino is somewhat overgrown. This is a level walk.
Refreshment: Nothing en route.
Accommodation: Locanda della Galleria Rosazza (for those who choose to remain on the GTA): 1622 m, mid-June–mid-Sept., mid-April–Oct. at the weekends, 20 B, tel. +39 337/24 74 40. – **Santuario di Oropa:** 1184 m, open year-round, DR (34 €) up to 4-bed dorms (50 €), capacity 571 persons, a number of restaurants, tel. +39 015/ 25 55 12 00 or 255 51 11, www.santuariodioropa.it. – **Capanna Renata:** 2391 m, 8 B, tel. +39 015/204 37. – **Rifugio Savoia:** see Stage 21.
Shopping/Services: Oropa: Shops, cash dispenser, pharmacy, post office.
Public transport: Bus line 2 provides hourly service from Oropa to Biella, 14 km. away (timetable: www.atapspa.it).
Tip: A viewing point par excellence is the Capanna Renata just below the Monte Camino. If you arrive early enough in Oropa, you can take the cable car at 3:30 p.m. to the mountain station Oropa-Sport, and then catch the last scheduled run of the antiquated basket lift which will take you directly to the hut. Stunning view of the Matterhorn & Co, and the evening lights of the Po Valley.
Information: ATL Biella, tel. +39 015/35 11 28, www.atl.biella.it.

From the **Santuario (1)**, take the road for a stretch then turn left onto the old trail towards Bele, where a few houses in the »Swiss Chalet« style are standing. Meet up with the main road once again and follow this to a right-hand bend with a white house. Turn left onto the GTA, which is also the Alta Via della Fede. After crossing over two stream courses, the GTA forks off to the right while the Tracciolino continues to the left. Along a broad track, not always maintained, follow the same level of height at first through woods, then through the open *alpe* terrain below the Monte Cucco. At the **Colle Cucco**, 1247 m, you find yourself standing with the Po Valley and Biella lying directly below you. On this spot in 1987, by the way, the environmental protection organization, Mountain Wilderness, was founded as the result of a proposal made by Reinhold Messner. The trail now leads into the valley of **Oropa**, soon entering a wood, and then reaches the broad promenade ending at the **pilgrims' complex (4)**, the immensity of which is a true marvel.

> *Oropa:* almost like a little city – shops, souvenir boutiques, pharmacy, restaurants, cafés and accommodation ranging from a Spartan attic room to a luxury suite. 800,000 pilgrims visit the shrine every year and more than 100 processions are held here. In the evening, the hustle and bustle subsides and the more contemplative spiritual ambience is revealed. The focus of worship is the Black Madonna. This is displayed in the ancient basilica, which seems rather modest when compared to the Baroque architecture of the 80 metre high, domed church which towers over everything around it (3000 worshippers can find space inside). Next to this monumental grandeur, the Sacro Monte, with its 12 chapels hidden away in a wood, is hardly noticeable. Since 2003, the pilgrimage site, along with other Sacri Monti of the Piedmont and Lombardy, has been declared a UNESCO World Heritage Site.

Oropa.

6.30 hrs.
↑ 860 ↓ 1280

Oropa – Trovinasse | 21

A rugged trail into the Canavese

Boulder fields and a secured path along a sharp ridge highlight the route to the Colle della Lace. When the weather is clear, the stretch is accompanied by an extraordinary panorama. The Alps beyond, in the Canavese region, are still intensely farmed. Cattle have seriously roughened up the trail along some stretches.

Starting point: Oropa, 1148 m, alternatively Oropa-Sport, 1870 m.
Destination: Trovinasse, 1453 m.
Length: 14.9 km.
Grade: Well-marked; only one leg is lacking in markings, between the Colle della Lace and the Alpe Druer. Until reaching the Rif. Coda, there are numerous boulder fields to cross; there's a stretch along a ridge to Colle della Lace (sure-footedness and an absolute head for heights required), although the route is well secured by a wire cable and steps. The descent is easier along *alpe* trails.
Refreshment: Rifugio Coda.
Accommodation: Mountain station Oropa-Sport: Rifugio Rosazza, 1850 m, CAI, 33 B, Claudia Comello, tel. +39 0339/460 21 33. Rifugio Savoia, 1870 m, 40 B, HB 40 €, Fabrizio Bazzocchi, tel. +39 015/849 51 31, both open daily June–Sept., May/Oct. at the weekends. – **Rifugio Coda:** 2280 m, CAI, beg. July–beg. Sept., mid-May–mid-Oct. at the weekends, 53 B, HB/AV 44/35 €, Christina Chiappo, tel. +39 015/256 24 05. – **Alpe Quartiere delle Trovinasse:** 1453 m, Agriturismo Belvedere, 18 B, HB 35 €, accommodating family business, fantastic food, Simona Nicoletta, tel. +39 0125/65 87 31 or +39 333/ 241 58 16. – **Rifugio Mombarone:** 2312 m, mid-June–Sept. at the weekends, mid-July–end Aug. daily, 25 B, tel. +39 015/40 19 60.
Shopping: Cheese at the Alpe Druer.
Public transport: Oropa see Stage 20.
Information: ATL Biella, tel. +39 015/35 11 28, www.atl.biella.it.
Notes: Funivie Oropa: June 9–20/Sept 8–28 Tues–Fri 8:30 a.m.–12:30 p.m., 1:30 p.m.– 5 p.m., Sat/Sun until 5:30 p.m. July 21–Sept. 7 Mon–Fri until 5:30 p.m., Sat/Sun 7:30 a.m.–9:50 p.m., tel. +39 015/245 59 29, www.funivieoropa.it. – if you prefer not taking the cable car, you should take two days for this stretch and spend a night in the Rifugio Coda (4.30 hrs.).
Alternative: From the Colle della Lace, at the ridge, continue on to Mombarone, the last peak facing the Po Valley, to enjoy a mind-boggling view. Descent: continue via the Alpe di Mombarone to the *agriturismo* of Trovinasse; same walking time.

From the **mountain terminus of the cable car**, 1870 m, pass the **Rifugio Savoia (2)**, and shortly before reaching the Lago di Mucrone at the Fonte del Bersagliere, turn right to climb up to the **Bocchetta del Lago (4)**, 2026 m. Descend slightly, then traverse through the valley head of the Valle Elvo, over a field of boulders. The route steepens (a couple of tricky spots are secured) and leads to the **Rifugio Coda (5)** west of the trail, and onto the ridge that separates the Biellese from the Aosta region. A 5-min. excursion to the Punta della Sella, 2315 m, presents a view of the Monte Rosa. Otherwise, you can feast on the Gran Paradiso or on the food at the hut, served by Christina. If you are wondering why the sugar cubes in the large preserve jars on the shelves above the bar do not dissolve, the answer lies in the hard alcohol therein. When you put one of these *Zuccherini* on your tongue, you'll enjoy the most amazing flavour combinations. Be sure to try one tasting of clove!

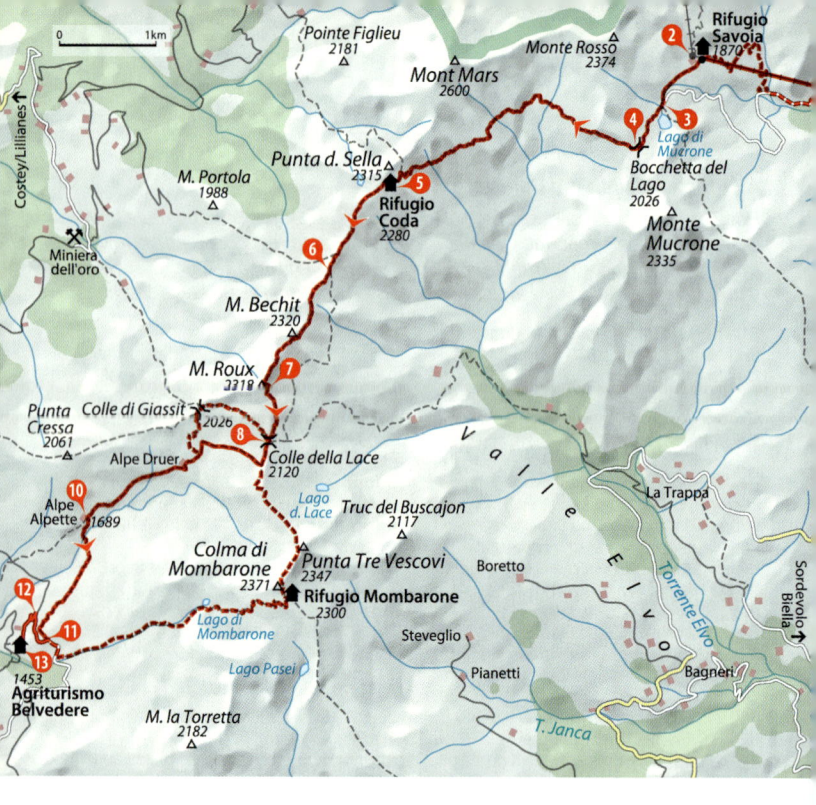

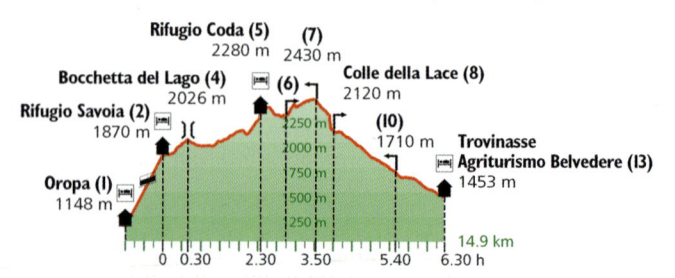

98

Continue along the ridge to reach the Colle di Carisey. When the GTA forks off to the left shortly after, ignore it. The trail has become so overgrown and tricky in the meantime that the ridge route, marked in yellow (Alta Via della Valle Aosta 1) and blue (AV delle Alpi Biellese), is a better bet. Although mostly secured just like a *via ferrata*, this stretch lacks safety measures in a couple of spots. At the **Colle della Lace (8)**, 2120 m, meet up again with the GTA, which, however, does not follow the same route as the yellow-marked AV1 to the Colle di Giassit. From the pass, the GTA descends directly westwards to climb down to the Alpe Druer. This unmarked stretch is scheduled to be restored.

Past the **Alpe Druer**, head down the valley until reaching the Alpe Alpette, 1689 m. Because the *Posto tappa* in Maletto is closed, turn left towards Trovinasse. This route is also marked red/white/red. Climb down to the stream. Past the bridge, pick up a *mulattiera* to traverse southwards. Afterwards, descend through the woods to a house on a road only to find that the markings have disappeared once again. Turn right onto the road to descend, and at the first fork, turn left onto the track to reach the **agriturismo (13)**.

Rifugio Coda.

22a Trovinasse – Quincinetto

3.00 hrs.
↑30 ↓1180

Gateway to the Aosta Valley and the lowest height of the Piedmont

The mulattiera which leads into the valley of the Dora Baltea awaits us with idyllic passages. You will cross through archaic hamlets and scattered tumbledown, stone-built houses in a chestnut forest. At last, the climate becomes more Mediterranean. Grape vines are entwined like garlands around pergolas, and porticos span terrace after terrace along the slope. The ancient methods of cultivation, going back to the Romans, lend the landscape a very extraordinary aspect. Here, one of the very best Nebbiolo wines is produced. At 295 metres above sea level, you will not get any lower for this journey on foot, that is, apart from your final destination on the Mediterranean seacoast.

Quincinetto.

Starting point: Agriturismo Belvedere, 1453 m.
Destination: Quincinetto, 295 m.
Length: 7.8 km.
Grade: The waymarkers (trail No. 854) are not always easy to spot. If you lose the trail, you will always automatically meet up again with the road and return, further down, along the true trail. The IGC map is useless for this stretch. Ideally, you would have the map Alpi Canavesane 02, MU edizioni for reference.

Refreshment: Nothing en route.
Accommodation: Quincinetto: 295 m, Hotel Praiale near the church, 8 DR, breakfast only, DR 50 €, tel. +39 0125/75 71 88, www.hotelpraiale.it. B&B Cascina Salet, 1 km towards Tavagnasco, DR 60 €, tel. +39 340/556 49 70, www.cascinasalet.com.
Shopping: Quincinetto: Shops, restaurants, cash dispenser, pharmacy, post office.
Public transport: Bus line 22 Quincinetto – Carema – Ivrea – Torino (timetable: www.sadem.it).

From the **agriturismo (1)**, straight down and, at the parking place, along the broad and grassy trail which turns left into the woods and continues on to Trovinasse. A trail short-cuts the grassy trail and then crosses over two very lovely Roman bridges, but the turn-off to the right past a house is easy to miss. Just past the church from **Trovinasse**, 1374 m, turn left onto the trail No. 854 heading towards Torredaniele. The trail crosses over the road time and again; the waymarkers are often not easy to spot; you have to keep a good eye out. Afterwards, a longer stretch through the woods until reaching the street at Sengie, 419 m. Descend a short way down the street until, in a left-hand bend, the trail to Airale forks off to the right. From **Airale** descend to the main road, but shortly before reaching it, turn left onto the footpath that runs parallel. Continue until you see a white house and then turn off to the right to reach the intersection. Cross over the bridge to reach **Quincinetto (4)**.

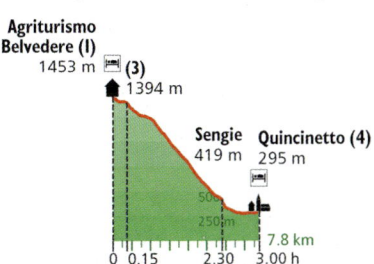

The Canavese and the wild side of the Gran Paradiso National Park

The Dora Baltea valley separates the Valaisian Alps from the Graian Alps, whose highest peak is the Gran Paradiso.
King Vittorio Emanuele II, at the time, the regent ruler of Savoy and Piedmont, and later, king of the newly founded country of Italy, worried about his favourite pastime and so ordained a strict ban on hunting in the last refuge of the alpine ibex around the Gran Paradiso, and in 1856, proclaimed this area as his exclusive hunting grounds. That environmental protection did not play the slightest role in the king's concern for the pending total extinction of the ibex is made evident by the fact that when Switzerland was asked to sell young animals to the king to populate the area, a firm refusal was the answer. The result was a cloak and dagger operation in the summer of 1906 whereby, with the help of poachers, ibex kids were stolen from the strictly

protected preserves and then smuggled over the border. Hence, the ibex was successfully reintroduced to other Alpine regions.
The king's successor, Vittorio Emanuele III, made a present of the royal hunting grounds in the end – in 1919, he gave it to the Italian government, under the condition that the area would be made into a national park. Three years later, an area measuring 703 square kilometres, shared just about equally by the Piedmont and Aosta regions, was declared the first national park in Italy. While the Aosta side of the national park is well-developed for tourism, and in summer, a bustling business is underway, the GTA penetrates into the untamed, little-known opposite side of the nature reserve. This route provides pure solitude, bold pass crossings and villages in the back of beyond. Only in Ceresole Reale can you find a pulsing tourism, but even there, just in August. Vittorio Emanuele II liked to spend some nights there which is why Ceresole bears a royal title.

Lago Agnel, Lago Serru (Stage 28, see Tip).

22b *Quincinetto – Le Capanne*

4.00 hrs.
↑1110 ↓0

A change in flora – from Mediterranean to Alpine

Through vineyards, we ascend to the heights again. The mulattiera is sometimes artfully cobbled. If the weather is hot, you will enjoy the pleasant coolness of the forest. At the end, we are greeted by open alpe terrain where an overnight in an agriturismo awaits us.

Starting point: Quincinetto, 295 m.
Destination: Le Capanne, 1400 m.
Length: 5.8 km.
Grade: Well-marked, mostly a broad mule track. Strenuous ascent.
Refreshment: Nothing en route.
Accommodation: Agriturismo Le Capanne: 1400 m, beg. April–beg. Nov., 15 B in a dormitory HB 30 €, 4 DR HB 40 €, Monetta familiy, tel. +39 0125/75 73 97.
Shopping: In Quincinetto.
Public transport: Quincinetto is on the bus line No. 22 Torino-Carema (www.sadem.it).
Information: www.comune.quincinetto.to.it.

Past the **church**, turn right into the passageway and continue ascending through the village. Now cross through vineyards and enter a wood. The unspoiled *mulattiera* winds steeply to a rocky viewing point with a wayside shrine. An excursion into a **quartz mine** presents a cool break. After about 1 hr., the mule track meets up with a road. Short-cut the bends and then reach the hamlet of **Preghera**, 780 m. Continue to the

Santa Maria.

A quartz mine on the side of the trail above Quincinetto.

chapel of **Santa Maria (2)**, 915 m. Head along the road until you reach a **shelter with a madonna (3)**. Turn left to cross the bridge, pick up the *mulattiera* and sometimes ascend quite steeply. Before Frera inferiore, meet up again with the road and short-cut this. At the trail junction above Frera, do not turn right towards Scalaro; instead, turn left onto the country lane to climb up to the recently modernized **Agriturismo Le Capanne (4)** (IGC map: Le Cavanne).

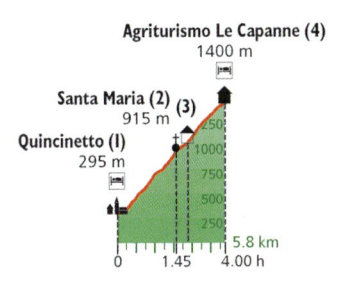

23 Le Capanne – Fondo

6.00 hrs.
↑850 ↓1170

Milk: the Alpine energy drink

This is a panoramic route featuring entertainment at the Alpe Chiaromonte where Giorgio and Maria enjoy serving trekkers polenta, cheese and fresh milk. The two free spirits lead a life as it was a century ago. They are only here for about a month, however, starting from around the end of July. The descent into the Val Chiusella leads through steep, exposed grassy slopes and requires your close attention. Starting at the hamlet of Cappia, you can relax again while walking a quiet, high mountain trail.

Starting point: Le Capanne, 1400 m.
Destination: Fondo, 1074 m.
Length: 13.8 km.
Grade: Not always well-marked. The stretch to the Rif. Chiaromonte is incorrectly drawn on the IGC map (correct route on map No. 02/MU edizioni). Starting at Fumà inferiore, the trail to the Alpe Chiaromonte is simple, then somewhat trickier as it leads through steep grassy slopes, demanding absolute sure-footedness.
Refreshment: Alpe Chiaromonte.
Accommodation: Rifugio Chiaromonte: 2015 m, self-catering hut, 14 B, 5 €, open during *alpe* season July/Aug., then you can get an evening meal in the neighbouring *alpe*, Maria & Giorgio Marino, Alpe Chiaromonte, tel. +39 0338/276 46 07. –
Fondo: 1074 m, Trattoria del Ponte, open year-round, 2 R with 3 B, HB 32 €, tel. +39 0125/74 91 24. Beautifully situated, next to the arched bridge, but, unfortunately, rather unkempt; the meals are good though. If booked out, guests will be transported to the B&B La Traleua (+39 0125/74 90 87) 7 kms away, managed by Luci-

Alpe Chiaromonte, Giorgio milking.

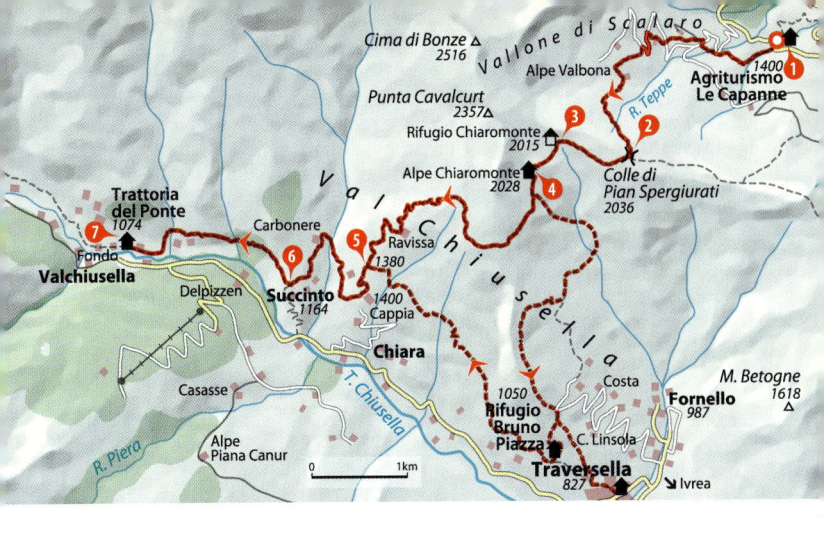

ana and Luigino Beratto's daughter Rosanna, private mineral museum. – **Rifugio Bruno Piazza:** 1050 m, mid-July–beg. Sept., otherwise at the weekends, 25 B,HB/AV45/36 €,tel. +39 0125/74 92 33.
Shopping: In Traversella shop, post office.
Public transport: GTT bus line Traversella – Ivrea (www.comune.torino.it/gtt/intercomunale/percorari.shtml).
Alternative: From the Alpe Chiaromonte, you could choose instead to descend to the village of Traversella (3 hrs.) where you can find comfortable accommodation and good food at the Albergo Miniere, tel. +39 0125/74 90 05, www.albergominiere.com. Interesting mining museum (May–Sept., Sat. 2–6 p.m., Sun. 10 a.m.–12 p.m. & 2–6 p.m.) includes mineral exhibits and a tour through the mine shafts (www.gmv.traversella.com). The next day, continue along the Sentiero delle Anime to Cappia to pick up the GTA (4 hrs. to Fondo).

Ascend behind the barn of the **agriturismo (1)**. Caution: cow paths can lead you somewhat astray: look out for waymarkers which lead above and to the right of the stream and, on the opposite side of the Rio Teppe, to the house at

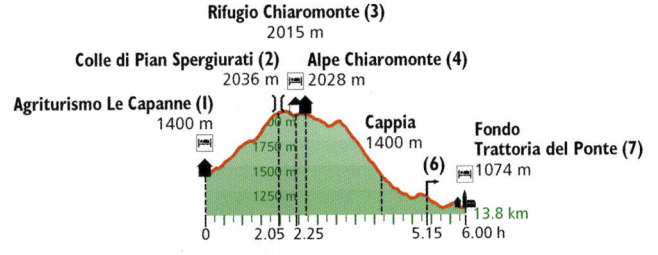

107

Fumà inferiore. Be sure to ascend to the house itself and the *alpe* road, otherwise you'll miss the trail sign. Then, the route continues without a problem. Head westwards over the meadow to Alpe Fumà superiore and on to Cavanna Nuova. Now a short stretch along the *alpe* road, then left onto the path to reach the **Alpe Valbona**. Climb up to the ridge. What do we see below?

> *La Serra Morenica:* Europe's largest moraine wraps around Ivrea like a snake. What a stage setting! This ring of wooded hillocks reveals the glacial flow of the Dora Baltea glacier which, during the last ice age, stretched from Mont Blanc far into the plain of the Po Valley. The British alpine pioneer, Edward Whymper, was so fascinated by the area that he began to make some calculations: during his era, the mid-19th century, from the rock faces of Mont Blanc to the valley floor, he measured a distance of about 128 kilometres; If the glacier moved about 121 metres per year, the debris must have taken at least 1055 years to reach this point; he noted this in »Scrambles amongst the Alps«. The ice sheet must have been around 500 metres thick. – A fascinating bird's-eye view of this can be enjoyed from the ridge.

Beyond the **Colle di Pian Spergiurati (2)**, 2036 m (nameless in the IGC map), the path crosses to the northwest and drops down into the alpine basin to the **Rifugio Chiaromonte (3)**, 2015 m. Some minutes later, meet up with the **Alpe Chiaromonte (4)**. A couple of metres below the huts, the trail continues in a south-westerly traverse. At a trail junction, you could turn left to descend to Traversella. The GTA, however, keeps to the same height for the moment. As an extremely narrow, sometimes overgrown path, the route leads around the southern ridge of the Punta Cavalcurt, crossing precipitous grassy slopes before descending steeply to pass the *alpe* huts of Binelli, Pertusa and Ravissa.

At the first houses of **Cappia** the waymarkers are irritating; we do not continue to the right along the red/white marked trail, but instead, descend between the houses over the mountain ridge until meeting up with a fork; turn right here. Passing under rock faces, continue on to a rise with a shrine for the Madonna and enjoy a marvellous view of Succinto. The *mulattiera* drops down northwards to a stream where a rock pool provides a refreshing break. Now ascend in a traverse to **Succinto (6)**, 1164 m, where a couple of holiday homes give evidence of people present. The high mountain trail leads to **Fondo**, mixed with surprising stretches of ascent. Immediately at the photogenic arched bridge, you will find an **accommodation (7)**.

The medieval arched bridge at Fondo's Posto tappa.

24 Fondo – Piamprato

6.30 hrs.
↑1350 ↓870

From Val Chiusella into the Soana Valley

Ornate arched bridges and giant boulders left over from landslides lend the valley floor a special flair. Climbing ever upwards from alp to alp, a fantastic view will open up. Beyond the Bocchetta delle Oche is no man's land. Rocky stretches are followed by bushy undergrowth; if you are lucky, the stretch has been cleared by the GTA's maintenance team in the meantime. The route then becomes a tad more romantic as the trail leads through a narrow gorge with a thundering waterfall at the eastern edge of the Gran Paradiso National Park.

Starting point: Fondo, 1074 m.
Destination: Piamprato, 1551 m.
Length: 13.5 km.
Grade: Well-marked, beginning at the upper *alpe* terrain, the trail is no longer very distinct; long ascent; the descent demands sure-footedness since uneven ground with holes is hidden by the undergrowth; a couple of tilted plates of rock, slippery when wet; the chains securing the route are not always placed in the most logical positions.
Refreshment: Nothing en route.

Accommodation: Piamprato: 1551 m. Agriturismo Aquila Bianca, 12 R with 4 B, HB 45 €, very good food, Renza Zanfra and Roberto Chiolerio, tel. +39 0124/81 29 93 or 683 22. Posto tappa (8 B, 8 €) in the old village school, very neglected in the past, now managed by the agriturismo and better maintained as a result.
Shopping: Travelling vegetable and fruit stand in Piamprato Tues/Fri starting around 9 am.
Public transport: Bus service Piamprato – Ronco July–Sept. 9:20 a.m. and 5:30 p.m.

Start with a leisurely route along a *mulattiera* flanked with dry stone walls, which leads along the right bank of the stream. Stone-built huts are scattered between rocky boulders. Cross through the archaic **Tallorno (2)**, 1214 m, and then continue to the Alpe Pasquère, 1486 m. A little later, at an

Bridge near the Alpe Pasquère.

arched bridge, keep to the right bank of the stream and do not change over to the other bank until you pass the **Alpe Pra**, 1625 m. The route steepens as you cross the *alpe* terrain, rutted by stream courses, in a north-westerly direction, then reach **Bocchetta delle Oche (4)**, 2415 m. The descent over sometimes rocky, sometimes meadow-blanketed terraces begins easily enough but soon becomes rather unpleasant. A couple of perilous plates of rock must be negotiated as the maw of a gorge nips at your heels. Alder bushes provide a mock sense of security in the event of a tumble but are quite annoying when they tangle up the trail. Finally, reach the stream where the steep descent comes to an end. After crossing over the stream, a tight-rope act continues along a partially secured rock face trail which leads through the gorge. Now continue north-westwards over meadowland to a high tension pylon and then through the woods, then descend to **Piamprato (6)**.

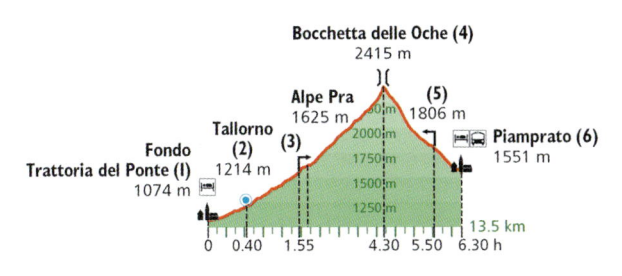

25 Piamprato/Ronco – Talosio

6.15 hrs.
↑1180 ↓900

Highs and lows at the edge of the Gran Paradiso National Park

The Cima Rosta ridge.

Since the GTA follows long stretches of the road as it crosses through the Soana Valley to Ronco, you may prefer to take a bus instead. The Alps pioneer, Francis Fox Tuckett, who circuit-walked the Gran Paradiso in 1859, was, even then, unable to find a kind word for the only (even today) Posto tappa in Ronco: »An inspection of the inn was terrible.« Nevertheless, the settlement exhibits a certain charm. It is only a pity that the mayor seems to be so blasé about tourism, but maybe this will all change in the future. Via a panoramic ridge, we will change over into the Val di Ribordone. Here, too, not a trace of tourism is to be found. You will have to spend the night in the old schoolhouse in Talosio.

Starting point: Piamprato, 1551 m, or Ronco, 948 m.
Destination: Talosio, 1225 m.
Length: 14 km.
Grade: Well-marked but the trail is sometimes not very distinct. Cow paths sometimes confuse the route.
Refreshment: In Ronco.
Accommodation: Ronco: 948 m, Albergo Centrale, B&B, 3 DR, 40 €, tel. +39 0124/81 74 01. – **Valprato** (see »Tip«): 1116 m, Locanda Alpina, 5 DR, 50 €, tel. +39 0124/81 29 29. – Talosio: 1225 m, Posto tappa in the old schoolhouse, the key (and meals as well) can be had in the Trattoria Grisolano, the village's only restaurant, 17 B, HB 40 €, bountiful breakfast, Marina and Alberto Grisolano, tel. +39 0124/81 80 15 or +39 340/91 91 958. A Posto tappa (8 B, kitchen) has been set up in the **Santuario di Prascondù** (opening planned for 2013).

Shopping/Services: Ronco: Shop, bank, pharmacy, post office, restaurants (Lo Moderno: good Pizzeria, Rock Café with live music, www.lomoderno.it). Talosio: you can buy groceries in the Trattoria.
Public transport: Bus service Piamprato – Ronco July–Sept. 9:20 a.m. and 5:30 p.m. GTT bus line from Ronco and Talosio to Pont (www.comune.torino.it/gtt/intercomunale/percorari.shtml).
Tip: A marvellous insight into a virtually unknown area of the Gran Paradiso National Park can be experienced along the well-marked route from Piamprato via the Colle della Borra into the Valle di Campiglia (4.30 hrs), the same route that so thrilled the Alps pioneer Francis Fox Tuckett in 1859. After reaching Campiglia Soana, you have to pay the piper with a couple of kilometres of tarmac road: 2.8 km to Valprato and another 3 km to Ronco.

From **Ronco (1)**, 948 m, descend along the main road until crossing over the bridge. At the second street, turn right and pass the hamlet of Bosco, 900 m. Continue along several kilometres of tarmac until the road ends near **Masonaje (3)**, 1201 m. For the next two days, the GTA shares the same course with the Alta Via Canavese (AVC). Cross through the hamlet and then head south-westwards up the valley. Past the woods, livestock paths confuse the course of the route. Bearing left, cross over a secondary stream and then ascend to the **Alpe Cavanis (4)** (spring). Skirt around with the *alpe* to your right and then reach the Alpe Goie lying to the north. Now the route steepens as it continues westward onto a broad meadow-blanketed ridge. Before the ridge breaks off into the neighbouring valley, cross the Pian delle Masche. Keep right to ascend onto the southern ridge of the Cima Rosta. Traverse the steep grassy slopes below the summit while enjoying an overwhelming view to the Po Valley plain; reach the **Colle Crest (8)**, 2040 m. Descend along zigzags in a southerly direction to reach the **Alpe Rocco (10)**, 1812 m (spring). Descend to the right then traverse to the left to reach a saddle; continue to the right. Past a patch of woods, left to the ruins of Barlan. Once there, you will find that you have missed the GTA, but a path descends to the stream below where you can meet up with it again. After crossing the stream, soon reach the **Santuario di Prascondù**, 1321 m. Although the GTA follows the road to **Talosio (11)**, the old *mulattiera* along the left bank is a far prettier choice.

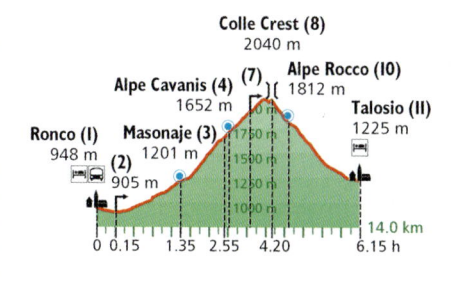

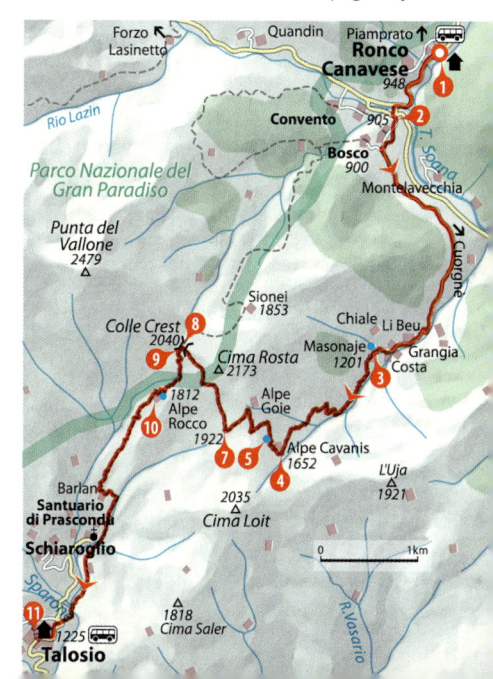

26 Talosio – San Lorenzo

7.30 hrs.
↑ 1370 ↓ 1550

The wild side of the Gran Paradiso National Park

To be honest, the ascents inbetween are not exactly pleasant but the impression left by the landscape is simply fabulous. This already begins below the Monte Arzola at the Redentore, a statue of »the Savior«, stretching his hands out to heaven. Also stunning is the downward view into the Orco Valley, as well as the one taking in Gran Paradiso with its rugged flanks.

Starting point: Talosio, 1225 m.
Destination: San Lorenzo, 1045 m.
Length: 15.4 km.
Grade: Well-marked, mainly indistinct trail with rocky stretches, numerous ascents in between; final descent long and wearisome.
Refreshment: Nothing en route.
Accommodation: Bivacco Blessent Redentore: 1976 m, 5 mins. away from the trail, always open, 3 mattresses, no cooking facilities. – **San Lorenzo:** 1045 m, Albergo degli Amici, open year-round, 20 B, HB 35 €, pretty, but very damp lodging, sweaty clothing hard to dry here; Ernesta Procarione and Adriano Pezzetti, tel. +39 0124/80 01 95 or +39 349/217 25 88. Trattoria San Lorenzo, 4 B, Simone Reale is a guide for the Gran Paradiso National Park, tel. +39 0124/80 02 13 and +39 340/126 03 43, www.sanlorenzotrattoria.it. The Posto tappa here (7 B, without running water), showed signs of neglect on our last visit.
Shopping: Talosio and San Lorenzo.
Public transport: Bus service from Talosio and San Lorenzo into the main valley.

We recommend an early start. From the **restaurant (1)**, take passageways to reach the church, pass through an archway in the row of houses above the church, and finally, along a *mulattiera*, reach the road further above. Waymarkers do not appear until reaching this point. Climb up the road then turn left through the Frazione Posio. Now along a good *alpe* trail, reach the huts at **Arzola** to continue along the southern ridge of the Monte Arzola. A path forking left leads, in some minutes, to the pilgrimage chapel of Madonna della Neve and the **Cristo Redentore**. Otherwise, keep bearing right, but not onto the intersecting trail with the hope of saving some height since this path peters out later on. The GTA, on the other hand, climbs the Monte Arzola,

View from Monte Arzola taking in the Orco Valley.

2158 m, not going quite the whole way but passing somewhat below the peak along the summit ridge to a nameless **pass (4)**, 2175 m. There is a more precipitous descent to the northwest to the reservoir in view. At the end, you have to struggle with a few metres of height since, unfortunately, you cannot cross over on the dam wall; instead you must go below and around it. Not until reaching the rearmost point do you cross over a stretch of the dam wall. Now descend along a broad track road. About 15 mins. later, the GTA turns off to the right. At the beginning, the tree-lined route is lovely, then it climbs steeper up the slope north-westwards to reach the saddle at the **Alpe di Colla (7)**, 2171 m, where a tidy hut, belonging to the national park, is standing. Behind the hut, there is a water tap and a mirror! Traverse to the **Alpe Praghetta (9),** and before reaching the *alpe* huts, descend steeply. At the outset, the waymarkers are not easy to spot. The maintenance team showed deference to the most direct way and not to the old *mulattiera*. Not until we are further down does the route follow the better laid mule track. After negotiating many zigzags, reach the cascades of a stream and, afterwards, a fork in the trail. Turn left here to descend to **San Lorenzo (11)**.

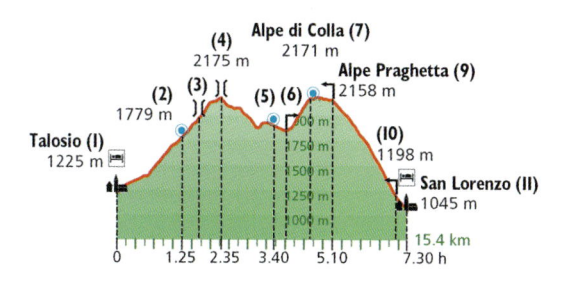

115

| 27 | **San Lorenzo – Noasca** | 5.30 hrs.
↑810 ↓790 |

Vanished alpes above the Valle dell'Orco

For many years, the GTA was interrupted here, but finally, the overgrown stretches have been cleared away again. This panoramic route leads along the edge of the Gran Paradiso National Park, then drops down into the valley and, along a Sentiero Natura, enters a village at a waterfall. The Noaschetta Falls cascading down between dark cliffs was already an attraction in the early days of tourism.

Starting point: San Lorenzo, 1045 m.
Destination: Noasca, 1058 m.
Length: 13.4 km.
Grade: Well-marked, newly laid trail; an easy high mountain and valley walk.
Refreshment: Nothing en route.
Accommodation: Noasca: 1058 m, Albergo Gran Paradiso, open year-round, 26 B (DR and Posto tappa), HB 40 €, very good meals, tel. +39 0124/90 18 10 and +39 340/472 93 34.
Shopping: Noasca: : Shops, post office.
Public transport: GTT bus line Torino – Pont – Locana – Noasca – Ceresole – Colle del Nivolet (www.comune.torino.it/gtt/intercomunale/percorari.shtml).

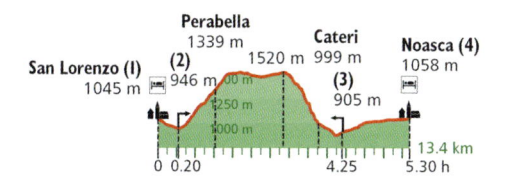

From **San Lorenzo (1)**, descend along the street. Past the hamlet of Rocci, the GTA forks off to the right (westwards) via Bertodasco, 1176 m, to reach **Perabella**. At the hamlet, ascend steeply to the right (north-eastwards); following the line of height, reach **Meinardi** with the pilgrimage chapel of Sant' Anna. Continue westward in a traverse to the Rio della Frera and, on the other side of the stream, descend. Passing Coste and Carbonere, reach Fé. Now descend to the main road. Take this to the right, then cross over the Orco to the opposite bank and, finally, continue from Prà to **Cateri**, 999 m. Cross over a stream, follow the road to the left until the Sentiero Natura forks off to the right and then take this via Borno, 1013 m, to **Noasca (4)**.

Photo left: Noasca; photo right: Albergo degli Amici, San Lorenzo.

28 | Noasca – Ceresole Reale

4.30 hrs.
↑ 980 ↓ 550

High mountain trail through ghost towns

This is an easy route allowing plenty of time to explore tumbledown hamlets. From the final height, a view opens up to the broad valley of the Ceresole, where the snow-covered peaks of the Levanna tower above. The first-class alpinists from the year 1859 were thrilled to the bone when they found a comfortable hotel in the Swiss style; Tuckett himself could sleep in »the king's own bed«. Vittorio Emanuele II deigned to spend a night in the Hotel Levanna (no longer in operation today) when he came here to hunt. Three years before this point in time, the king had purchased the hunting rights for the area around the Gran Paradiso and thereby laid the groundwork for the future creation of the national park. Even back then, it was a »must« to visit the mineral springs whose healing properties were known since the 1820s. Nowadays, you will be greeted on the spot by the Rifugio Fonti Minerali where you can stock up on the iron- and arsenic-rich spring water to take along on the next day's march.

Starting point: Noasca, 1058 m.
Destination: Ceresole Reale, 1494 m.
Length: 11.1 km.
Grade: Well-marked, distinct trail, an easy high mountain trail.
Refreshment: Nothing en route.
Accommodation: Ceresole Reale: 1494 m, Rifugio Fonti Minerali below the reservoir wall, May–end Sept., 20 B, HB 35 €, Daniela Chiri and Pierre-Franco Nigretti, tel. +39 0124/95 31 17 or +39 347/711 03 09, www.fontiminerali.com. Much more lodging in various village districts of Ceresole, among which, the Fonti Miner-

The ghost town Cappelle.

ali proved also to offer very good meals. The second best recommendation: Chalet del Lago, a few metres away from the lakeshore, 8 DR, HB from 45 €, tel. +39 0124/95 31 28, www.chalet-ceresolereale.it.

Shopping/Services: Shops, cash dispenser, pharmacy, post office.

Public transport: GTT bus line Torino–Pont – Locana – Noasca – Ceresole – Colle del Nivolet (timetable: www.comune.torino.it/gtt/intercomunale/percorari.shtml).

Information: Tourismusbüro I.A.T. in the Casa di Gran Paradiso at the spacious open area on the lake, tel. +39 0124/95 31 86, www.casa-granparadiso.it. Visitor centre for the Gran Paradiso National Park in the former Grand Hotel, with an interactive exhibition, tel. +39 0124/95 31 66, www.homoetibex.org. List of accommodation: www.ceresolereale.com.

Tip: Since you are so close to the »Cuore del Parco«, you should treat yourself to an extra-excursion by taking the bus to the Colle del Nivolet. From the top of the pass, it is a thirty-minute walk to reach the lake-dotted plateau – a real highlight of the Gran Paradiso National Park. Especially beautiful is the way the Laghi Trebecchi nestle in front of the icy Titans of the Grivola, Gran Paradiso and Ciarforon.

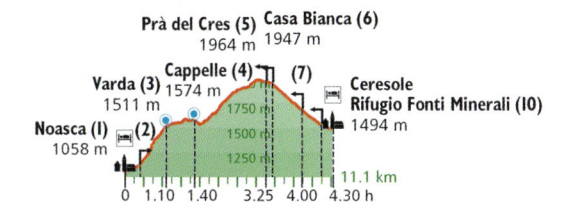

From **Noasca (1)**, take the main street, at first climbing up along four bends. At the bus stop past the stream, turn right onto the GTA. Ascend along zigzigs and pass the car park at Balmarossa. The *mulattiera* climbs further up for a steep stretch and then follows the line of height to reach Varda, Maison, Mola, **Cappelle (4)**, villages which were once inhabited year-round. At Potes, cross over the stream and then ascend to the chapel at Borgo Vecchio. Continue uphill, heading south-eastwards through woods, and then, with an open view, traverse to **Prà del Cres (5)**. At the *alpe* huts, turn left, crossing pastureland, to **Casa Bianca (6)**, and skirt around to the left of it. Along a *mulattiera*, pass through woods to reach the main street of **Ceresole**.

Waymarkers lead to the left, descending along the street then turn right to the **Posto tappa Fonti Minerali (10)**. The gigantic reservoir wall looming over the GTA hostel is kind of scary-looking.

> *i* Since the 1930s, the **Valle dell'Orco** has acted as a kind of surge tank. A total of six reservoirs, 50 kilometres of pressure pipeline and five hydroelectric energy plants combine to produce cheap electricity at night and expensive peak power during the day. What will happen when the glaciers are no longer there? Only a small amount of glacial ice blankets the mountains now.

Lago di Ceresole.

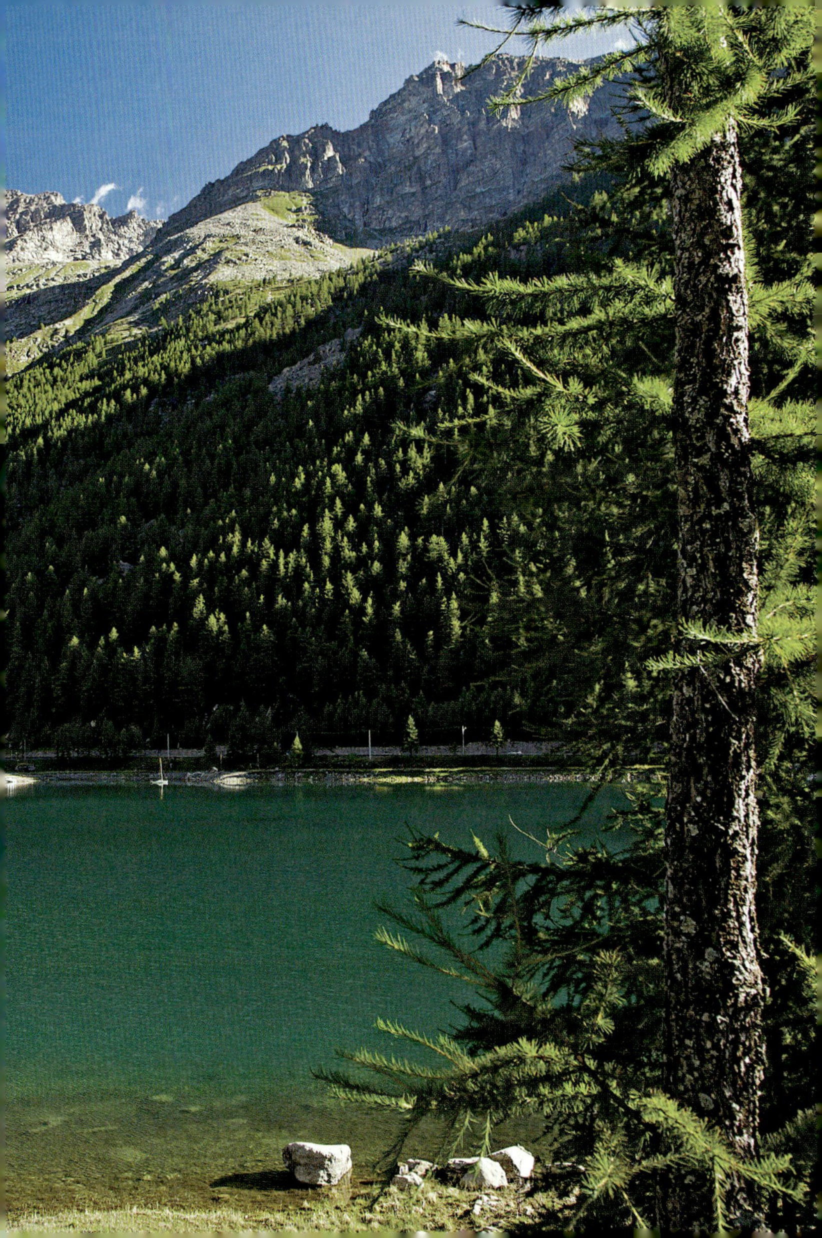

Through the Lanzo valleys – Turin's former summer holiday retreat

From the ridge which acts as the French-Italian border, three valleys run parallel to each other, cutting their way deep into the mountains before they unite in Lanzo.

When tourism first began, because of their proximity to the capital city of the Piedmont, the *Valli di Lanzo*, especially the Ala di Stura valley, became popular summer holiday destinations for the *bel mondo*, the »high society« of Turin. This area is considered the cradle of Italian mountaineering because the first activities of the Alpine Club (CAI, founded in 1863) focused on the mountain landscape round the romantic valley. The village of Balme a mere 55 kilometres from Turin, presented the perfect starting point for touring. The village, with a long history of trading with the neighbouring region, Maureinne, located on the other side of the glaciated border ridge, provided competent local guides, familiar with the terrain. A good example is Antonio Castagneri's sister, who could, it was said, march for eight hours with a 30 kilo sack over her shoulder as she crossed over the border to France while scrambling and negotiating icy passages – without ever having to take her pipe out of her mouth. But, at the end, it was always the men who were engaged as guides. Antonio Castagneri, who was called Tòni dij Toùni, had especially distinguished himself. The museum in Balme is even named after him. More than forty first ascents were attributed to him, not only in the Lanzo valleys but also in the bordering regions. He found his way up the Matterhorn and onto Mont Blanc, where he finally disappeared during a storm with his friend, Jean Maquignaz, and a guest walker in August 1890. Their bodies have never been found. Guido Rey, who initiated a number of new routes with Castagneri (amongst which, the 1500-metre sheer, southern face of the Uia di Ciamarella in 1883 and also, over the north ridge onto the Bessanese in 1889), wrote a biography of the heroic guide and W.A.B. Coolidge wrote a poignant epilogue to him in the British *Alpine Journal*.

Despite the craggy barrier, the relationship between the two villages of Balme und Bessans were even closer than those to the neighbouring villages; this is reflected in the traditions and dialects that they share. It wasn't until 1861, when the new country of Italy was founded, that the border to France was set at the alpine main ridge. Naturally, this not only influenced the close contact that the two villages once had, but from now on, some things had to be done in secret. From being traders to being smugglers, and from being smugglers to becoming, at the end, mountaineering guides, was the chain that followed. Walking tours became more and more in demand along the bordering ridge and over to Bessans on the other side, where a couple of rooms at the Bessans Hotel Cimaz were always reserved for the wealthy Italian clientele. Among the special guests listed, the name Achille Ratti, who would later become Pope Pius XI, is found. Of course, the avid mountaineer couldn't easily be recognized as a priest while he was walking the mountains, which once brought the village priest of the neighbouring Lanslevillard into an embarrassing situation: in 1899, he demanded that Ratti show him his papers identifying himself as a priest before he would allow the man to hold a mass in his church. Ratti's gratitude towards the services of the mountaineering guides from Balme, who had accompanied him in his youth, was expressed in an invitation to Rome.

Except for a few stately mansions, there is nothing today to remind you of the golden age of tourism in Balme. The lucrative mountain guide enterprises have moved to the higher mountains and the *bel mondo* have turned away to seek out other destinations. The guestbook of the Antico Albergo Camussòt, which includes not only entries for the mountaineering elite, but also for the tabloid darlings, is securely stowed away in the Museo Nazionale della Montagna in Turin.

Along the walk through the deeply-cut Valli di Lanzo and into the Susa Valley, the differences in height are especially brutal, but the impressions called up by the landscape are unique. At the very end, the walker must meet the challenge of the Rocciamelone heraus. Europe's highest-lying mountain pilgrimage site is a real must, but only if the weather is good.

Ascent to the Rocciamelone, overlooking the sea of lights marking Susa (Stage V33).

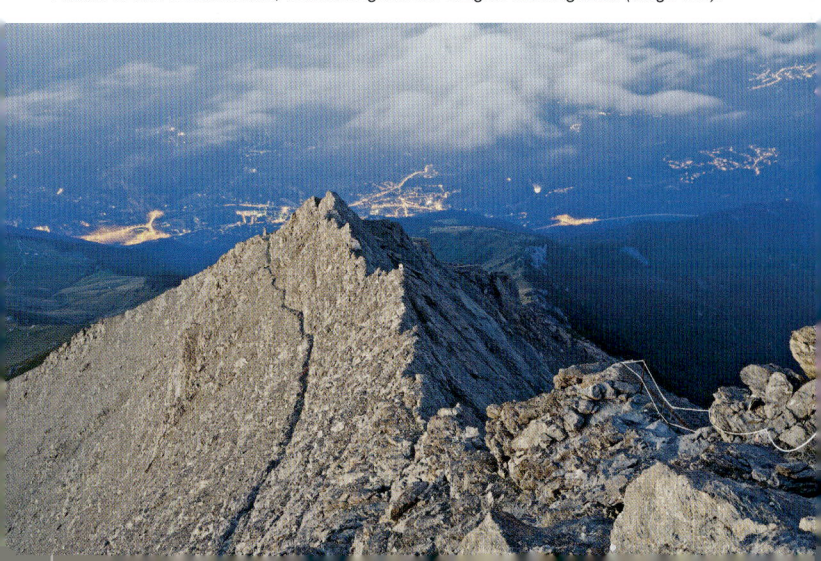

29 Ceresole Reale – Pialpetta

6.30 hrs.
↑1170 ↓1610

A delightful view of a summit

Through larch forests to idyllic alpine plateaus which open striking views all the way to the Gran Paradiso massif, to the western-lying peaks of the Levanna and to the Vanoise. The descent into the Val Grande is accompanied by a view of the Uia di Ciamarella, the landmark for the Lanzo valleys. The locals call the extraordinary peak »Clessidra« because it resembles an hourglass.

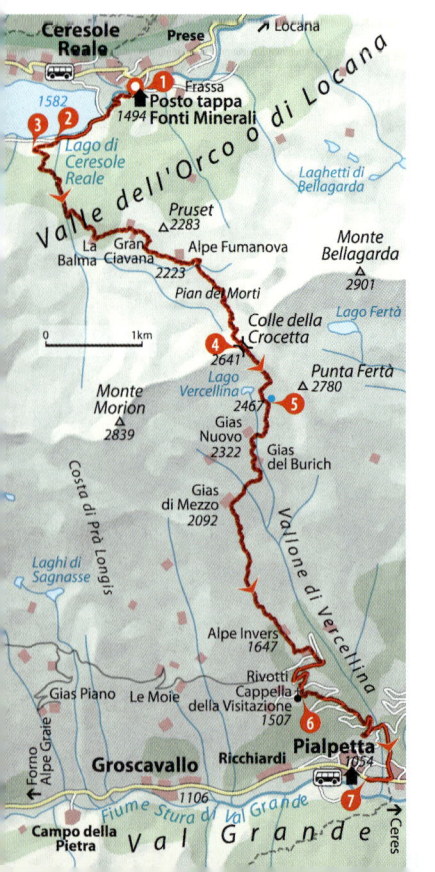

Starting point: Ceresole Reale, Rifugio Fonti Minerali, 1494 m.
Destination: Pialpetta, 1054 m.
Length: 15 km.
Grade: Well-marked, mostly a distinct trail. During the final ascent to the pass, through fields of boulders.
Refreshment: Nothing en route.
Accommodation: Pialpetta: 1054 m, Albergo Setugrino, May–Oct., 6 DR, 1 R with 1B, HB 45 €. Posto tappa, a couple of mins. away, 18 B, HB 40 €, Giuseppe Berardo, tel. +39 0123/810 16. Albergo Pialpetta, year-round, 15 DR, 70 €, Berardo Battista, tel. +39 0123/810 44.
Shopping: Shop, post office in Pialpetta.
Public transport: Bus service to Ceres and Torino (timetable: www.vigobus.it/autolinee.php).

Take the trail behind the **Rifugio (1)** to ascend through woods, then a stretch along a reservoir until the GTA forks off to the left. (Note: if you spent the night in the village, you will meet up with the GTA after you've negotiated the dam wall). Pick up a broad forest trail, then turn off to the left along a steeply ascending path, while enjoying the shade, to enter an idyllic mountain valley. Bear left to ascend along the slope on the opposite side of the stream and pass the tumbledown

Colle della Crocetta.

alpe hut of La Balma, as you cross from *alpe* plateau to *alpe* plateau. Starting from the Piano dei Morti, traverse a boulder field onto the **Colle della Crocetta (4)**, 2641 m. While descending, first pass the **Lago Vercellina**, 2484 m, then the Gias Nuovo, the Gias del Burich and the Gias di Mezzo. At the Alpe Invers, cross over a service road and, further below, meet up with a street. In front of the pretty church at **Rivotti (6)**, back to the meadows and left of the church, descend along the *mulattiera* to the next stretch of street. The GTA short-cuts the road to **Pialpetta (7)** time and again, but the turn-offs are not always easy to spot.

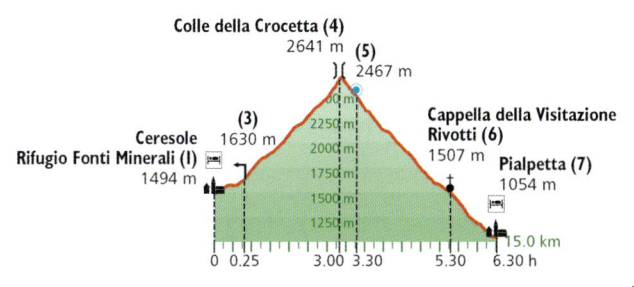

30 — Pialpetta – Balme

8.00 hrs.
↑ 1670 ↓ 1230

A welcome from the »Matterhorn« of the Lanzo valleys

From Pialpetta to Balme.

This is a classic ascent from alpe to alpe. The Trione lakes draw you to a romantic repose before the steep ascent to the pass demands its toll. Starting from here, the view of the Uia di Mondrone will accompany us; the »Matterhorn« of the Lanzo valleys, with a steep and craggy peak towering over Balme, was a powerful attraction for the Turin alpinists, Alessandro Martelli and Luigi Vaccarone. Along with the legendary guide, Antonio Castagneri, they negotiated a winter ascent of the peak, the first such ascent in the history of mountaineering in the Lanzo valleys. On Christmas Eve of 1874, they could congratulate each other on the summit and could still return the entire way back to Balme, arriving safe and sound.

Starting point: Pialpetta, 1054 m.
Destination: Balme, 1500 m.
Length: 17.5 km.
Grade: Well-marked but with a couple of small gaps. On the upper stretches, the trail is somewhat overgrown with alder thicket. A tough climb. The descent route is confused at the Alpe Valsuera (the route, in the IGC map, is drawn incorrectly).
Refreshment: Nothing en route.

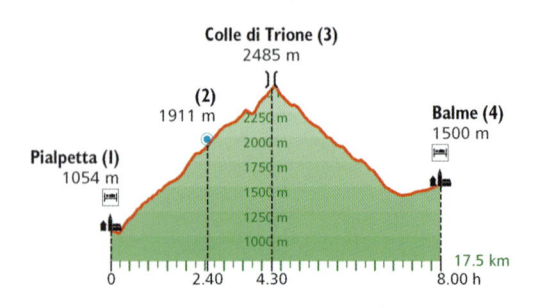

Colle di Trione (3) 2485 m
(2) 1911 m
Pialpetta (I) 1054 m
Balme (4) 1500 m
17.5 km
0   2.40   4.30   8.00 h

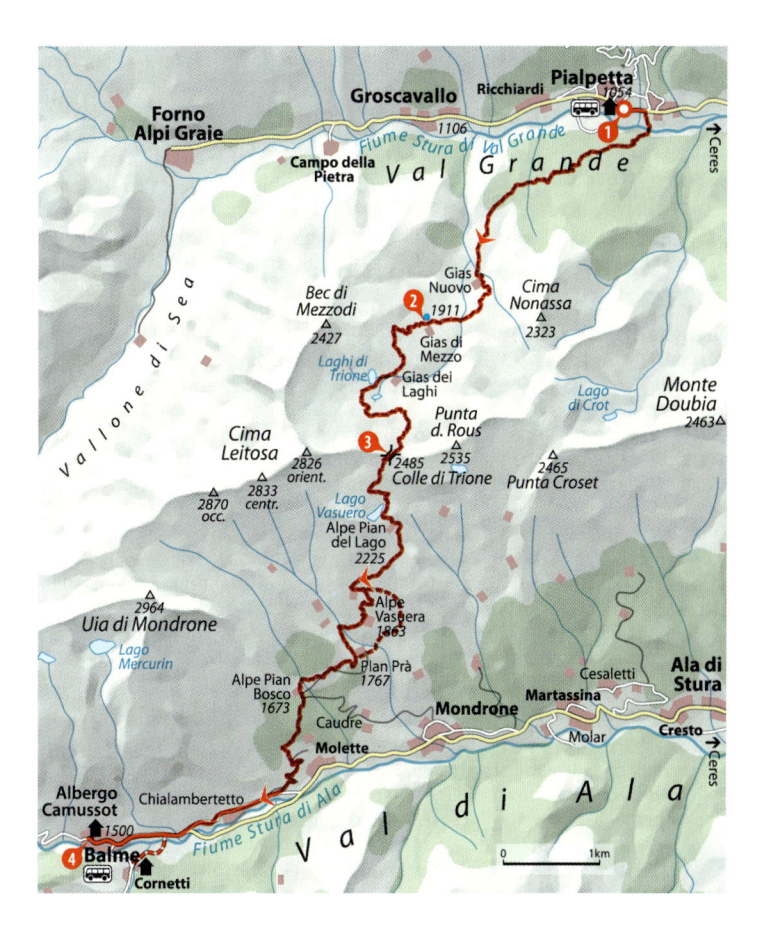

Accommodation: Balme: 1500 m, Albergo Camussot, temporarily closed. – **Cornetti:** B&B Gloria, tel. +39 338/247 13 76. Posto tappa »Les Montagnards«, tel. +39 0123/23 30 73 or +39 347/363 40 82, www.lesmontagnards.it.
Shopping: Shop, post office in Balme.
Public transport: Bus service to Ceres. In the holiday season, a bus also goes to the valley head Pian della Mussa. Every Sun., an express service Torino – Pian della Mussa. Balme – Torino Sun./holidays beg. July–beg. Sept. 5:40 p.m. (timetable: www.vigo-autoindustriale.com).
Tip: Ecomuseo delle Guide Alpine di Balme, July–Sept. Sun. 3:30–5:30 p.m., in Aug., also on Sat, or by appointment, tel. +39 0123/829 02, www.ecomuseobalme.it.

Balme.

From the **Posto tappa (1)**, turn left along the main street until, just after the village sign for Migliere, the GTA descends to the right, down to the river. On the other side of the bridge, do not turn left; instead, head straight on into the forest but then immediately take the path on the right to ascend. Continue via the Gias Nuovo and the Gias di Mezzo to reach the Gias dei Laghi, situated between the Trione lakes. Above the huts, head past the lake along a sweeping loop, skirting around a rocky outcrop. Afterwards, climb steeply through a boulder field and debris onto the **Colle di Trione (3)**, 2485 m. After the first steep section, cross through hilly terrain. Continue to the left of the Lago Vasuero (usually dry) to reach the huts of the **Alpe Pian del Lago**, 2225 m. In the area around the Alpe Vasuera, cow paths confuse the route but even the waymarked trail leads completely illogically to the left of the *alpe*, through a stream bed overgrown with alders. The best course is to ascend from the upper huts, directly over the meadow to the lower huts. The trail then leads westwards, crossing a stream, then descends again to the **Alpe Pian Prà**, where you meet up with a new *alpe* road that does not appear on the map. The GTA short-cuts the bends time and again. Later on, descend along the tarmac road coming from Molera to reach the old, unused valley road. Take this road via Chialambertetto to reach **Balme (4)**. The Posto tappa is located in the lower village district, Cornetti.

---

i ***Balme:*** *One of the most noteworthy houses is the Haus Routchàss on the main street in the upper village. The oldest house in Balme is very much like a cavern: a maze of covered corridors, stairways, storage rooms, stables and living quarters – convoluted like a fortress. Before a part of the old village had to give way to the construction of a street in 1909, this sort of building plan allowed easy access to the well, the bake oven, the wash-house and the chapel, especially during the snowy winter months. To find a particularly beautiful fresco – a portrayal of the famous Shroud of Turin – seems a labyrinthian search. In 1535, the precious relic, endangered by religious and political conflicts, was smuggled to safety via secret routes over the bordering ridge between Bessans and Balme. Later on, in 1578, the mountain inhabitants would again be astounded by a very unusual caravan of Christian dignitaries, accompanied by mules and military men, as they struggled through ice and snow over the alpine barrier towering more than 3000 metres over sea level, to carry the precious relic to its final destination; the Savoian dynasty had transferred their seat of power from Chambéry to Turin. By the way, some of the motifs in Bessan's frescos are also anchored in the legends of the Shroud.*

6.30 hrs.
↑1120 ↓1350

Balme – Usseglio 31

Some lakes, two passes and a steep descent

The crossing to Usseglio is very beautiful but also very strenuous. You should avoid the temptation to dawdle during the ascent since the extremely steep descent which follows demands concentration and therefore more time, especially if you want to avoid wear and tear on your knees.

Starting point: Balme, 1500 m.
Destination: Usseglio, 1265 m.
Length: 11.8 km.
Grade: Well-marked but the trail around the pass is not very distinct. The descent through steep, grassy slopes requires sure-footedness and concentration. Very dangerous when wet.
Refreshment: Nothing en route.
Accommodation: Bivacco Gino Gandolfo: 2200 m, always open, 6 B, no oven or gas. – **Usseglio:** 1265 m, Albergo Grand' Usseglio, beg. June–Oct., 20 R (45 B), DR HB 53 €, GTA-HB 42 €, we cannot recommend the food, tel. +39 0123/837 40, www.hotelgrandussseglio.com. Albergo Rocciamelone, year-round, 15 DR, HB 50 €, tel. +39 0123/837 43 or 837 89, www.albergorocciamelone.com. – **Villaretto:** Hotel Furnasa, 8 R (12 B), HB 45 €, year-round, tel. +39 0123/837 88, www.hotel-ristorantefurnasa.com. The same owners also manage a new hotel, Stella Alpina, between Usseglio and Villaretto.
Shopping: Shop, post office in Usseglio.
Public transport: Bus service to Lanzo (www.comune.torino.it/gtt/intercomunale/percorari.shtml).
Tip: One phone call is all it takes to be picked up by the Rifugio Vulpot (destination Stage 32). This will save you the long slog along the road Usseglio – Morgone; a lovely location on the Lago di Malciaussia; a very warm welcome and good food, tel. +39 0123/837 71 or +39320/840 70 78, www.rifugiovulpot.com.

Making butter in the traditional way.

Passo Paschiet (3)
2435 m

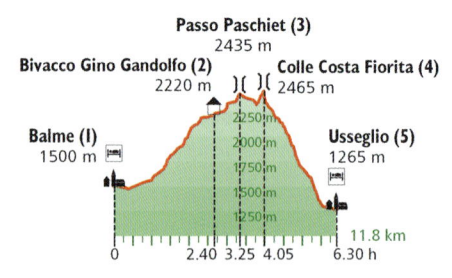

Bivacco Gino Gandolfo (2)   **Colle Costa Fiorita (4)**
2220 m   2465 m

Balme (1)   **Usseglio (5)**
1500 m   1265 m

11.8 km

0   2.40   3.25   4.05   6.30 h

The descent from the Colle Costa Fiorita to Usseglio.

From **Balme (1)** or **Cornetti**, follow the narrow road to Frè. Below the hamlet, turn left to cross the bridge then pick up the trail leading upstream. Pass the *alpe* huts of Pian Salè and Garavela through a gorge-like closure in the valley. Somewhat above the Alpe Pian Buet, turn right to cross the stream and head southwards to the Laghi Verdi, nestled between gigantic crags. The refreshing waters offer a worthwhile invigorating dip before the route begins to sap your strength. At a small, isolated meadow only a little further up, the **Bivacco Gandolfo (2)** has been placed in a lovely location. The course of the GTA turns to the left, continues climbing up and then traverses a scree-blanketed slope onto the **Passo Paschiet (3)**. On the other side, a short descent follows which leads to a trail junction; turn right onto a meadowland plateau. Here, at a large boulder, turn right for another ascent to the **Colle Costa Fiorita (4)**. At the pass, the course of the trail is somewhat unclear. Old GTA waymarkers would have you heading directly into the abyss. However, we keep to the S.I. (Sentiero Italia) waymarkers, bearing more to the left at the edge of the cirque, descending along a mountain ridge and then we meet up with a meadow-blanketed ridge and a sign: Colle Teina, 2200 m. Now traverse to the left to reach the meadowland plateau **Pian Venaus**, 1930 m. Afterwards, a somewhat tricky stretch must be negotiated. The path descends almost vertically, is only a little trodden-down and extremely slippery when wet. After a traverse to the wood, the descent becomes easier; remaining, however, quite steep. Pass the sheer rocky precipice Brech dla Rama, 1725 m, and at Giench dla Roccia, 1465 m, reach a gully for a stream course where you can descend along the protective wall to reach a meadow trail. The trail merges a little later into the valley road for the Val di Viù. Turn right to reach **Useglio (5)**.

32 | *Usseglio – Rifugio Vulpot*

3.00 hrs.
↑ 580 ↓ 30

Through the Val di Viù

Enjoy a day of rest before sweating out the strenuous mountain passes of the Valli di Lanzo. Unfortunately, longer stretches of the route follow the road. Much more exciting is the Decauville, a high mountain trail following an old railway line which runs along the rock faces of the right-hand slopes of the valley. Unfortunately, the first stretch of trail is already somewhat overgrown.

Starting point: Usseglio, 1265 m.
Destination: Rifugio Vulpot, 1820 m.
Length: 10.9 km.
Grade: Both routes are well-marked. The GTA is easier and shorter but with long stretches of tarmac; the Sentiero Italia requires sure-footedness.
Refreshment: In Margone.
Accommodation: Villaretto see Stage 31.
– **Rifugio Vulpot:** 1820 m, mid-June–mid-Sept., 35 B (also DR), HB 39 €, very good meals, Gianni and Ileana Bruno, tel. +39 0123/837 71 or 320/840 70 78, www.rifugiovulpot.com.
Shopping: Nothing available.
Public transport: Bus servise to Margone (timetable: www.comune.torino.it/gtt/intercomunale/percorari.shtml).

Usseglio.

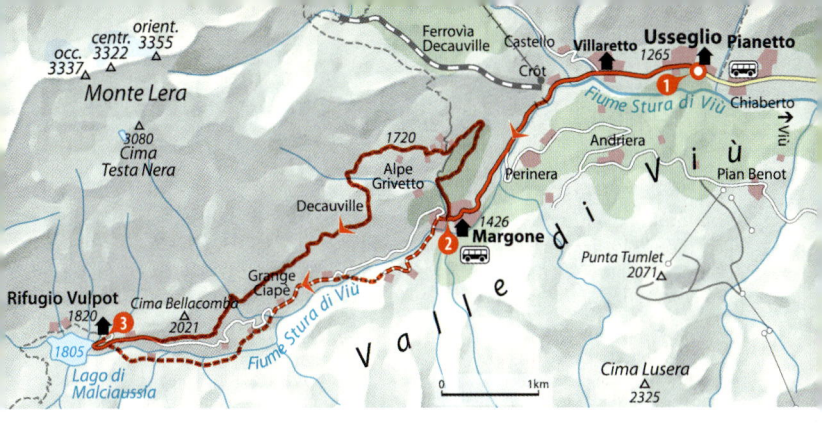

Unfortunately, you have to follow the road (3 km) to **Margone (2)**. There is only a bus service at the weekend. Starting at Margone, you have two options:

GTA: In Margone, descend along the narrow street to the stream, then ascend along the left bank. The trail continues on the opposite side and follows the road. At the right-hand bend, from the Grange Ciapè, the GTA forks off to the left, leading along the right flank of the valley, then along the left-hand side. Before reaching the dam wall for the Lago di Malciaussia, cross over the stream, climb steeply to the road and turn left to reach the **Rifugio Vulpot (3)**.

S.I.: the Sentiero Italia, the much more adventurous route, ascends at the Trattoria in Margone to the right, following trail No. 118. Soon pass a fountain on your right-hand side, enter a wood and then, crossing the slope, continue northwards until reaching an *alpe* hut. From here, turn left, following white waymarkers to reach the **Alpe Grivetto**; now follow the traces of a path westwards through the meadows to reach **Decauville**, the railway line along the slope is easy to spot. At the outset, the high mountain trail is somewhat overgrown with alder thicket and, from time to time, the route is blocked by a tree. Later, the trail is cleared again, leading in an exciting stretch through rockslides, then through a tunnel (head torch recommended). At the end, along a rock face that is made more secure by steps and cable, reach the road; turn right here to reach the **Rifugio Vulpot (3)**.

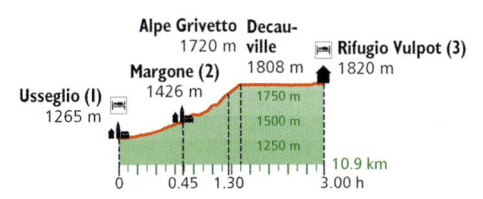

33 | *Rifugio Vulpot – Il Trucco*

5.00 hrs.
↑820 ↓930

In a semi-circle rounding the Rocciamelone

This route is very panoramic. At the Colle Croce di Ferro, the view sweeps into the Po Valley plain, to the Monviso and all the way to the mountains bordering France. With the Susa Valley below your feet, the trail winds through the south face of the Rocciamelone to land in the »eagle's nest«, Trucco.

Starting point: Rif. Vulpot, 1820 m.
Destination: Il Trucco, 1706 m.
Length: 15.5 km.
Grade: Well-marked, distinct trail.
Refreshment: Capanna Sociale Aurelio Ravetto.
Accommodation: Capanna Sociale Aurelio Ravetto: 2545 m, mid-July–end Aug., in Sept. when the weather is good, at the weekend, 20 B, HB 37 €, Franco Vigna, tel. +39 011/627 04 41 or +39 338/900 78 13 – **Il Truc (Trucco):** 1706 m, Posto tappa, beg. June–end Sept, 12 B, HB 37 €, delicious meals, Katerina Giorsa, tel. +39 0122/329 63 and +39 347/778 44 16, www.rifugioiltruc.com.
Shopping: Alpe Costa Rossa (cheese).
Public transport: None.

From the **Rifugio Vulpot (1)**, take the gravel track along the shore of the Lago di Malciaussia, cross over the inflow point and then ascend to the left (southwards). Ignore the turn-off higher up to the left which leads Lago Nero; in a pleasant ascent along a sometimes cobbled *mulattiera*, reach the **Colle**

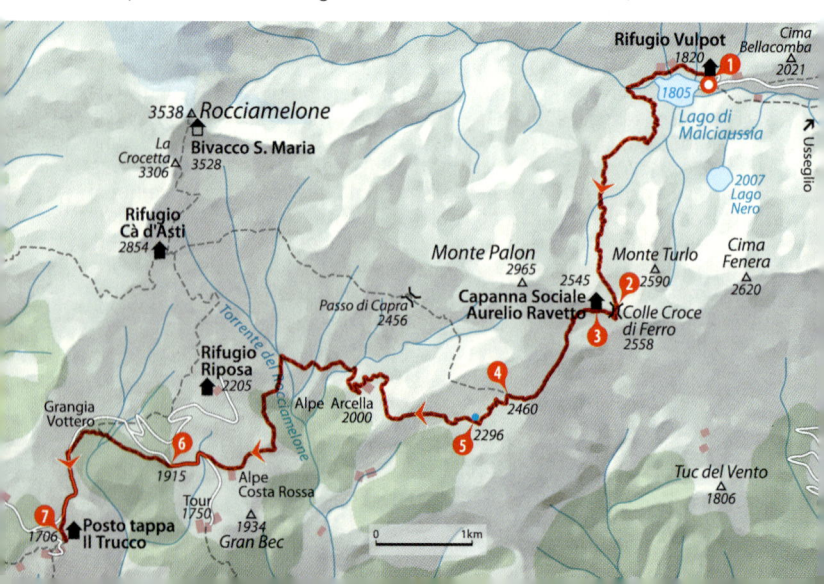

Lago di Malciaussia with Rocciamelone.

Croce di Ferro (2), 2558 m. Below the crest of the pass lies the **Capanna Sociale Aurelio Ravetto (3)**, 2545 m, a former military barracks. On the level now, the GTA traverses the eastern flank of the Monte Palon and crosses over to the southern flank where the view sweeps all the way to the glacier-blanketed Ecrins peaks. After a short descent, a cairn marks the turn-off to the right which leads to the Rifugio Cà d'Asti. The GTA, on the other hand, heads down the valley and, at the **Alpe Arcella**, 2000 m, meets up with an *alpe* road. This leads on the level to the **Alpe Costa Rossa** and also a little further until, at a patch of woods, the GTA forks off to the left **(6)**. A romantic, grassy trail passes larch trees and leads along a *suone* (ancient watercourse). In the area around the Grangia Vottero cow paths may lead you to the farmyard. Before that point, on the other hand, the GTA descends to the left; we missed this turn-off, but nonetheless, discovered a lovely trail in the process. A pleasant forest trail at a solitary stone-built house leads along an irrigation channel. Just before meeting up with the road, cross over this watercourse and then head straight ahead over a meadow to reach the **Posto tappa (7)**.

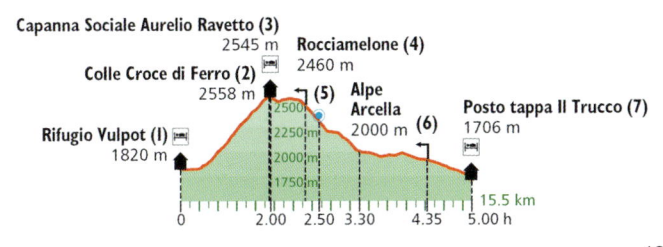

V33 Rocciamelone

2 days
↑ 1900 ↓ 2000

The highest-lying pilgrimage site in the Alps

When the weather is clear, an excursion here is almost a »must«, even when you have to spend the night in the Rifugio Cà d'Asti, which isn't exactly one of the best huts. Sunrise on the Rocciamelone is a sight that you will never forget. Three thousand metres above the Susa Valley, enjoy a splendid 360° view.

A certain Bonifacio Rotario d'Asti is given credit as the first man to climb to the summit. On 1 September, 1358, he even erected a triptych with a Madonna on the peak. The alleged crusader was said to have once fallen into the hands of the Mussulman and had pledged, if he were liberated, to place a shrine on a summit which opens the best 360° view. His ascent is actually documented, but he could not have been a crusader because in his lifetime, the Crusades were long since past. But indeed, legends are known to be the fuel for myth and help make the pilgrimage site even more attractive. This is also made manifest in the countless votive pictures in the summit chapel and again on the well-constructed trail that, at the weekend in the summer months, is choked with crowds of pilgrims, especially during the annual pilgrimage which take place on August 5. This is the commemorative day for Our Lady of the Snow; since 1899, her mighty bronze statue raises the summit by another 3 metres and her benevolent smile lights up an endless sea of mountaintops.

Starting point: Rif. Vulpot, 1820 m.
Destination: Il Trucco, 1706 m.
Length: 21 km.
Grade: Mostly well-marked. The traverse along the Alta Via Val di Susa to the Rifugio Cà d'Asti can present orientation problems when conditions are foggy, since waymarkings have faded and the path is not very distinct. To the summit, the terrain is sometimes exposed and the craggy peak is guarded by a cable.
Refreshment: Capanna Sociale Aurelio

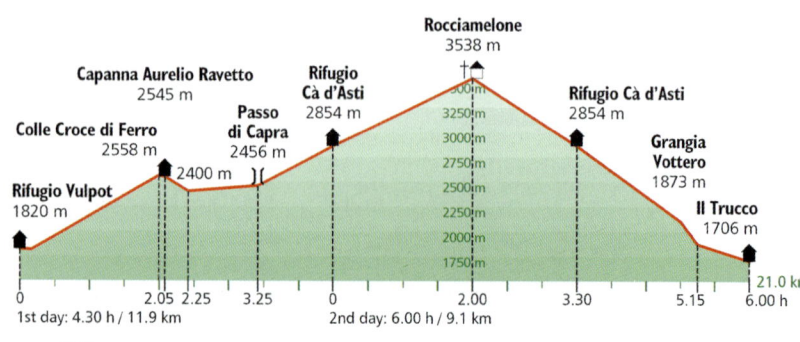

136

Ravetto, Rifugio La Riposa.
Accommodation: Capanna Sociale Aurelio Ravetto: see Stage 33.
– **Rifugio Cà d'Asti:** 2854 m, CAI, beg. July–mid-Sept, 90 B, Fulgido Tabone, tel. +39 0122/331 92. – **Rifugio La Riposa:** 2205 m, beg. July–mid-Sept.,72 B,tel. +39 338/844 45 07. – **Bivacco Santa Maria:** 3528 m, always open, 14 B, no water. – **Il Trucco:** see Stage 33.
Shopping: Nothing available.
Public transport: None.

Day 1: Rifugio Vulpot – Rifugio Cà d'Asti (4.30 hrs.)
Until reaching the fork at about 2460 m, see Stage 33 for the route to the **Capanna Sociale Aurelio Ravetto**. At this point, turn right onto the white/red-marked Alta Via Val di Susa. The path requires some concentration because the waymarkers are not always easy to spot. In a short stretch of up-and-down walking, the path keeps more or less at the same height and leads westward, crossing through numerous stream gullies (sometimes slippery), towards the **Rifugio Cà d'Asti**, 2854 m, which is visible already from afar.
Below the shelter, the pilgrimage chapel, built in 1798, still stands. In the past, the pilgrim's mass was held here. However, since the precipitous summit trail was improved in 1895, the annual pilgrimage on August 5 is celebrated on the peak of the Rocciamelone.

Day 2: Rifugio Cà d'Asti – Rocciamelone – Il Trucco (6 hrs.)
If the weather forecast is favourable, there is usually quite a hustle and bustle going on at the hut and, therefore, we recommend making the ascent to the summit before the official breakfast hour to avoid ending up in a walker's jam. Until reaching the secondary peak, **La Crocetta**, 3306 m, ithe trail is just very steep. From this point on it is also precipitous, but you can now use cables to hold on to and thus easily reach the southern ridge of the final summit of **Rocciamelone**, 3538 m. Apart from special celebrations, the chapel at the peak is closed (the key is held by the warden of the Cà d'Asti hut), the bivouac, on the other hand, is always open.
The descent to the **Rifugio Cà d'Asti** follows the approach route.
From there, continue along the well-trodden trail No. 558 to descend to the military road coming from La Riposa. A path to the right short-cuts the bends and then meets up with an intersecting road coming from the Alpe Arcella and the Costa Rossa. At the **Grangia Vottero**, head towards a house located somewhat below and to the right, then continue along a level forest trail which leads above a *suone*. Afterwards, turn right to cross the watercourse and then over a meadow to reach the settlement of **Trucco**.

34a Il Trucco – Susa

3.00 hrs.
↑10 ↓1220

Downward view of a Romanesque town

Enchanted trails through woodland and passing stone-built houses. Here and there, a striking view of Susa. If we could only fly! The valley, that is decried as spoiled by construction presents quite a contrary impression as the route leading to the city is by no means a confused plod through a concrete jungle. The old town is sheer poetry, especially at night when the historical buildings are posed in stage spotlights. If you take a good look at the legendary triptych in the church of San Giusto, you will easily see that Bonifacio Rotario d'Asti was a banker who had absolutely nothing to do with any Crusades. More likely, the legend was spurred by a power struggle in his home town of Asti. When the problem was resolved, he climbed the Rocciamelone to show his gratitude and left the triptych, actually produced in Bruges, at the peak.

Starting point: Il Trucco, 1706 m.
Destination: Susa, 494 m.
Length: 8.1 km.
Grade: The waymarkers are not always easy to find, but the trails are distinct. A steep descent.
Refreshment: Nothing en route.
Accommodation: Susa: 494 m, Hotel du Parc, DR 80 €, tel. +39 0122/62 22 73. Hotel Susa & Stazione, DR 78 €, tel. +39 0122/62 22 26, www.hotelsusa.it. L'Archivolto della Terrazza, B&B 33 €, www.bb-laterrazza.com.
Shopping/Services: In Susa: shops, post office, cash dispenser, pharmacy, restaurants (best pizza and good ambience: the Pizzeria Italia in the old town).
Public transport: There's a train from Susa to Torino (www.trenitalia.com).
Alternative: The more direct trail, No. 558, is also very nice and the stretch of tarmac to Susa is somewhat shorter (2.30 hrs. total time).

From the **Posto tappa (1)** take the right-hand path to the road, then descend immediately to the left. Past the holiday homes, reach a fork: to the left, trail No. 558 (Alternative); the road straight ahead, that is, to the right, is the GTA. If you prefer the GTA, you must keep a good eye out along the road since the turn-off to the left that follows a little later isn't very easy to spot. Descend to the meadowland clearing of Praletto, then continue to climb down steeply. After you cross over a road, the route leads you to the houses of **Pietrabruna (2)**. Continue the steep descent to reach the ruins of Castagneretto, where you ignore the Sentiero dei Monaci to your left. At the next trail junction, the continuation of the GTA is not distinct. If you turn left, you'll end up at the church from Marzano again (a roundabout way), so, do not turn left at the trail junction but turn right instead to continue to San Giuseppe. From there, take the road to **Susa (4)**.

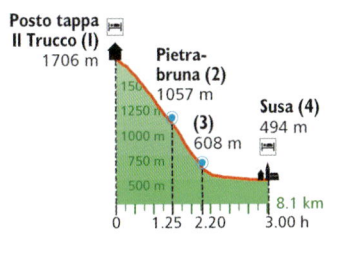

Susa, Porta Savoia.

Occitania and the birthplace of the Waldensians – from the Susa Valley into the Po Valley

The Susa Valley separates the Graian Alps from the Cottian Alps. The broad trough where the Dora Riparia flows has always been an important alpine crossing – for the armies under the command of Augustus, of Charlemagne, Napoleon, Hannibal ... for the pilgrims along the Via Francigena, for tradesmen, smugglers and partisans. The strategic importance for the military is obvious. Countless fortresses occupied valley clefts and mountain ridges. One of the most impressive installations, the Forte di Fenestrelle, will be met on the second day of this leg. Time after time, the border between France and Italy was moved to and fro until, in 1947, it was finally fixed at the main ridge of the Alps. Until 1713, both the upper Susa Valley as well as the Chisone Valley belonged to the »Grand Escarton«, the »League of Briançon« – valley regions which had fused together around the Mongenèvre Pass and were governed democratically. Because of this, more money flowed into their own coffers, which today, is reflected in the elegance of the villages (see Stage 44).

Starting at the Susa Valley, we enter into the Occitan lingual and cultural region, which stretches from the valley heads of the Piedmont over the entire south of France and all the way to Catalonia. From this point on, you will often spot a bright red flag with the yellow cross of the Cathar and, furthermore, you will enjoy Occitan delicacies and hear the unusual musical strains of this region. Occitan (*Lingua d'oc*), one of the oldest Romance languages, evolved in the early Middle Ages in the region of southern France. Renowned poets, such as Dante Alighieri, and also minstrels (or troubadours), such as Daniel Arnaut, found fame even beyond their own borders. Since the crusades against the Cathar faith in the 13th century, the language was suppressed on the French side of the alpine central ridge and continued its existence only in spoken form. Only since 1999 has the language been officially recognized and protected. An organization, Chambra d'Oc, is striving for the language to be included in the UNESCO World Heritage list. On the Italian side of the ridge, Occitan has never been banned and is therefore better preserved.

The valleys of Chisone, Germanasca and Pellice are home to the Waldensians (*Valdesi* in Italian), a Protestant religious community founded near the end of the 12th century by Petrus Valdes (a merchant from Lyon), that has undergone persecution over the centuries. The Waldensian movement sprang from criticism centred on the power abuses of the Catholic Church. Followers accepted only the writings of the Bible, rejected all ecclesiastical authority and renounced swearing oaths of allegiance to the feudal lords. Conflict with the Church and the ruling classes was thus inevitable. Excluded from the Church as heretics and blasphemers, followers found refuge in the Cottian Alps where the valley communities, due to their recognition of individual freedom, did not insist on controlling religious belief. The Waldensians joined the Reformation movement in 1532 when they officially and publicly announced themselves as a church, but this only drew more suppression and torturous handling. It appeared that the impending downfall of the Waldensians peaked in 1685 with the repeal of the Edict of Nantes, which, up until then, had guaranteed freedom of religion to the Protestant movements. Many thousands fled into Switzerland but some returned to their homeland valleys again in 1689 (known as the »Glorious Return«). Not until 1848 would Carlo Alberto, the King of Piedmont and Sardinia, once again guarantee freedom to practice their religion. But during the fascist period from 1922 until 1945, the Waldensians found themselves again under government control. It was not until 1984 that they finally achieved full recognition. More than 800 years of persecution and suppression had finally been put to an end. The intensity of the repression that took place during this time is well illustrated in the fact that, until the 19th century, the *Valdesi* was the only Evangelical Christian religion in all of Italy.

The Conca del Prà with the Rifugio Jervis, Valle Pellice (Stage 40).

34b Susa – Meana di Susa

0.45 hrs.
↑120 ↓20

Most walkers hurry through much too quickly

Surprisingly enough, you can actually find pleasant walking routes through the Susa Valley. The wide-spread construction found in this important transportation corridor can be avoided to the point of being invisible. Instead, you can wander through vineyards and orchards, meadows and woodland.

Starting point: Susa, 494 m.
Destination: Meana di Susa, 595 m.
Length: 2.6 km.
Grade: Well-marked, broad, level trails.
Refreshment: Nothing en route.
Accommodation: Meana di Susa: 595 m, Albergo Bellavista, open almost year-round, 20 B, HB 42 €, an old aristocratic villa with nostalgic flair, Nina Ghrone, tel. +39 0122/391 62.
Shopping/Services: In Susa and Meana di Susa.
Public transport: While Susa is a terminus station, Meaná di Susa has international railway connections (www.trenitalia.com).

The Arch of Augustus in Susa – erected by the Celtic King Cottius.

In Susa's historic centre.

Past the church of San Giusto in the centre of **Susa (1)**, cross over the bridge and ascend straight ahead. The Via Norberto Rosa becomes the Via Monte Grappa. Continue to the left via the SS24 into the Via Colle delle Fenestre. Not until reaching this point do waymarkers reappear. The street soon becomes an unpaved trail, leading mostly through open woodland.

Finally, a slight descent leads past vineyards. With a view of the railway station at **Meana di Susa** meet an intersecting street and turn left, following the Via Pian Barale to reach the **Albergo Bellavista (2)**.

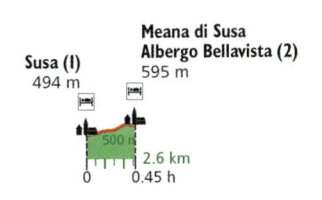

Susa (I) 494 m
Meana di Susa Albergo Bellavista (2) 595 m
2.6 km
0.45 h

35 Meana di Susa – Alpe Toglie

4.30 hrs.
↑ 1070 ↓ 130

Hamlets, forests & game

Along the pleasant trail through the upper villages of the Susa Valley, you will enjoy a view of the striking Rocciamelone time and again. In the gardens, vegetation is abundant, sometimes even including banana trees. Then the steep mulattiera passes through dense forest onto alpe terrain where very different temperatures await us.

Starting point: Meana di Susa, 595 m.
Destination: Alpe Toglie, 1534 m.
Length: 10.6 km.
Grade: Waymarking is insufficient, especially junctions lack signs. Some tarmac walking at the outset, otherwise, track roads and mule tracks.
Refreshment: Bar Le 4 Strade in Gillo near Menolzio.
Accommodation: Posto tappa Alpe Toglie: 1534 m, June until end Sept./beg. Oct, 12 B, cooking facilities, 7,50 € a night, also an evening meal can be arranged in advance 15 €, Guido Agli, tel. +39 347/032 45 16.
Shopping: At the Alpe Toglie, you can purchase cheese, sausage, wine, beer and sometimes even fruit and vegetables.
Public transport: By rail to Meana di Susa.

Borgata Suffis.

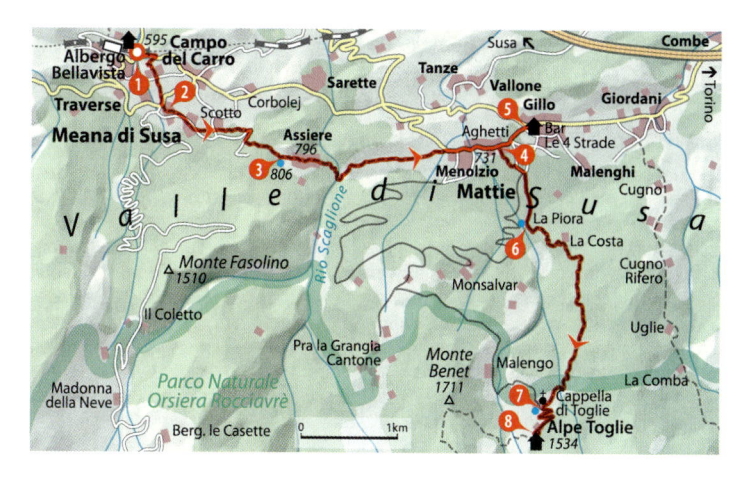

From **Bellavista (1)**, turn left onto the street then right, crossing under railway tracks, and ascending. Soon, turn right onto the *mulattiera* towards Grangia. From the Via Grangia onto the Via Durante, then pass through the next set of houses. Turn left onto the second intersecting street. Pass a fountain and cross through the *Borgata* Suffis. Pass a playground in a wood and descend to a street. Turn right onto the street to ascend (a path short-cuts the bends in the street) and reach **Assiere**, 796 m. Now the street becomes a country lane. Continue through a stream bed. At the shrine to the Madonna, turn left onto the country lane towards **Menolzio**, 731 m. Cross through the village, then over the bridge onto the Via Aghetti. Past house No. 23, turn right onto the *mulattiera*. You can find a **bar (5)** 5 mins. down the street in **Gillo**. Cross through a chestnut forest to reach the street that leads to a picnic place. Here, turn right onto the road towards the Alpe Toglie. About 1 km on, at a waterworks, turn off from the road onto a path. Now head steeply through the wood to reach a clearing. Here, do not turn right, but instead, keep straight on to ascend to an unpaved road which soon climbs up to the **Alpe Toglie (8)**.

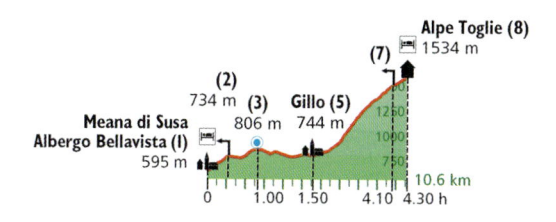

145

36 Alpe Toglie – Usseaux

7.30 hrs.
↑ 1340 ↓ 1430

A stroll through the Orsiera Rocciavrè Nature Park

The bulk of the Rocciamelone, towering 3000 metres over the valley, catches the eye during the ascent to the Colle dell'Orsiera. At the pass, the Monviso joins in to create a unique panorama. After a steep descent, take a high mountain trail through the upper villages of the Chisone Valley. The trail follows the same route as the Plaisentif trail which connects the Plaisentif chesse makers. Plaisentif cheese is rare; only produced in the Val Chisone and only during the month-long flowering of the violets flourishing here in the alpine terrain; these lend the cheese a special aroma. Usseaux, heralded as one of the »Borghi più belli d'Italia«, the »most beautiful spots in Italy«, is renowned for its murals. The life-size wall frescoes depict different professions. Didiero, the destination for the following day, is dedicated to music.

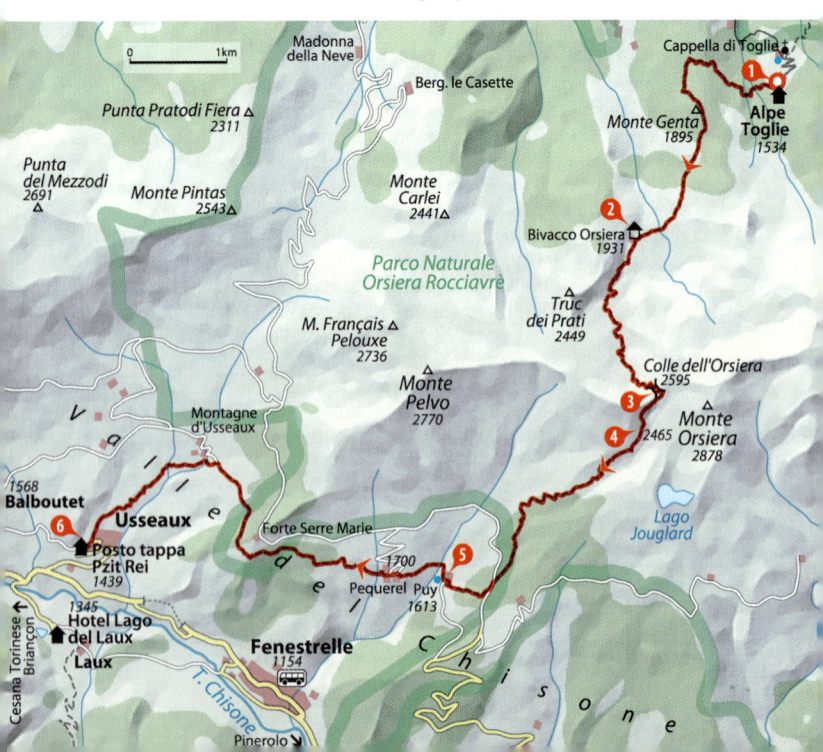

Starting point: Alpe Toglie, 1534 m.
Destination: Usseaux, 1439 m.
Length: 17.1 km.
Grade: Well-marked trail but not always distinct; sometimes very steep. The high mountain trail through the Chisone Valley leads more up and down than expected. During the descent to Puy, you will lose some precious height gain and have to slog back up again afterwards.
Refreshment: Nothing en route. Trattoria La Placette in Usseaux, not open on Thursdays, www.trattorialaplacette.com.
Accommodation: Bivacco Orsiera: 1931 m, open June–Sept., 10 B with blankets, oven, gas stove, fountain, shower. – **Usseaux:** 1439 m, Posto tappa Pzit Rei, open year-round, 20 B, HB 44 €, rustically comfortable, fantastic food, Anna Jahier and Claudio Challier, tel. +39 0121/838 76, www.pzit-rei.it. B&B Titòt, DR 70 €, tel. +39 338/326 63 13, www.casatitot.it. – **Hotel Lago del Laux:** 1345 m, open almost year-round, 8 DR à 126 €, specialty: polenta, fresh trout, Marinella and Franco Canton, tel. +39 0121/839 44, www.hotellaux.it (a short stretch past Usseaux, see Stage 37).
Shopping/Services: In Fenestrelle: shops, post office, cash dispenser, pharmacy.
Public transport: Bus line Sestriere – Fenestrelle – Pinerolo – Torino (timetable: www.sadem.it).
Information: www.comune.usseaux.to.it.
Tip: From the GTA, you will miss gaining an impression from the Forte di Fenestrelle. Above Puy, an excursion would not be far, but that entrance to the fort is closed when approaching from above. Since a visit is absolutely worthwhile, you really should spend an extra night (in Usseaux or, more expensive, at the Lago Laux). From Laux, a lovely path leads to Fenestrelle (45 mins.). Fortress: open daily in July/Aug (9 a.m.–6 p.m.), Sept.–June, only Thurs–Mon; info office (closed 12–14.30 p.m.) tel. +39 0121/18 36 00, www.fortedifenestrelle.com.

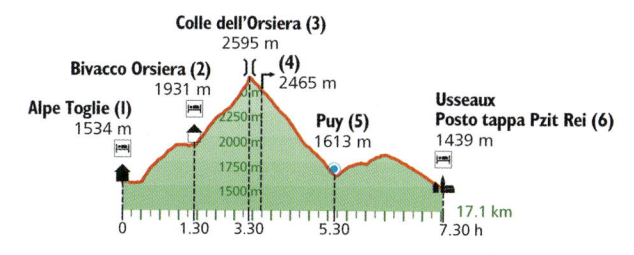

Murales in Usseaux.

Descent from Colle dell'Orsiera into the Val Chisone.

From the **Alpe Toglie (1)**, climb up past the cow shed and a short stretch along the slope, then turn right onto the well-marked path. After making a traverse, ascend steeply through the wood and, via Monte Benet, reach Monte Genta. Now traverse through open terrain southwards to reach the **Bivacco Orsiera (2)**, 1931 m. Starting at the hut, ascend south-westwards along the slope. Further up, the trail is somewhat overgrown by alder thicket. Cross over open *alpe* terrain again on the Pian Marmote. Now head south along bends that become steeper as they lead to the **Colle dell'Orsiera (3)**, 2595 m; a wall and trenches are a reminder of the battle of 1747 (see also Stage V36). On the other side, descend south-westwards through a little valley onto the *alpe* terrain in the Chisone Valley. Afterwards, through open wood, climb steeply down to the Finestre road at Prà Catinat, then continue along the path to the right to reach the village of **Puy (5)**, 1613 m. Now to the right in a bend through a stream bed and ascend once again to **Pequerel**, 1700 m. An avalanche wedge, built in 1716, still stands bravely as protection while the village itself is falling into ruin. Once, like Puy, a flourishing farming community, today, also like Puy, only visited for a couple of weeks at a time by the families who are now commuters.

Ascend along the road to the first bend and then turn left onto a path. Climbing up north-westwards, the route levels out somewhat and then continues, sometimes exposed, just below the Forte Serre Marie. Now descend onto the *alpe* terrain of the Montagne d'Usseaux. Before reaching the huts, climb down to the left along the stream to the road to **Usseaux (6)**. By the way, the wooden signs sporting proverbs along the last stretch of trail were erected by the host of the Posto tappa in Usseaux. Claudio is a wood carver and, together with his wife Anna, displays his talents in the creation of a cosy inn.

> *Directly at the terrace of the Posto tappa, you have a view of the **fortress of Fenestrelle**, which runs along a rocky ridge almost like the Great Wall of China. A covered flight of 4000 steps (Scala Coperta) and a 2500-step exterior stairway (Scala Reale) connect the various bastions with one another along a three kilometre stretch with a height difference of 635 metres. Especially when it is dark, this presents quite a sight when the largest fortress fortification in the Alps becomes a string of lights.*

Forte Fenestrelle, the »Great Wall of China« for the Alps.

V35 Salbertrand – Rifugio Arlaud

2.00 hrs.
↑770 ↓30

Ecolodge in the Gran Bosco di Salbertrand nature park

The route over the Assietta high ridge is extremely scenic as it follows the trail for the »Glorious Return«. At the same time, you could touch upon a 3700-hectare woodland area which, because of the unusual abundance of European spruce for this part of the Western Alps, has been made into a nature reserve since 1980. The Rifugio Arlaud is one of the first alpine huts to be awarded an Ecolabel. Its energy supply is met exclusively with solar power and wood; the food served here consists of locally-produced organic products.

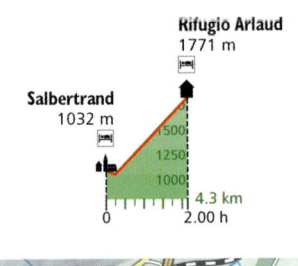

Starting point: Salbertrand, railway station, 1032 m.
Destination: Rifugio Arlaud, 1771 m.
Length: 4.3 km.
Grade: Well-marked, distinct trail.
Refreshment: Nothing en route.
Accommodation: Rifugio Daniele Arlaud: 1771 m, end of May–Oct., as well as Jan.–April at the weekends, 16 B, HB 40 €, Elisa Pecar, tel. +39 335/40 16 24, www.rifugioarlaud.it.
Shopping: Nothing available.
Public transport: Salbertrand is situated on the railway line Torino – Bardonecchia.
Note: The stretch of the GTA between Susa and Salbertrand is somewhat spoiled by the construction of a motorway and is therefore not included in the route description presented here.

From the **railway station**, turn left to ascend along the street and then turn left again onto the Via Flavio Arlaud. Cross over the tracks and then the river; now turn right and cross under the motorway through the underpass. Afterwards, the trail to the visitor's centre for the nature park forks off to the left. To the right, the route continues toward the Rifugio Arlaud. Through woods and passing various tumble-down houses, reach the *alpe* settlement of **Montagne Seu**, 1771 m, perched on a panoramic clearing. Here you also find the **Rifugio Daniele Arlaud**.

The hamlet of Seu with the Rifugio d'Arlaud.

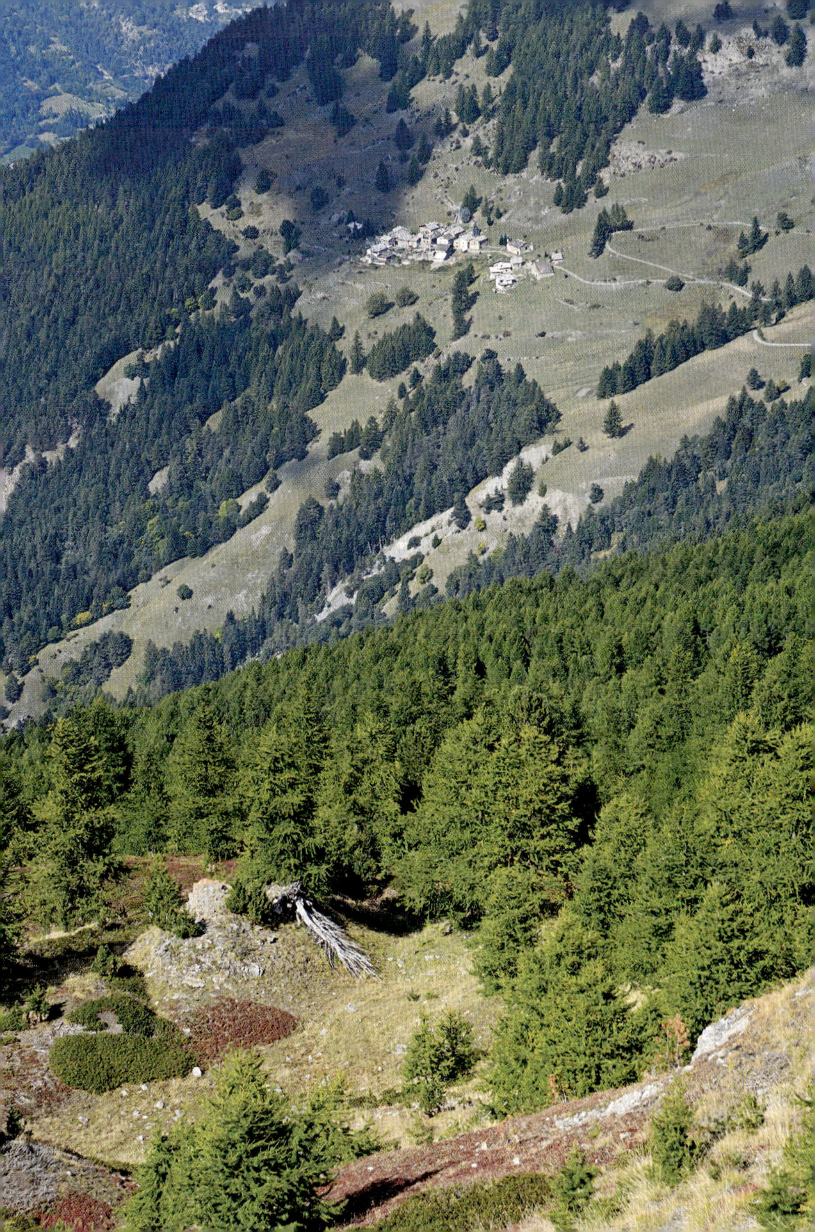

V36 — Rifugio Arlaud – Usseaux

6.00 hrs.
↑800 ↓1130

Battlefields in the »Olympic« mountains

Over the ridge between the Susa and the Chisone valleys, the Strada dell'Assietta, an unpaved track about 60 kilometres in length, connects Sestriere, the Piedmont's most famous winter sports resort, with the Colle delle Finestre; in 1932, the track was constructed along an important strategic line of defence. Today, this is a fantastic panoramic route which is, unfortunately, also a favourite for motor tourists. Ideally, you can plan your route for days when the road is closed to traffic (July/August, every Wednesday and every Saturday 9 a.m.–5 p.m.).

In the battle of 1747, French and Spanish forces tried to invade the Piedmont by skirting around the fortresses at Exilles and Fenestrelle. Already aware of the plan, the defending forces (the Piedmontians were also supported by Swiss mercenaries and Austrian battalions) came out the winners in this slaughter. On the Testa dell'Assietta, you can still see the military positions and the trenches very clearly. And when you look more carefully, you can also see, far below, the »battlefield« of the 2006 Winter Sport Olympics, including the tumbledown ski jumps at Pragelato.

Starting point: Rifugio Arlaud, 1771 m.
Destination: Usseaux, 1439 m.
Length: 19.2 km.
Grade: Well-marked paths and military trails. Until reaching the Assietta ridge, the trail is not very distinct.
Refreshment: Trattoria Nido dell'Aquila (closed Mon.) and Agriturismo Edelweiss in Balboutet.
Accommodation: Balboutet: 1568 m, B&B La Maison, tel. +39 0121/39 65 57 or 340/074 14 19. – **Usseaux:** see Stage 36.
Shopping/Services: See Stage 36.
Public transport: See Stage 36.
Information: www.stradadellassietta.it.
Tip: Every year in mid-July, the battle at the Colle dell'Assietta is recreated in historical costumes. Info: Associazione »Festa del Piemont al Còl ed l'Assietta«, tel. +39 011/99 61 14.

The Bergerie Assietta on the Assietta ridge road.

From **Montagne Seu**, at first, ascend north-eastwards along the slope, then cross over a clearing towards a raised hunter's hide. A little later, pass a ruin while ascending slightly to the left (southeast) to reach the next clearing where you ignore the path to the right leading to the Alpe Selle. Continue in the direction of »Strade dei Cannoni«. Cross the next meadow by bearing slightly to the right. Above the tree line and to the left, the path soon becomes a reinforced cannon track and then reaches the broad Assietta ridge.

Along a wide military track, head north-eastwards to pass below the Testa di Mottas to reach the **Testa dell'Assietta**, 2566 m, crowned with an obelisk. Shortly before the road junction on the **Colle dell'Assietta**, 2472 m, the GTA forks off to the right. Crossing over meadows through a little valley which becomes narrower, pass the *alpe* and **Bergerie Assietta**, then descend to Cerogne, 1740 m, and continue via **Balboutet** to reach **Usseaux**.

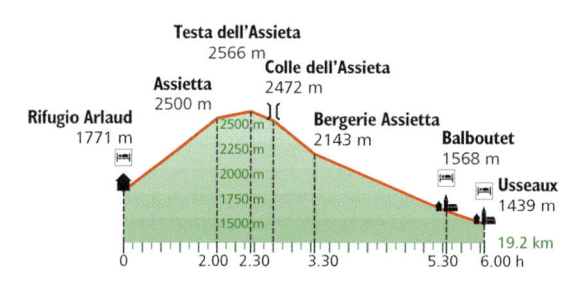

37 Usseaux – Basiglia/Didiero

7.30 hrs.
↑ 1380 ↓ 1450

Witch's trail and a fateful route

Vallone del Laux, Via delle Masche.

Witch's work? It appears as if creatures are creeping out of the trees. A stretch towards the Colle dell'Albergian is accompanied by the fantastic wooden figures of the »Via delle Masche«. What would it take to negotiate this stretch in winter when it is already so strenuous in summer? During Christmas 1440, 80 Waldensian children failed to do so as they fled from their pursuers from the Chisone Valley into the Germanasca Valley. On the pass, they met a miserable death by freezing. Also during the winter of 1689/90, in Balsiglia, the Waldensians suffered hardship, barricading themselves from enemy troops: 360 resistance fighters against 4000 Frenchmen.

Starting point: Usseaux, 1439 m.
Destination: Basiglia, 1370 m, alternatively Didiero, 1245 m.
Length: 20.6 km until reaching Balsiglia.
Grade: Well-marked, mostly distinct trail.
Refreshment: at the Lago Laux.
Accommodation: Hotel Lago del Laux: see Stage 36. – **Balsiglia:** the Posto tappa, (open July/Aug), is self-catering (but no grocery store in the village!). – **Didiero:** 1245 m, Agriturismo La Miando, open year-round, rooms (28 B) HB 50 € and Posto tappa (10 B) HB 45 €, delicious food, Renata Brunet & Pierluigi Bertalotto, tel. +39 0121/80 10 18 or +39 339/276 32 15. – also **La Foresteria di Massello:** 1157 m, Località Molino, about 2 km before Didiero, year-round, DR à 80 €, dormitory (10 B) 28 €, Mario & Isabella, tel. +39 0121/80 86 78, www.foresteriamassello.it.
Shopping/Services: Nothing available.
Public transport: None.

Note: On the evening before, at the very latest, you have to reserve in Didiero for the transfer from Balsiglia. Otherwise, after the long crossing over the pass (7.30 hrs.) to Didiero, you'll have to walk another 2 hrs. or 4 kms on tarmac to reach the Foresteria. Pierluigi, from the Agriturismo La Miando, is happy to pick up his guests from Balsiglia; he can also organize the key for the Museum of Balsiglia, which is worth a visit.

Tip: The Waldensian Museum in Balsiglia thoroughly documents the courageous resistance put up against the French army by the Waldensians after their return from Switzerland. A visit is only by appointment through Edda Tron, tel. +39 349/181 33 64. Guided tours, also in English, can be organised through the Waldensian tourist office »il barba«, tel. +39 0121/95 02 03, www.fondazione-valdese.org.

Usseaux
1439
Posto tappa
Pzit Rei
Balboutet
1568
Pourrières
1418
Cesana
Torinese
Briançon
Fraisse
1421
Forte Serre Marie
Pequerel
Puy
1613
1345
Hotel Lago
del Laux
Laux
Fenestrelle
1154
T. Chisone
Pinerolo
Mentoulles
1071
Pinerolo
Valle del Chisone
Bergerie del
Laux
M. Ciabertas
2748
1828
Vallone dell'Albergian
M. Albergian
3041
2116
Rocca
degli Angeli
2231
Becco
delle Masche
2452
Punta
Belvedere
2630
Monte
Gran Miuol
2974
Laghi dell'Albergian
Bric Rosso
3026
Colle dell'Albergian
2713
Becco dell'Aquila
2809
Fea Nera
2946
Truc Cialabrie
2936
Valle di Massello
Cascata del Pis
Bergerie
del Lauson
T. Germanasca di Massello
Pleine
1895
Clot del
Mian
Punta Raccias
2205
Eidut
Monte
Pelvo
2803
Balsiglia
1370
1257
Aiasse
Gros Passet
Porte
Roberso
1188
Porrence
Massello
Bric Ghinivert
3037
M. Laparè
2198
Bergerie
del Ghinivert
Ciaberso
Perrero/Perosa Argentina
T. Germanasca
Campo la Salza
1090
Parco Naturale
Val Troncea
Monte
Fournet
2737
Serre
M. Cucoulioun
1471
Monte
Peolioso
2886
Salza di Pinerolo
Didiero
1245
Meinier
0
1km
1
2
3
4
5
6
7
8
9
10
11
12

From **Usseaux (1)**, descend along the street, turn right via the SS 23, then turn left onto the narrow street to the Lago Laux (Occitan, Laus = lake). Shortly after the popular trout pond, the street ends at the entrance to **Laux (3)**, 1345 m. It's well worth a walk around the archaic Waldensian village where notice boards point out interesting information. At the end of the street, continue to the right while ascending into the *Vallone* along a track road. When the unpaved road exits the wood and levels out, the GTA forks off to the right and leads along the old *mulattiera* to reach the last still usable building on the *alpe* terrain of the **Bergerie del Laux**. Afterwards, enjoy the lovely wood carvings along the edge of the trail produced by Daniel Giovanni of Fenestrelle. Pass the Fontaine des Chamois with its four *Holzkännel* (hollowed-out tree trunks), then continue along a very steep stretch, crossing through a forest. It soon opens up to give views to the pass and into the Chisone Valley. Further up, a sign marks the turn-off to the Laghi Albergian. On the **Colle dell'Albergian (6)**, 2713 m, a sweeping view takes in the Barre des Écrins, Pelvoux and Mont Chaberton, as well as the Colle Finestre to Rocciamelone and Monte Rosa. From the pass, traverse the left-hand slope towards the two prominent military ruins and pass these by skirting left to reach the next higher terrain. A long traverse leads eastward to the Bergerie del Lauson, where the trail above the huts takes a sharp hook to the west and the **Cascata del Pis** comes nearer and nearer. The waterfall is especially im-

Balsiglia.

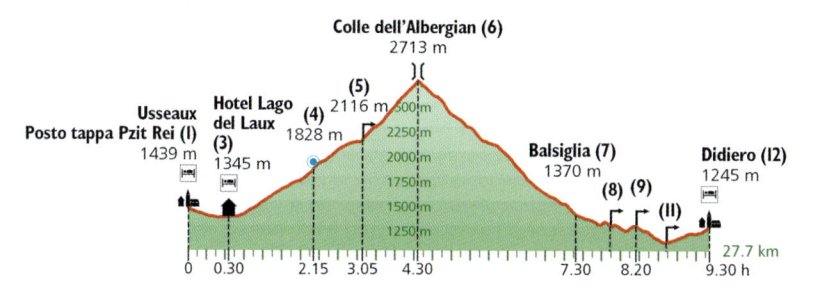

pressive when viewed from the valley floor. On the left-hand side, cross over the Germanasca stream whose lovely rock pools are a temptation to take a break, then reach the ruins of Clot del Mian. A little later, reach **Balsiglia (7)**.

> *Balsiglia is a »fortress« of the Waldensian resistance. This is hard to imagine if you haven't visited the museum in the old school. At the »Quattro Denti«, the Valdesi had set up an entrenchment. The »four teeth«, above the furthermost region of the Massello Valley, presented a natural fortress here. Again and again, the Valdesi effectively beat back the French troops and they kept it up for an entire winter. 360 defenders against an attacking force of 4000. When French reinforcements arrived, accompanied by cannon, it seemed that their fate had been sealed. On May 24, a fog set in and with it, the darkness of nightfall. Silent, shadowy figures crept past the soldiers, then negotiated »almost vertical mountain slopes by lying on their stomachs and pulling each other by the hands.« (from the memoirs of L'Ombraille, the governor of Pinerolo). Along breakneck trails, they managed to escape into the Angrogna Valley. Two days later, a message of peace arrived: religious freedom had been granted. The Piedmont had declared war on France.*

From Balsiglia, continue on foot or get picked up by Pierluigi Bertalotto and be driven to **Didiero (12)**. Only 20 people live here year-round. When Pierluigi doesn't have any guests, he sells his crusty bread, baked in a wood-fired oven, and canned vegetables that the »Cugina« in the »Cucina« (his cousin Renata in the kitchen) conjures up, in the markets in Pinerolo and Turin.

> *Didiero, too, has a museum in the old Waldensian schoolhouse (since 2012, a Posto tappa on the 1st floor). The classroom reflects the hard life of the children. Trekking to school was long and strenuous, especially in winter. Responsible for heating the school, each child had to bring a log along with him every day. If anyone forgot, the teacher would simply toss the child's »Zoccoli«, his wooden shoes, in the fire instead. This punishment was certainly a splendid »fuel for memory«.*

38 | Didiero – Ghigo di Prali

4.30 hrs.
↑ 730 ↓ 520

Woodstock & Waldensian villages

In 1985, the first music festival was celebrated here, and with such success, that 1988, even some stars performed and the little secluded hamlet of Didiero, as a result, was transformed every year into a virtual »Woodstock« at a June weekend. Parallel to this event, the »Murales« were created; a painter's tribute to the Salza Music Concerti. At the Agriturismo, you should take one of the maps for the Murales, so that you can find the individual frescoes and also discover to which song they are dedicated. During the ascent, you can, for example, recognize a song by Bob Marley and one by Bob Dylan. The GTA follows the same route as the »Glorious Return«, the Valdesi, however, only travelled by night. In Rodoretto and in Ghigo, Waldensian museums tell their story.

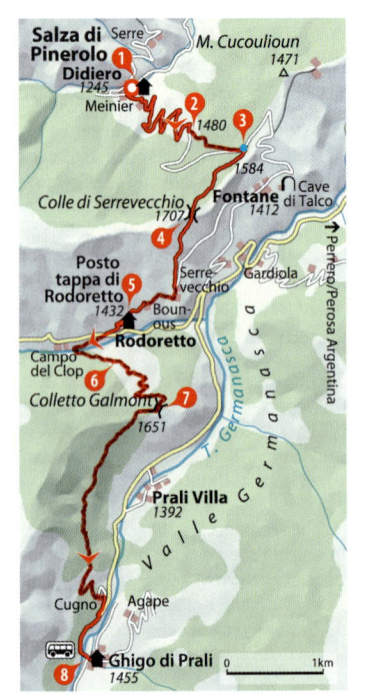

Starting point: Didiero, 1245 m.
Destination: Ghigo di Prali, 1455 m.
Length: 12.6 km.
Grade: Well-marked track roads and distinct paths. An easy walk.
Refreshment: Osteria da Mafalda in Rodoretto, tel. +39 0121/80 77 16.
Accommodation: Posto tappa di Rodoretto: 1432 m, self-catering, 15 B, you can get the key in the house opposite, tel. +39 340/429 06 98. – **Ghigo di Prali:** 1455 m, Albergo delle Alpi, except for November, open year-round, rooms (40 B) HB 65 € and Posto tappa (10 B) HB 43 €, Angelo Giuliano, tel. +39 0121/80 75 37 or 80 61 08 or +39 333/740 78 62.
Shopping/Services: Shop, cash dispenser and pharmacy in Ghigo di Prali.
Public transport: Bus line Torino – Pinerolo – Prali Ghigo – Seggiovie 13 laghi, timetable: www.sadem.it.
Tip: In case you have to sit it out for a day in Didiero or Ghigo due to bad weather, you can make use of the time by visiting the exciting *Scopriminiera*, the largest talc mine in Europe. The mine is located on the main road below Fontane; guided tours also in English; open March–November 9.30 a.m.–12.30 p.m. and 1.30 p.m.–5.00 p.m.; www.scopriminiera.it.

At the **village limits (1)**, turn left to cross the bridge. If you are looking for the Murales, stroll through the hamlets of Inverso and Meinier. If not, ascend directly along the road towards Meinier. Then continue on, short-cutting a couple of bends en route, to the **Colletto delle Fontane (3)**, with a fountain and a lovely picnic place. Keep to the right along the ridge to reach the **Colle di Serrevecchio (4)**, then left along the southern slope to descend via ancient hamlets to **Rodoretto (5)**, 1432 m. From the village, head up the valley (only for a short stretch), then turn left onto the gravel trail to descend to the stream and climb up once again. The GTA, which short-cuts the bends, is barely waymarked, so it's easier to follow the forest track. From the **Colletto Galmont (7)**, 1651 m, for a little while

Rodoretto.

along the crest of the ridge, then turn left to descend along a trail which is also marked as an MTB track. In Cugno, meet up with a tarmac road which, just before reaching **Ghigo di Prali (8)**, leads to the valley road.

> [i] The **Tempio Valdese** (Waldensians didn't use the word »church«, but instead, the word »temple«) was the only one not destroyed during the war of 1686. It was also here that the priest, Henri Arnaud, leader of the »Glorious Return«, held his first sermon after the group left from Lake Geneva. Within these walls, dating from 1556, a museum has been established (open July/Aug. except Mon. 3 p.m.–6 p.m., on holidays 11 a.m.–12.30 p.m., otherwise, also request, tel. +39 0121/80 75 19).

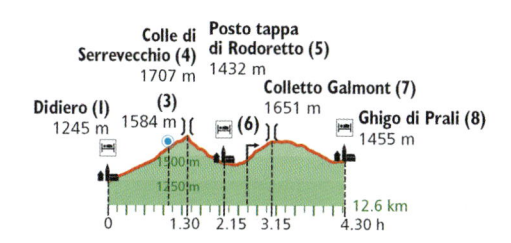

| 39 | *Ghigo di Prali – Villanova* | 4.45 hrs. ↑330 ↓1520 |

The Conca dei 13 laghi – highlight in the Germanasca Valley

The plateau of the 13 lakes is very popular; one reason for this is because a chairlift brings you comfortably up to it. A viewpoint opens up a sweeping panorama that reaches all the way to Monte Rosa. A wonderfully laid military trail traverses to the Colle Giulian, where you will be surprised by the close-up view of the Monviso. Usually, this peak sticks out from a line of clouds like a rocket appearing ready for take-off. The descent into the Pellice Valley is not so pleasing to the eye since a new alpine road has been crudely cut into the slope.

Military trail, Conca dei 13 laghi.

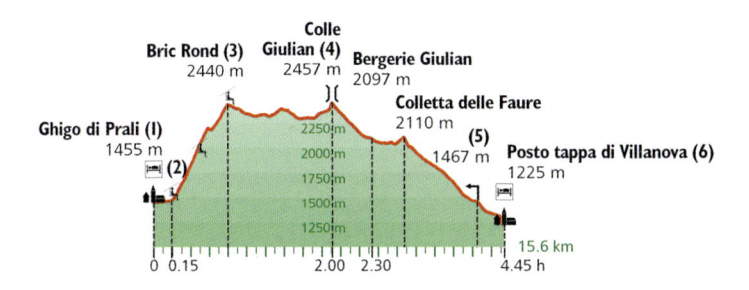

Ghigo di Prali (1) 1455 m — **Bric Rond (3)** 2440 m — **Colle Giulian (4)** 2457 m — **Bergerie Giulian** 2097 m — **Colletta delle Faure** 2110 m — **(5)** 1467 m — **Posto tappa di Villanova (6)** 1225 m

15.6 km / 4.45 h

Starting point: Ghigo di Prali, 1455 m, alternatively, the mountain terminus for the chair lift Bric Rond, 2440 m.
Destination: Villanova, 1225 m.
Length: about 16 km (excluding the stretch with the lift).
Grade: Well-marked, pleasantly laid military trails. Tough descent into the Valle Pellice, sometimes along a road.
Refreshment: Nothing en route.
Accommodation: Posto tappa di Villanova: 1225 m, end May–end Oct., 10 B, HB 38 €, Elda Rostagnol, tel. +39 340/329 74 28 or +39 0121/95 78 50. – Alternative route: **Rifugio Lago Verde:** 2583 m, CAI, 56 B, Guido & Silvia, HB 39 €, tel. +39 348/600 99 20, www.rifugiolagoverde.it. – **Alpe Crosenna:** 1654 m, Agriturismo La Porziuncola, 10 B, HB 35 €, tel. +39 0121/59 02 88 or +39 349/373 72 83.
Shopping: Bobbio Pellice: shop, post office.
Public transport: Chair lift in Malzat, just past Ghigo; June only Sun., July/Aug. daily, at the first 3 weekends in Sept. 8 a.m.–5 p.m., one-way trip to the mountain terminus Bric Rond 6 €, www.nuova13laghi.com. Bus line Bobbio Pellice – Pinerolo, timetable: www.sadem.it. From Pinerolo, continue by rail. The railway station at Torre Pellice is no longer in service.
Information: www.ghironda.com/vpellice/comuni/bobbi.htm.
Note: If you wish to abort the trek in the Valle Pellice, after passing the Bergerie Giulian, turn off onto the trail leading directly to Bobbio Pellice (about 2.30 hrs.), since there is no bus service from Villanova.
Alternative: If you prefer a more alpine experience, there is a lovely alternative route via the Rifugio Lago Verde, from Ghigo 4.30 hrs. The next day, cross over the Colletto di Gran Guglia. At the trail junction which follows, turn right (the route noted in the map as the GTA turning left to the Colle Giulian is no real gain and is also very long, many ascents and descents) and head directly along the ridge to the Punta Cerisira. Now descend towards the Alpe Bancet, then right via the Col Content to the Alpe Crosenna, 3.30 hrs. Here, do not descend into the valley to Villanova, but instead, keep to the high mountain trail (sure-footedness required!) to the Rifugio Jervis (see Stage 40), 3 hrs.

From **Ghigo (1)**, head for a short stretch along the road until reaching the valley station of the chairlift (2) in **Malzat**. The chairlift consists of two sections; at the Pian dell'Alpet, transfer to the mountain station for **Bric Rond (3)**, 2440 m. On a clear day, be sure to take the very rewarding excursion to the left which leads to a viewpoint (Monte Rosa, Rocciamelone, and more). From the chairlift, head right to the **Conca dei Tredici Laghi**, where you catch a view of three of the 13 lakes. At the prominent military ruins past the

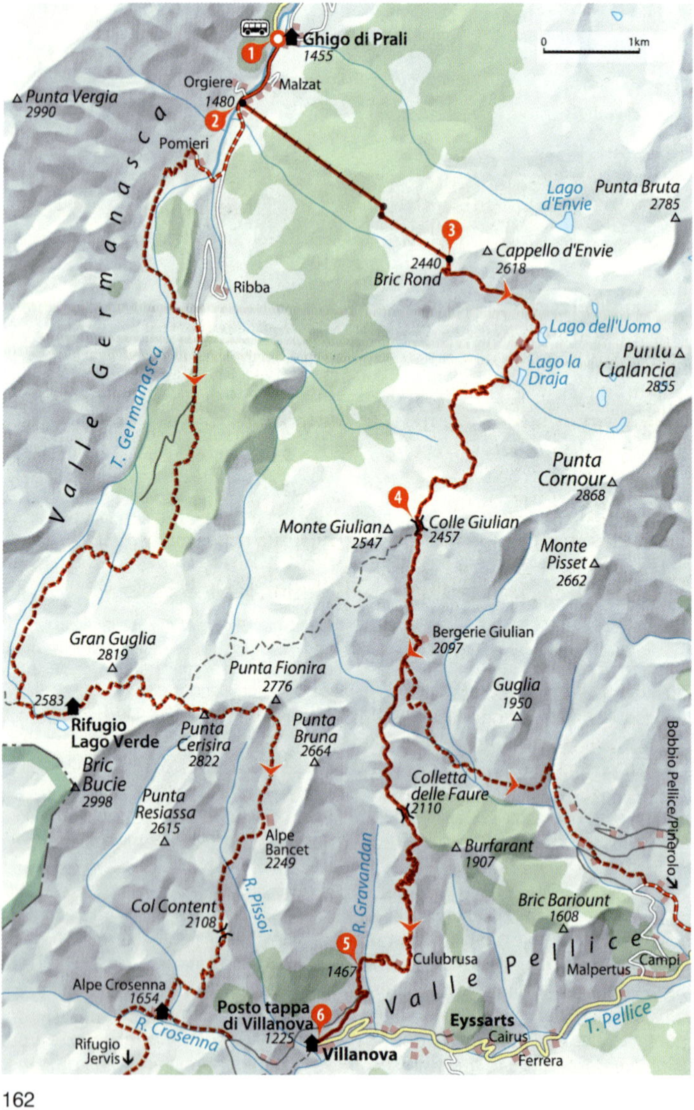

Ghigo di Prali
1455
0
1km
Orgiere
1480
Malzat
Punta Vergia
2990
Pomieri
Valle Germanasca
Ribba
T. Germanasca
Lago d'Envie
Punta Bruta
2785
2440
Bric Rond
Cappello d'Envie
2618
Lago dell'Uomo
Lago la Draja
Punta Cialancia
2855
Punta Cornour
2868
Monte Giulian
2547
Colle Giulian
2457
Monte Pisset
2662
Bergerie Giulian
2097
Gran Guglia
2819
Punta Fionira
2776
Guglia
1950
2583
Rifugio Lago Verde
Punta Cerisira
2822
Punta Bruna
2664
Bric Bucie
2998
Punta Resiassa
2615
Colletta delle Faure
2110
Alpe Bancet
2249
Burfarant
1907
Bobbio Pellice/Pinerolo
R. Pissoi
R. Gravandan
Col Content
2108
Bric Bariount
1608
Culubrusa
1467
Valle Pellice
Malpertus
Campi
Alpe Crosenna
1654
R. Crosenna
Posto tappa di Villanova
1225
Villanova
Eyssarts
Cairus
Ferrera
T. Pellice
Rifugio Jervis

Conca dei 13 laghi.

Lago dell'Uomo, continue to the right, pass the Lago la Draja, then cross over a stream. Now along a partially paved military trail, traverse the western side of the ridge until, at the **Colle Giulian (4)**, 2457 m, you cross over to the other side. Head southwards to the **Bergerie Giulian**, 2097 m, from which you then follow a track road. This leads for a fairly long stretch, keeping to the same height, and has pretty much destroyed the lovely, old walking trail. After yet another ascent (an easy one, but not a very welcome one at this point), to **Colletta delle Faure**, 2110 m, the road then plunges down in steep zigzags into the valley. Not until reaching the huts of Randulire are we able to leave the track behind. The barely trodden path leads through a steep, grassy slope to the huts at Culubrusa and then meets up again with the track; take the track to cross over the Rio Gravandan.
When you ascend once again, pay close attention so as not to miss the footpath that descends to the left (only marked with a single cairn); this shortcuts the track so that, at the end, you only have to descend for a short way along the dusty road to reach **Villanova (6)**.

40 Villanova – Rifugio Barbara Lowrie

5.00 hrs.
↑1210 ↓680

A gorge, some military trails and a botanical garden

Established in 1976, Oasi del Barant is the name given to the 4000 hectare nature reserve at the valley head of the Valle Pellice where two attractive mountain valleys merge. Alpine ibex, deer and mouflon were reintroduced here. The rare Lanza's Alpine Salamander is endemic to this region. Among the botanical rarities is the insect-eating plant, »Pinguicula Alpina« (alpine butterwort), which you may find in the botanical alpine garden on the Colle Barant. This is a pristine, historically interesting landscape. In the gorge, ascending to the Conca del Prà, Waldensians had to fight for their lives; an avalanche buried a group of people here in 1655, as revealed in the name Piano dei Morti. A sweeping panorama accompanies us into the neighbouring valley where the annual mountain race, »Tre Rifugi Val Pellice«, takes place every year in July.

Starting point: Villanova, 1225 m.
Destination: Rif. Barbara Lowrie, 1753 m.
Length: 13.7 km.

Grade: Well-marked *mulattiera*, military trails. The »short-cuts« are always very steep.
Refreshment: Rifugio Jervis, and the Locanda Ciabotà del Prà, next door.
Accommodation: Rifugio Jervis: 1732 m, CAI, open year-round, 80 B, HB 35 €, very good meals, Roby Boulard, tel. +39 0121/93 27 55 or +39 338/638 56 77, www.rifugiojervis.it; reservation required. – **Locanda Ciabotà del Prà:** 1732 m, June–Oct., 15 B, tel. +39 0121/95 34 77. – Rifugio Barant is closed. – **Rifugio Barbara Lowrie:** 1753 m, CAI, , beg. May–end Sept., and the weekends in Oct., 26 B, HB 35 €, very good meals, Roberto Pascal, tel. +39 0121/93 00 77, www.rifugiobarbara.it.
Shopping/Services: Nothing available.
Public transport: None.

Pass through **Villanova (1)** and follow the ancient *mulattiera* high above the Torrente Pellice. At the hardly recognizable ruins of Fort Mirabouc (built in 1565 to keep the Waldensians under control, as well as the traffic over the pass; destroyed in 1794), the trail merges

Grange del Pis at the Rifugio Barbara Lowrie.

into the gravel track which leads to Conca del Prà. Pass the roaring Cascata del Pis and then the Piano dei Morti; now you can short-cut some stretches of the gravel track once again. As soon as the gravel track begins to lead to the valley cleft, the Colle della Maddalena, 1821 m, the *mulattiera* crosses a little knoll, thereby creating a shorter route which leads directly to the Conca del Prà, a marvellous high plain surrounded by a wreath of rugged mountain peaks. Now head straight on to the **Rifugio Jervis (2)**.

From the Rifugio, you can head directly eastwards over the meadow to reach the bridge at the opening to the Conca del Prà. On the other side, a trail sign points out the direction of the ascent along the western slope. The red/white-marked route short-cuts the military track time and again as it makes its way to the **Colle Barant (4)**. Just before the pass, you can visit the Giardino Botanico Peyronel. Immediately past the Colle Barant is the Rifugio Barant, 2373 m (closed due to water problems). Again, during the descent southwards, the trail short-cuts the sweeping bends of the military track. At the end, you must make another short ascent to the **Rifugio Barbara Lowrie (5)**.

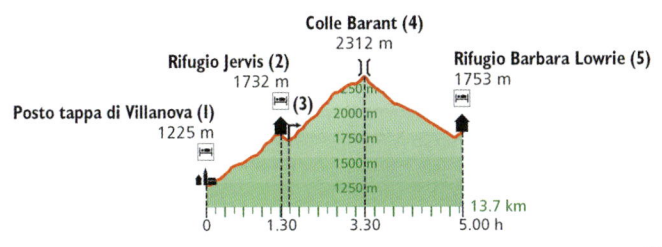

41 Rifugio Barbara Lowrie – Pian Melzè

4.00 hrs.
↑810 ↓810

The mighty Monviso

Because the original route for the GTA wasn't planned logically, a new, more direct route has been waymarked, which does more justice to the scenic landscape. Often, you can participate in a unique spectacle as the sea of cloud cover in the Po Valley confronts the mountainous barrier. On the Colle della Gianna, you meet up with the mightiness of the Monviso, and at the destination for this stage, awaits what is perhaps the best polenta in the entire Cottian Alps.

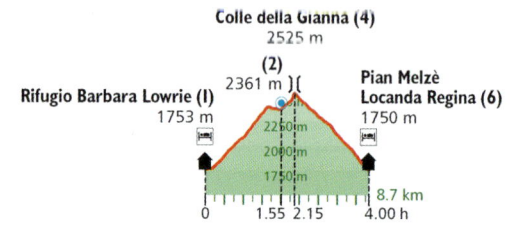

Colle della Gianna (4)
2525 m
(2)
2361 m
Rifugio Barbara Lowrie (I)
1753 m
Pian Melzè
Locanda Regina (6)
1750 m
8.7 km
0   1.55 2.15   4.00 h

Starting point: Rif. Barbara Lowrie, 1753 m.
Destination: Pian Melzè (Località Pian della Regina), 1750 m.
Length: 8.7 km.
Grade: Well-marked, narrow, but distinct path; in the uppermost heights, boulder fields and scree.

Refreshment: Nothing en route.
Accommodation: Locanda Regina (Baita della Polenta): 1750 m, open year-round, 7 DR, HB 60 €, and Posto tappa (20 B), HB 45 €, delicious antipasti and polenta, Gabriele and Roberta Genre, tel. +39 0175/949 07 or +39 333/314 29 36, www.pianregina.it, www.locanda-regina.com.
Shopping/Services: Crissolo: shop, post office, cash dispenser, pharmacy, accommodation.
Public transport: Bus line Pian del Re – Pian Regina (or Melzè) – Crissolo end June–end Sept. only Sat/Sun, timetable: www.vallipo.cn.it. The same bus company services the daily bus line Crissolo – Paesana: www.dossettobus.it. From Paesana to Saluzzo, Cuneo or Torino: www.atibus.it.
Information: Tourist office Crissolo, tel. +39 0175/94 01 31, www.comune.crissolo.cn.it.

Polenta in the Locanda Regina.

Behind the **Rifugio (1)**, cross over the level meadow. If you meet anybody carrying a mattress with them, no worries, you are walking along one of the most famous boulder fields in the Piedmont. At the trail junction, ignore trail No. 113 (GTA) and take trail No. 111 instead, which leads steeply through larch forest into the Vallone della Gianna. On the **Colle Proussera**, 2198 m, if you climb up the knoll to the left, you can enjoy a view of the Monte Rosa.

From the saddle, ascend a little, then the trail dips downwards, leading south-eastwards through blocky boulders to reach the source, **Mait di Viso (2)**; meet up again with trail No. 113 (GTA). Now a steep stretch brings you to the **Colle della Gianna (4)**, 2525 m.

Here, we leave the province of Torino and enter the province of Cuneo.

At the first trail junction, descend to the left, cross over the mountain meadows of the Cassera Sbiasere. A steep descent leads to an ascending road at **Pian Melzè (6)**; you can short-cut the bends.

Monviso, landmark of the Cottian Alps; the descent from the Colle Gianna into the Po Valley.

The Monviso country –
from the Po Valley into the Varaita Valley

Monviso, Monte Viso, Mont Visible – this peak, lying to the south of the Gran Paradiso, steals the show, towering more than 500 metres above all the surrounding summits on the border ridge of the southern Italian Alps. A solitary Titan at 3841 metres above sea level, the highest mountain of the Cottian Alps, a mere 30 kms. from the Po Valley plain and only 90 kms. from the sea. These facts explain why, for a very long time, people thought it was the highest summit in the entire Alps, and also why it earned the name »the visible mountain«. The waters that flow down from Monviso are the source for the Po River (»Sorgenti del Po«), which waxes from a little mountain creek to become the longest river In Italy before it finally empties into the Adriatic Sea. The Monviso is one of the first alpine summits given a name in the Roman era: Monte Vesulus. It also appeared early on in literature and the arts; both Vergilius and Dante wrote down descriptions of the mount. Leonardo da Vinci was the first artist to mention the name used today. In the 14th century, the mountain appeared in the Canterbury Tales by Geoffrey Chaucer and

Monviso, view from the Lanzo valleys.

caught the attention of the English. Nevertheless, it took a few centuries more before scientific interest and the pioneering spirit overcame the fear of the mountains. In August 1861, Edward Whymper (later on, the first mountaineer to climb the Matterhorn), attempted to climb the Monviso starting at the French side, but his efforts failed. Only a little later on, William Mathews and Frederic William Jacomb discovered a better approach from the Val Varaita, along with their guides from Chamonix, the brothers Jean-Baptiste and Michel Croz (who died in 1865 during the tragic first ascent of the Matterhorn), and became the first to stand on the summit on 30 August, 1861.

A milestone in the Alpine history in Italy was set with the expedition organized by Quintino Sella; at the

Bosco dell'Alevè (Stages 43 and 44).

time, the 36 year-old, considered the founder of the Italian Alpine Club, the CAI, was a geologist and a politician. On August 12, 1863, as he stood on the summit of the Monviso, the brilliant notion to create the CAI occurred to him. In August, 1864, the first women, Alessandra Boarelli and Cecilia Fillia, who was only 14 at the time, reached the peak via the »normal« route. Two years later, the first hut of the alpine club was erected on the Po Valley side: the Rifugio Alpetto. A rocketing demand led to the building of the Rifugio Quintino Sella, a craggy level higher, in 1905. By then, every rock face of the Monviso had already been climbed.

Because the Monviso counts as one of the most prestigious mountains, starting at the source of the Po, the action is somewhat more lively and international. On the IGC map, virtually all the routes around the mountain are marked as the GTA, causing confusion. We chose what is, in our opinion, the most beautiful route; by the way, this happens to be the best in the culinary sense as well. A large leg of the stretch leads through a fascinating, rocky wasteland replete with magical lakes. The might of the Monviso will amaze you, especially on a clear day when a sweeping view opens up over the Po Valley plain, reaching all the way to the Monte Rosa. During the descent into the Val Varaita, you will become acquainted with the Bosco dell'Alevè. With an area of 825 hectares, it is considered the largest Swiss Pine forest in the Alps. Here you can find gnarled specimens that are more than 600 years old.

42 Pian Melzè – Rifugio Alpetto

4.30 hrs.
↑1000 ↓480

Source of the Po and the King of Rock

Since there is a road leading to the Pian del Re and the source of the Po, the splendid mulattiera provides some solitude. The rest of the natural monuments are then enjoyed in group dynamics: the marvellous lakes, which are ideal for swimming, and the Re di Piedra. The higher you climb, the easier it is to understand why the Monviso is called the »King (made) of Rock«. Since it is almost always chaotic at the Rifugio Quintino Sella, the base camp for a summit attempt of the Monviso, an overnight in the Rifugio Alpetto instead will prove much more pleasant. Although you will lose a couple of metres of altitude, the lovely landscape more than makes up for it

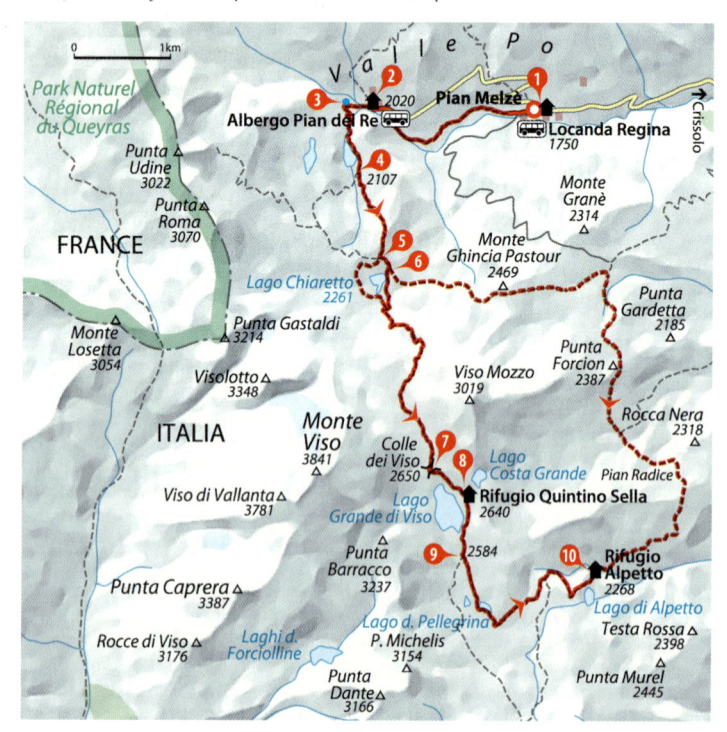

Starting point: Pian Melzè, 1750 m.
Destination: Rifugio Alpetto, 2268 m.
Length: 11.9 km.
Grade: Well-marked, distinct trail. Before reaching the Colle del Viso, you have to cross a boulder field.
Refreshment: Albergo Pian del Re, Rifugio Quintino Sella.
Accommodation: Albergo Pian del Re: 2020 m, mid-June–end Sept., rooms+dormitory (50 B), HB 48 €, Aldo Perotti, tel. +39 0175/949 67 or +39 349/531 59 21. – **Rifugio Quintino Sella:** 2640 m, CAI, end Jun–end Sept., 83 B, HB/AV 43/33 €, Fam. Tranchero, tel. +39 0175/949 43, www.rifugiosella.it. – **Rifugio Alpetto:** 2268 m, CAI, mid June–mid Sept., 32 B, HB/AV 42/32 €, Andrea and Alessandro Casassa, tel. +39 0340/ 513 07 92, www.rifugioalpetto.it.
Shopping/Services: Nothing available.
Public transport: From Torino with the bus, via Saluzzo to Paesana (timetable: www.atibus.it); bus line Paesana – Crissolo (timetable: www.dossettobus.it). Shuttle bus Crissolo – Pian Regina (alternatively Melzè) – Pian del Re from end June–end Sept. only Sat/Sun (timetable: www.vallipo.cn.it).
Alternative: At the huge rock after the steep stretch towards the Lago Chiaretto, turn left in the direction of the Rifugio Alpetto, then descend to the lake, but, once there, be sure to leave the trodden path by turning left and following the waymarkings along the traces of a path which leads eastwards through a low spot and

The mulattiera from the Pian Regina to the Pian del Re at the source of the Po.

head towards the ridge of the Monte Ghincia Pastour. This new route to the Rifugio Alpetto is not drawn on the IGC map, but is well-marked; about 2.30 hrs.

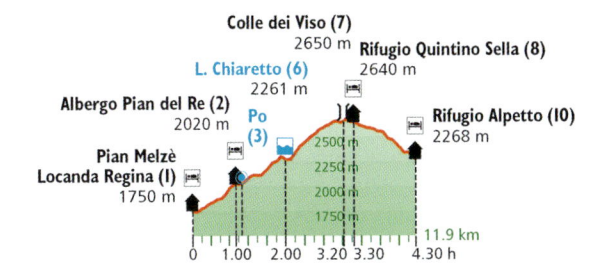

Sunrise at the Rifugio Alpetto.

From the **Locanda Regina (1)**, take the trail at the war memorial and head to the Convento Pian della Regina. The track road becomes an old *mulattiera* and leads, on the level, to a steep section crowned by a chapel, along which, you reach the Pian del Re. Passing the very conspicuous **Albergo Pian del Re (2)**, reach the **source of the Po (3)** where you can fill your water bottle. Now the GTA is identical with the Giro del Viso. Ascend to the left along the slope, pass the Lago Fiorenza and then reach the turquoise **Lago Chiaretto (6)**. If you are disturbed by all the hustle and bustle, you can pick up the alternative route here which leads over the ridge of the Monte Ghincia Pastour. The main route leads in a semicircle above the lake, through a stony cirque parallel to a lateral moraine, and constantly gains in height. Now traverse to the right along the moraine and through blocky boulders onto the **Colle dei Viso (7)**, 2650 m. At your feet lies the Lago Grande di Viso. To the left above the lake, the **Rifugio Quintino Sella (8)**, 2640 m, with a front-row view taking in the Po Valley plain and the mighty eastern face of the Monviso.

Pass the hut, then descend southwards to the lake below. Ignore the right-hand turn-off which leads to the Passo delle Sagnette. At the trail junction by the next pool, turn left. Past the Lago della Pellegrina, the route skirts eastwards around the mountain ridge, Balze di Cesare, to enter the mountain valley of the Rio dell'Alpetto, which winds through the plateau like a serpent and appears to jump off directly into the Po Valley plain. Bearing right, cross over the plateau to a saddle, where you can enjoy a splendid view of the Lago di Alpetto. Turn left to cross the slope above the lake to the **Rifugio Alpetto (10)**. At the historic hut next door, built in 1866, a museum is being established.

| 4.30 hrs. | **Rifugio Alpetto – Rifugio Bagnour** | 43 |
| ↑610 ↓860 | | |

Cairns and the largest Swiss Pine forest in the Alps

The crossing from the Valle Po into the Valle Varaita is a very scenic highlight – starting in the morning at the Rifugio Alpetto, when the red ball of the sun peeks out from the haze of the Po Valley plain. On a clear day, during the descent, a backwards view opens up all the way to the Monte Rosa. The mountain valley at the Passo Chiaffredo is a real work of art: a sea of cairns, created by diligent pass walkers, with cobalt-blue tarns nestled in between. Quite a contrast with the rocky wasteland is presented by the final slope: gnarled Swiss Pines and the Rifugio Bagnour set in a clearing with a moorland biotope.

Rifugio Alpetto at Monviso.

Monte Rosa, view from Passo Gallarino at Monviso.

Starting point: Rif. Alpetto, 2268 m.
Destination: Rifugio Bagnour, 2017 m.
Lenght: 11 km.
Grade: Well-marked; during the descent, there is a stretch of trail that isn't very distinct.
Refreshment: Nothing en route.
Accommodation: Bivacco Bertoglio: 2760 m, always open, 9 B with blankets. – **Rifugio Bagnour:** 2017 m, Comunità Montana Valle Varaita, mid-June–end Sept., and at the weekends, 20 B, HB 40 €, Livio Martino & Elisa Tosco, tel. +39 320/426 01 90, www.rifugiobagnour.it.

Shopping/Services: Maddalena (a village district of Pontechianale).
Public transport: Castello and Maddalena (a village district of Pontechianale).
Note: Pontechianale (1.30 hrs. from Bagnour) is a good place for a starting or ending point but is not suitable as a stop for a Stage. The only hotel is closed and the Posto tappa Ai Forest offers neither a meal nor drinks in the evening and a table in the Pizzeria Quetzal (with a rather unfriendly innkeeper) is only available by reservation (tel. +39 0175/95 01 41). (See also Stage 44.)

From the **Rifugio Alpetto (1)**, return along the approach route to the little waterfall at the Rio dell'Alpetto. Only a little higher up from the cascade, turn left onto the trail and cross over scree and patches of meadow to reach the main trail just somewhat below the Passo Gallarino. From the **Passo Gal-**

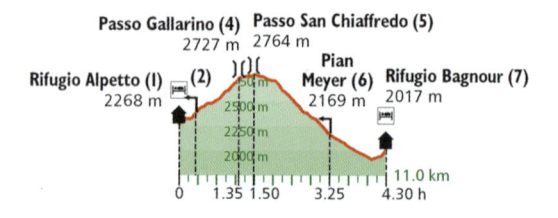

174

larino **(4)**, 2727 m, cross over (on the level) to the **Passo San Chiaffredo (5)**, 2764 m, while enjoying a lovely view of the Maritime Alps.

Pass the Lago Lungo to reach the Lago Bertin, above which, the **Bivacco Bertoglio** is enthroned on a hillock. Countless cairns flank the path and create a work of art in the middle of the rocky wasteland. Cross through a small gorge to the Gias Fons. The terrain is greener; a forest appears. The Bosco dell'Alevè, blanketing an area of 825 hectares on the eastern side of the Varaita Valley, is considered the largest Swiss Pine forest in the Alps. Thanks to the steep terrain, and also because it serves the valley as a barrier to avalanches, the forest has not fallen victim to clearing and the gnarled, century-old trees have been preserved. At the trail junction, **Pian Meyer (6)**, leave the Giro del Viso behind by turning left and then dive into the heart of this magnificent forest. Follow signs to the **Rifugio Bagnour (7)**.

Since 2004, the former forester's house has been converted into a cosy rustic inn, trumped only by the fine food served there. The adjacent Lago Bagnour is well-known to biologists because of a species of shrimp found only there. This endemic shellfish, »Branchipus blanchardi«, has its home in the moorland tarn.

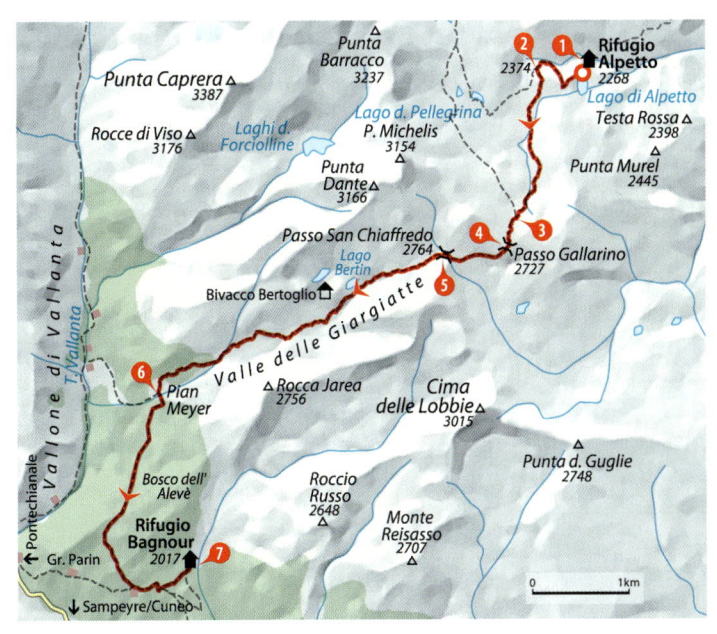

44 | Rifugio Bagnour – Chiesa/Chiazale

5.30 hrs.
↑ 860 ↓ 1170

To the splendid farming villages of the Bellino

The settlements in the upper Varaita Valley (which divides into two valleys – the Pontechianale and Bellino) belonged once to the »Grand Escarton«, a political organization quite similar to the Swiss Confederation. Five regions around the Mongenèvre Pass (Queyras, Briancon and Oulx in the upper Susa Valley, Pragelato in the Val Chisone and Casteldelfino in the upper Varaita Valley) joined together in the 12th century to form a kind of peasant republic by buying the rights from the feudal lord, the dauphin Humbert II, and then establishing self-government. The stately properties are evidence of the economic upswing that followed, but the Treaty of Utrecht, which redefined the borders, put this autonomy to an end in 1713. The »Grand Escarton« was dissolved and the three escartons, Oulx, Pragelato and Casteldelfino (also known as Castellata), went to the Piedmont.

Starting point: Rif. Bagnour, 2017 m.
Destination: Chiazale, 1705.
Length: 16 km.
Grade: Mostly well-marked. A MTB route during the steep ascent, a military track during the descent.
Refreshment: Bars in Maddalena.

Accommodation: Rifugio Grongios Martre: (between Bagnour and Castello), 1736 m, always open, 4 R, tel. +39 340/069 27 05, www.grongiosmartre.com. Rifugio Alevè: 1600 m, on the main road just before Castello, open almost year-round, 47 B, HB 35/45 €, tel. +39 0175/

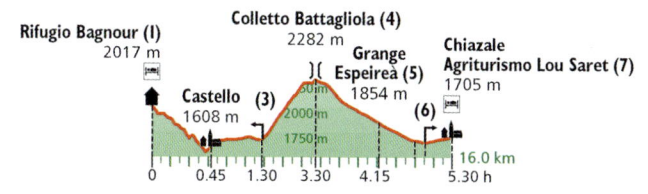

95 04 04 or +39 346/061 81 32, www.rifugioaleve.com. – **Pontechianale:** 1614 m, Meuble Ai Forest, always open, only B&B, Posto tappa 8 B, 20 € (shower 3 € extra), 4 DR, 30 € p.P., Tina Patrile, tel. +39 0175/ 95 01 61. – **Rifugio Savigliano:** 1743 m, 1 km above Maddalena, CAI, June–Sept., at weekends year-round, 50 B, C. & R. Isaia, tel. +39 0175/95 01 78 or +39 347/ 811 95 71. – **Bellino:** Trattoria del Pelvo in Chiesa, 1480 m, open year-round, 30 B, DR; Posto tappa, tel. +39 0175/ 95 60 26. Agriturismo Lou Saret in Chiazale, 1705 m, open year-round, 10 B, HB 50 €, O. Brun, tel. +39 347/975 38 99 or +39 0175/ 95 64 01, www.ghironda.com/vvaraita/pages/844152.htm. – **Rifugio Melezè:** 1806 m, mid-June–mid-Sept., with reservation, year-round 54 B, HB 40 €, B. Gallian, tel. +39 0175/ 953 38, www.rifugiomeleze.it.

Shopping/Services: Maddalena: shop, post office, cash dispenser, pharmacy; shops in Chiesa, Pleyne, Celle.

Public transport: Bus service Maddalena/Castello – Sampeyre – Saluzzo – Cuneo/Turin (timetable: www.atibus.it). A bus line services Mon–Fri the villages of the Bellino Valley (www.parolaviaggi.it). Dial-a-bus must be reserved the day before. Information: www.vallevaraita.cn.it.

From the **Rifugio Bagnour (1)** via the Grange Baciasot and Grange Parin, reach **Castello**. Pass through the village and then cross over the dam wall to a lovely shoreline trail which leads to Pontechianale. Maybe you would like to take a little stroll through the Frazione **Maddalena** where there are some bars and shops. The turn-off from the shoreline trail to the Colletto Battagliola is situated at the stream bed between the woods and the campsite. Ascend at the stream bed and then, on the opposite bank, continue steeply through the wood. That the trail is used as a MTB route is quite apparent. Much further above, the well-maintained trail leads through alder scrub. Reach a rise and then traverse along a panoramic stretch to meet up with the **Colletto Battagliola (4)**, 2282 m.

From the pass, you can climb a number of peaks by taking trails along the ridges. Otherwise, take the military trail to the left to descend. The GTA, which, starting at the first bend, short-cuts two more bends, is rather cumbersome, badly marked and sometimes damaged by land slips. At the **Grange Espeireà (5)**, the trail forks away from the military track and leads to Chiesa. If you want to spend the night in **Chiazale (7)** or in the Rifugio Melezè, continue along the track. Shortly before reaching Pleyne, meet up with the valley road. Take this up the valley and pass through the medieval villages of the Bellino region, which are chock-full of interesting bits and bobs (sundials, frescoes, stuccowork, colonnades, stone-carved grotesque faces, etc.).

The Dolomites of Cuneo – the valley heads of Varaita, Maira and Stura

This is a wonderful stretch: lofty limestone mountains create a landscape reminiscent of the Dolomites. Since tourism took hold in the Maira Valley, the epithet, »Dolomites of Cuneo«, has been commonly used here. This valley was once known as the »Black Hole« because during the era of emigration, it was particularly affected. Now more and more »emigrants« are returning to their homeland ever since new sources of income have been established.

A special role for the change was played by a German-Austrian couple, who has lived in the Maira Valley since 1980. By opening a language school, Maria and Andrea Schneider not only provided work for local teachers, but also boosted a touristic draw for the valley, inspiring business-minded locals to take their own initiative. In this way, Posto tappa operators were attracted and a circular walking route was worked out for the valley. Since Italians are not exactly known for their love of walking, writers and journalists were encouraged to spread the tidings to other countries, helping the Maira circuit become a popular one.

The GTA follows the same route as the yellow-marked Maira Trail or the Percorsi Occitani (P.O.) along numerous stretches (Stages 46, 47, V45, V46).

At the end, the Maira Valley has also become an El Dorado for mountain bikers. Nowadays, the Comunità Montana (mountain community) has to walk a slippery line between soft and not-so-soft tourism since more and more motocross hooligans are attracted to the area. Since the wheels of bu-

Centro Culturale Borgata and the Posto tappa in San Martino inferiore (Stage V45).

The dolomites of Cuneo, view from Campo Base (Stage 45).

reaucracy turn very slowly, each walker is encouraged to report encounters with anyone using a motorized vehicle on the walking trails. Also, a massive protest from locals, as well as from tourists, could lead to a ban on snowmobiles in winter.

In the meantime, the language school has developed into a real meeting place. In 1988, the Schneiders purchased the abandoned hamlet of San Martino inferiore and have converted a number of farmhouses into guest homes (accommodation for Stage V45). Since 2004, Maria Schneider, along with a team from the Centro Culturale Borgata, manages the project all by herself. In November, 2005, her husband was commemorated in San Martino with a plaque to honour his heartfelt commitment to the development of tourism in the Maira Valley.

For a long time, other valley communities have been keeping an eye on the success of the Maira Valley. Putting his convictions to work, Werner Bätzing (see page 10) could also bring them to fruition at the end, in the neighbouring Stura Valley. The concept of a circular walking route for the valley and the means to attract walkers to the marvellous countryside through lovely walking trails, tradition-oriented accommodation and »slow food« suddenly entered the picture. In summer 2008, the »Lou Viage« (in Occitan: »The Journey«) was inaugurated; we will become acquainted with this between Pontebernardo and Sambuco where two culinary highlights were established.

The alternative Stages, V45 to V48, follow the GTA eastern route, which once ran from the Susa Valley into the Stura Valley. Since the first stretch of the route has not been maintained for a very long time, we will describe the still usable stretch from Chiesa in Bellino to Sambuco in the Stura Valley, which can be combined with the main route to create a marvellous circuit.

45 Chiazale – Campo Base

6.30 hrs.
↑1190 ↓1240

Monuments of stone

Rocca Senghi.

The Rocca Senghi presents a natural monument which draws each and every eye. The mighty rock crag, clinging to the northern sheer face as if by magic, has inspired quite a collection of legends surrounding it. The Almighty Himself, at loggerheads with the Devil, is supposed to have smote him such that the Archfiend still clings to the rock. At the pass crossing into the Maira Valley, you could think that you had strayed into the Dolomites. And at the end of this Stage, the twin crags of Rocca Provenzale and Rocca Castello, with their »stone sail«, set a landmark.

Starting point: Chiazale, 1705 m, Rifugio Melezè, 1806 m, or Sant' Anna (bus station), 1882 m (30 min. shorter).
Destination: Rifugio Campo Base, 1650 m.
Length: 18.7 km.
Grade: Well-marked. During the descent from the pass, the trail has been somewhat damaged by motocross hooligans, and cow paths may lead you astray.
Refreshment: Rifugio Melezè.
Accommodation: Rifugio Campo Base: 1650 m, open almost year-round,

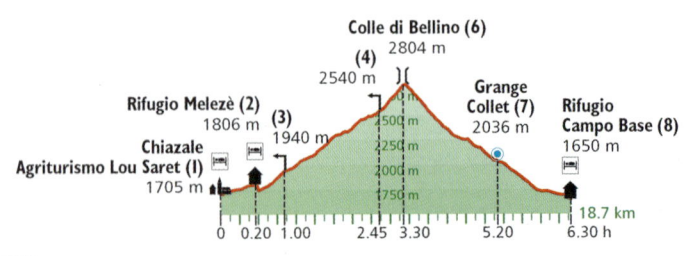

26 B, HB/AV 39/37 €, Stephane Le Goff, tel. +39 0171/ 990 68, www.campobase-acceglio.it. – alternatively, at the Hüttenkoller in **Saretto**: 1540 m, 40 min. away, Taverna di Diego, May 15–Oct. 17, 5 R (19 B), HB 45/52 €, Slow Food, Diego Pirotti, tel. +39 0171/990 54 or +39 348/ 932 11 53, www.dadiego.it.
Shopping/Services: Nothing available.
Public transport: Bus from Cuneo/Turin via Saluzzo to Sampeyre/Casteldelfino (timetable: www.atibus.it), then change to the bus line servicing the Bellino Valley (timetable: www.parolaviaggi.it).

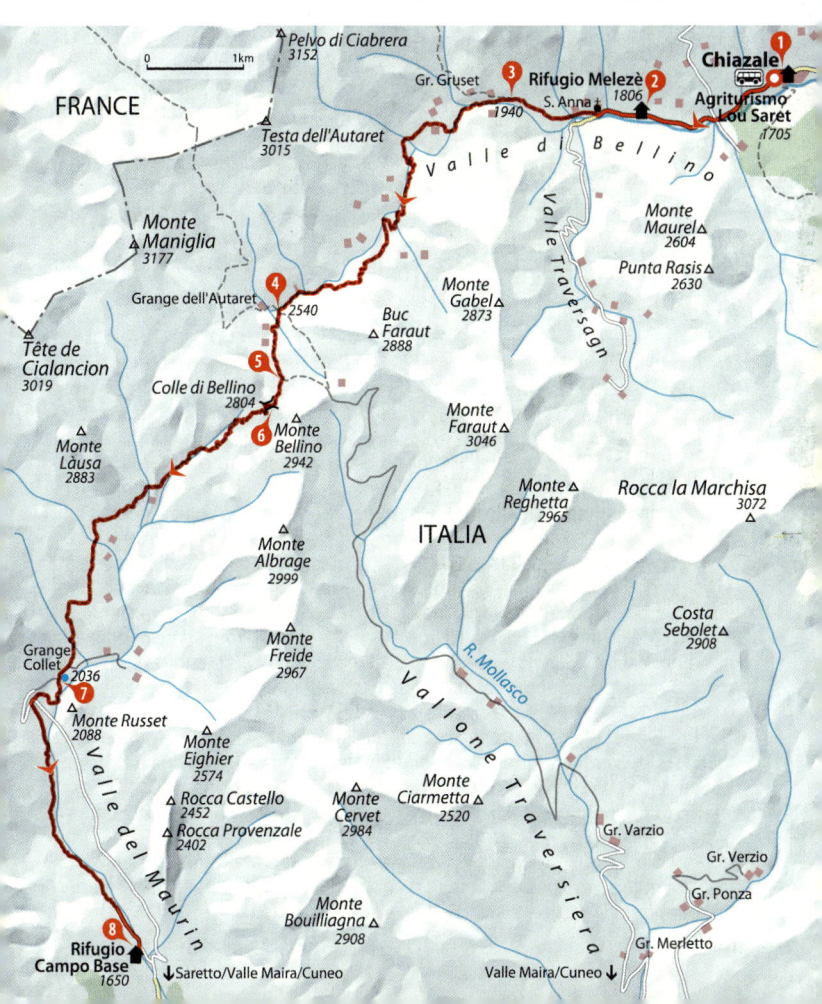

Colle di Bellino, with a view taking in Monviso.

The street ends just past the chapel of **Sant' Anna**; from the car park, follow the gravel trail to the right and cross over the stream to enter into the impressive valley head – to the right, the Rocca Senghi. At the **Grange Cruset**, turn left onto the *alpe* trail and follow this until it ends. A path then continues in a south-westerly direction over a meadow, heading towards a gorge. At the entrance, cross over the stream, then ascend through the narrow gorge (secured sections), passing through a still used *alpe* terrain. Along a good path, traverse south-westerly through the slope into the valley head, surrounded by mighty limestone rock faces. Above the huts of the Grange dell'Autaret, a trail sign points to the left. Ascend over scree, pass a bunker installation that has been blown up, then reach the **Colle di Bellino (6)**, 2804 m. The Monte Bellino blocks the view towards the Po Valley plain. You can conquer the mountain easily, but at the pass, you could also enjoy a splendid view.

At the outset, steep going through dusty terrain, then cross over *alpe* terrain to reach the Grange Turre where you meet up with a track road. At the **Grange Collet (7)**, 2036 m, the road forks. Turn left to continue and, past the houses, descend along the slope directly to the valley floor. The final stretch is level and meets up with the **Rifugio Campo Base (8)** where you can marvel at the rocky ridge of Rocca Provenzale and Rocca Castello, well-known to the rock climbing scene.

At this point, the GTA follows the same route as the Maira trail (P.O.), which has grown into a »classic« route in the meantime. Accordingly, compared to the recent past, you will meet many walkers en route.

5.30 hrs.	***Campo Base – Chialvetta***	**46**
↑810 ↓970		

Picturesque villages, the source of the Maira and a nostalgic museum

Chiappera is probably the most photographed village in the Maira Valley. The cluster of houses with the backdrop of the »stone sail« is simply perfection and is also an ideal spot for a cappuccino break in the bar. Along an idyllic trail, you traverse to the springs which provide the source waters of the Maira. Raspberries sweeten the ascent to the Colle Ciarbonet. Enjoying an open view, descend into the Vallone d'Unerzio, then pass through some hamlets into the picturesque Chialvetta, where Rolando Comba harbours a passion for collecting antiques. In his museum, you are sure to discover many a curiosity.

Starting point: Campo Base, 1650 m.
Destination: Chialvetta, 1494 m.
Length: 15.8 km.
Grade: Distinct, well-marked trail. The ascent to the pass is sometimes muddy. Descent along a military road, but afterwards, a lovely *mulattiera*.
Refreshment: Nothing en route.
Accommodation: Chialvetta: 1494 m, Osteria della Gardetta, end May–end Oct., HB 39 €, Rolando Comba, informal atmosphere, tasty meals, tel. +39 0171/990 17, www.lascurcio.it. And, directly opposite: La Locanda di Chialvetta, 6 R (18 B), open year-round except Nov., HB 65 €, tel. +39 0171/99 51 20, www.lalocandadichialvetta.it. – **Rifugio di Viviere:** after 7 years of renovation, reopened in March 2011, 3 DR, HB 65 €, tel. +39 347/745 12 89, www.rifugiodiviviere.com. – **Pratorotondo:** Rifugio Unerzio, 1639 m, self-catering accommodation without shower, the key can be picked up in the Osteria della Gardetta. – for the **Bivacco Bonelli** (Alternative) en route, you need to pick up the key (in the Rifugio Campo Base).
Shopping/Services: Nothing available.
Public transport: Sherpabus provided by Gianni Pilotto, tel. +39 348/823 14 77, luggage transport between Campo Base and Chialvetta for 7 €.

Alternative: A more alpine route leads over the Colle d'Enchiausa, 2740 m. The turn-off is at the source of the Maira. Only recommended when weather is good, 7.30 hrs.

Rolando Comba and his museum.

Chialvetta.

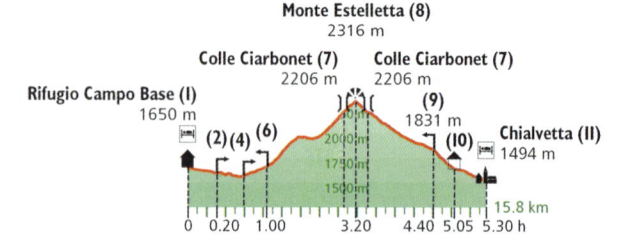

```
                    Monte Estelletta (8)
                         2316 m
         Colle Ciarbonet (7)  Colle Ciarbonet (7)
                  2206 m       2206 m
Rifugio Campo Base (I)              (9)
     1650 m                        1831 m
                                              Chialvetta (II)
        (2)(4) (6)     2000m    (10)            1494 m
                       1750m
                       1500m
                                              15.8 km
     0  0.20  1.00     3.20    4.40 5.05 5.30 h
```

From **Campo Base (1)**, at first, take the road down the valley and pass **Chiappera** until you reach the first downwards leading left-hand bend; here the trail turns off to the right **(2)**. Along this stretch, you can follow the yellow markings for the P.O. The path forks soon; turn left, at first somewhat in a descent and then ascending; through the woods, you catch glimpses of the Lago di Saretto. Afterwards, continue along a covered water conduit to reach the **Sorgenti della Maira (6)**. The clearing with karst springs is very popular for motorized excursionists. Cross through a campsite, along a lovely forest trail, south-eastwards onto the **Colle Ciarbonet (7)**, 2206 m. You can enjoy a better view when you turn left onto the path climbing the **Monte Estelletta (8)**, 2316 m (20 min.). A pleasant gradient along the military track brings you into the Vallone d'Unerzio. When you meet up with a tarmac road, the trail continues in the next bend by turning right. Pass **Viviere**, then cross through **Pratorotondo (10)**. Afterwards, at the village limits, turn right and then turn left onto a quiet *mulattiera* leading along a stream, to reach **Chialvetta (11)**. An excursion into Chialvetta is worthwhile and, in any case, preferable to the self-catering accommodation in Pratorotondo.

Chiappera with the Rocca Provenzale.

185

47 Chialvetta – Pontebernardo

6.15 hrs.
↑ 1160 ↓ 1340

Marmots, military bunkers and oceans of Edelweiss

The crossing from the Maira Valley into the Stura Valley presents a marvellous, multiform landscape. Marmots compete for the title of »best whistler« as they dig holes in the terrain, very much like the military once did here. If you have brought a head torch along, you might want to make a nerve-tickling exploration of one or the other fortification. From the Passo Gardetta until reaching the Passo di Rocca Brancia, you can hardly get your fill of views sweeping over the vast, high plain, or of the Edelweiss, strewn along the way leading to the turquoise-coloured Lago Oserot. A number of metres of altitude further down, lavender exudes its lovely scent and the gorge Barricate proves to be a real jaw-dropper.

Starting point: Chialvetta, 1494 m.
Destination: Pontebernardo, 1312 m.
Length: 19.2 km.
Grade: Well-marked military trails and paths. A couple of steep stretches. At the end, a stretch along a road (heavy traffic).
Refreshment: Rifugio Gardetta (15 min. diversion from the route).
Accommodation: **Rifugio Gardetta:** 2335 m, CAI, mid-June–mid-Sept., 45 B, HB/AV 32/40 €, Futura Barbero, tel. +39 348/238 01 58. – **Pontebernardo:** 1312 m, Pension Le Barricate, open year-round, DR and Posto tappa, 22 B, no longer offers HB, tel. +39 0171/966 16. Evening meal at the Osteria La Pecora Nera, creative meals, a reservation is absolutely necessary, GTA menu 16 € or à la carte, Lucio tel. +39 333/350 87 16.
Shopping/Services: Nothing available.
Public transport: Bus line Vinadio – Argentera: www.atibus.it.
Tip: The Ecomuseo della Pastorizia, located directly in Pontebernardo, is very interesting, documenting the valley's traditions, such as tending wandering sheep.

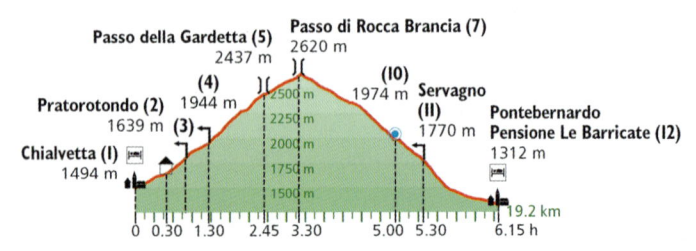

Return along the approach route From **Chialvetta (1)** to **Viviere**. Continue by heading up the valley, soon picking up a track road. Just before the road ends at the **Grangia Calandra (4)**, the trail turns off to the left. Now head steeply through the south-western flank, a magnificent alpine arena. The final slope, formed from bizarre gypsum hillocks, is riddled with fortification tunnels (home to marmots).

At the **Passo della Gardetta (5)**, a high mountain plain lies at your feet, surrounded by barren mountains. It only takes a short descent to bring us to the Rifugio Gardetta, 2335 m, a military barracks that has been converted to an Alpine Club hut (interesting flora). The direct route into the Stura Valley keeps on the level and follows a military road to the right and onto the **Passo di Rocca Brancia (7)**, 2620 m. Past the first bend, meet up with two military bunkers. Not as soon as it is drawn on the IGC map, but somewhat further on, the GTA forks off to the left. With a splendid view of the Maritime Alps, continue past the turquoise-coloured Lago Oserot, while heading down the valley. Further down, cow paths try to lead you astray, so keep a good eye out for waymarkers, especially at the tumbledown village of **Servagno (11)**, 1770 m. The marking on the solitary tree below the ruins is only visible for those ascending to this point.

So turn left and cross over the meadow, instead of to the right along the trodden path. At the end, reach the valley road and turn left to descend along it. At the half-tunnel, change over to the old road which opens an impressive view of the bottleneck of the Barricate. The final metres needed to reach **Pontebernardo (12)** are rather unpleasant because they follow the road.

48 Pontebernardo – Sambuco

3.00 hrs.
↑ 350 ↓ 480

Eco museum and »slow food«

Transhumance, in the form of sheepherding, has enjoyed a long tradition in the Stura Valley. The Ecomuseo della Pastorizia in Pontebernardo, established in 2000, focuses on this subject. The local breed of sheep, la Razza Sambucana, already threatened by extinction due to the major exodus of farmers, has recently enjoyed a revival through the increasing popularity of »slow food« (see also page 22, »Cuisine of the Piedmont«). You could test the high quality of this mutton yourself in the Osteria La Pecora Nera in Pontebernardo. Sambuco has also made a name for itself in the art of preparing this meat. Both »slow food« establishments are found along the Sentiero dell'Ecomuseo and are marked with the symbol of a black sheep on a white background; the trail follows the same route as the newly established, red-yellow-marked valley trail, »Lou Viage.«

Starting point: Pontebernardo, Kirche, 1312 m.
Destination: Sambuco, 1184 m.
Length: 9.5 km.
Grade: Poorly-marked until reaching the village of Castello, afterwards, easy to find the route. An easy Stage.
Refreshment: Nothing en route.
Accommodation: Sambuco: 1184 m, Albergo della Pace, always open, 14 DR (HB 65 €); Posto tappa (15 B, HB 37 €), sauna/wellness area 10 € extra, Bruna Family, tel. +39 0171/ 965 50, www.albergodellapace.com.
Shopping/Services: Shop and a post office in Sambuco.
Public transport: Bus service from Sambuco via Vinadio to Cuneo, www.atibus.it.

The starting point is the church of **Pontebernardo (1)** where there is also an information board. Follow the country lane which soon crosses over the

Adriano Fossati's Sambucana flock of sheep.

Stura. Continue to the northeast then cross over a dry stream bed to reach the Suort l'amant. At the beginning of this meadowland clearing, the path hooks off to the left. Through an open wood, meet up with a fork which lacks a waymarker; turn right here. The path follows outcroppings of rock through the southern slope while opening up lovely views. Reach **Castello (3)**, 1338 m, and take the track uphill. Now turn right onto a level trail from which a path soon turns off to the left. At first, steeply and then following the contour at the same height, merge into a country lane and turn right onto it. At the houses marking Moriglione San Lorenzo, 1414 m, turn left, keeping on the level, to pass the ruins of Moriglione di Fondo, 1400 m, following the stream bed and then south-eastwards to descend to **Sambuco (7)**.

---

*In the middle of the 19th century, over 1000 people lived in the stately village of **Sambuco**; now, a mere 85 inhabitants are left. The Bruna family counts as one of the few who have not abandoned their homeland for better job opportunities found in the cities in the plain. In the entranceway of the Albergo, a photograph is proudly displayed: Reinhold Messner next to Bartolo Bruna. The television channel, »Arte«, had devoted an entire programme to the village of Sambuco and also to the chef of the Osteria della Pace. With exceptional food and heartfelt cordiality, the Osteria has made quite a name for itself since it was founded in 1882, its fame reaching far and wide. In the meantime, the bar opposite is run by Bartolo's son, Daniele, the grocery store by his aunt and the bed & breakfast in the village district of Clauzio by his cousin. In this way, the family encourages other villagers to stay on.*

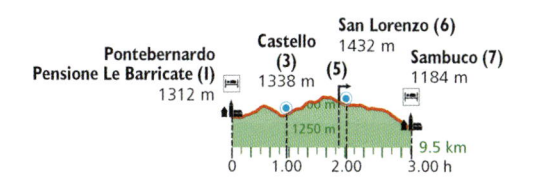

189

V45 Chiesa/Chiazale – San Martino

6.00 hrs.
↑1040 ↓1140

Curiosities of the Maira Valley

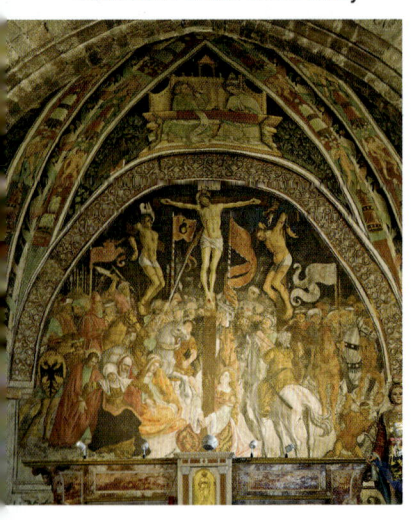

Frescos in the church at Elva.

From the Colle Bicocca, we are accompanied by a view of the striking Chersogno which, as a solitary crag, has earned the nickname of »the Matterhorn of the Maira Valley«. In Elva, inside the church which appears rather plain from the outside, you will be amazed by a detailed, true-to-life, cycle of frescoes which the Flemish painter, Hans Clemer, created at the end of the 15th century. But perhaps even more of a surprise is the Hair Museum. In the 19th century, as the valley began to open up to the outside world, new professions came into being to supplement the meagre income earned by farming. Thus, the villagers from Celle di Macra (see next Stage) began trading in anchovies (Acciugaio), while the villagers of Elva began to deal in human hair (Caviè). The cut-off locks were treasured as material for wigs, very much in fashion at the time, and brought in a good price. The English aristocracy, as well as the high society of Paris and America, were wearing wigs made of real human hair produced in Elva. The discovery of the means to make artificial hair in the second half of the 20th century put an end to the industry. The »Museo di Pels« in Elva, vividly documents the process of wig manufacture.

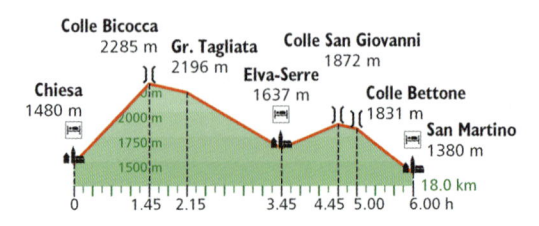

Starting point: Chiesa, 1480 m (alternatively Chiazale, 1705 m).
Destination: San Martino, 1380 m.
Length: 18 km.
Grade: Well-marked, distinct trail. Steep ascent.
Refreshment: In Elva.
Accommodation: Elva-Serre: 1637 m, Locanda San Pancrazio, open year-round, 55 B, rooms and Posto tappa, HB from 40 €, Edo & Caterina Loria, tel. +39 0171/99 79 86, www.lalocandadielva.it. Agriturismo L'Artesin, in the hamlet of Clari, open year-round, 8 B, HB from 40 €, tel. +39 0171/99 79 95. – **San Martino inferiore:** 1380 m, Centro Culturale Borgata, April–Nov., HB from 47 €, Posto tappa HB 39 €, Maria Schneider, tel.+39 0171/99 91 86, www.borgata-sanmartino.de.
Shopping/Services: Nothing available.
Public transport: Luggage transport by Gianni Pilotto, tel. +39 348/823 14 77.
Tips: You can get the key to the church at Elva in the Locanda nearby. – The Museo di Pels in Elva is open Weds–Sun 9–12 a.m., 3–5 p.m. as well as Tues afternoons, or by appointment, tel. +39 340/ 984 65 08. If you are starting the trek here, it would be better to walk the route in two separate days.
Alternative: The Colle Bicocca can also be approached from the Rifugio Melezè or from Chiazale via the well-marked U 24 which crosses over the Bric Rond (Bric Rutund), 2492 m, (3.45 hrs.).

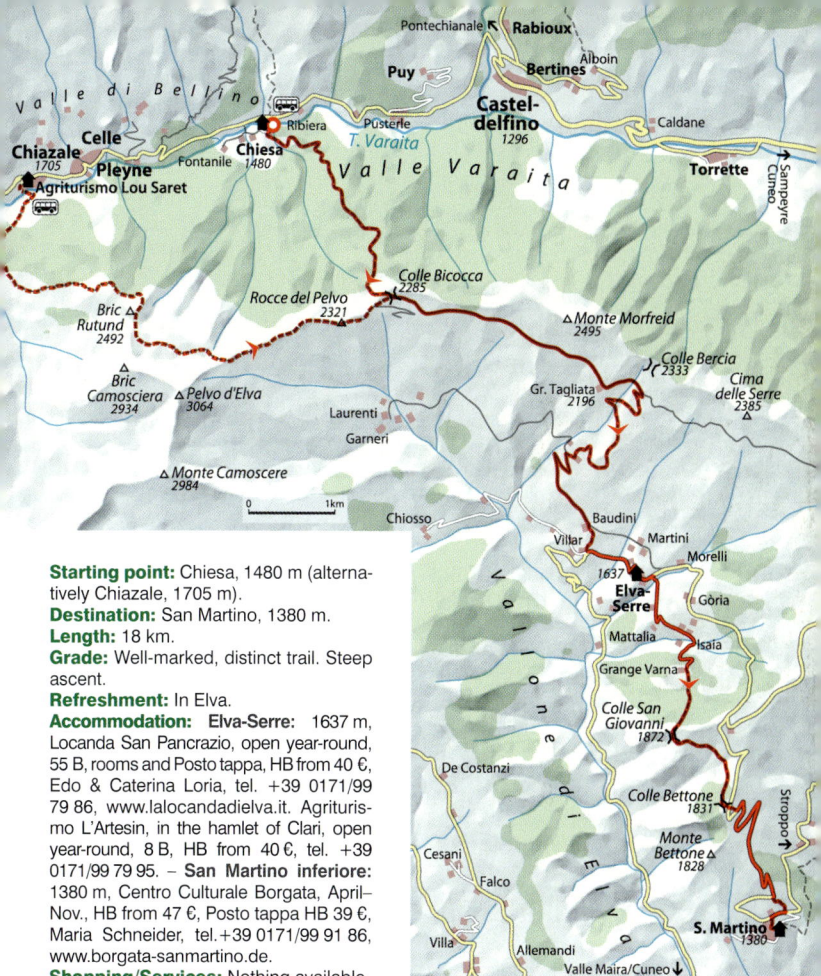

San Martino superiore.

From **Chiesa** until reaching the Colle Bicocca, the GTA follows the same route as the U 22. From the village, head south-eastwards and cross over the Cuculet stream, then continue more steeply through the wood onto the **Colle Bicocca**, 2285 m, to enjoy a marvellous view. A military track, which starts directly at the Po Valley plain, ends here. Continue along this track for a while. At the weekends, you might possibly have to eat the dust of cars driving by. At about the same height as the Colle Bercia and after passing an *alpe* hut, leave the track behind and take the old trail which runs somewhat below; this shares the same route as the new *alpe* road for a stretch. Before meeting a right-hand bend, keep heading in a south-easterly direction. Before the trail hooks towards Martini, a path turns off which short-cuts the way to **Elva-Serre**, 1637 m. Here, meet up with the P.O., the yellow-marked Maira Valley trail which follows the same route as the GTA eastern leg until it reaches Celle di Macra. Up until the 1930s, the footpath via San Martino was the only approach to the Maira Valley. Because the Conca of Elva, a marvellous broad, high mountain valley basin, is separated from the main valley by a gigantic gorge, settlements and trading were established primarily in the Varaita Valley instead. From Elva-Serre, take the narrow road to Mattalia and Isaia. At the Grangia Varua, turn left onto the trail leading to the **Colle San Giovanni**, 1872 m (chapel). High above the gorge, the trail drops to the **Colle Bettone**, 1831 m, and then short-cuts the bends for the road which is ascending from San Martino. At the end walk through the passageways of San Martino superiore, 1431 m, which is picturesquely enthroned on a craggy rock face, and descend to **San Martino inferiore**.

5.00 hrs.
↑780 ↓890

San Martino – Celle di Macra V46

Mysterious villages with a salty past

If you were wondering why salty anchovies have found a niche in traditional alpine cookery, we will let you in on a little secret. The Museum Seles at Celle di Macra, is devoted to a rather unusual profession with which the villagers from the central Maira Valley used to augment their livelihood. With a carretto (barrow), these men would travel in winter through the Po Valley plain, loudly proclaiming their wares: the very popular »acciughe«. From these travelling tradesmen, market stalls and speciality shops finally evolved. Many of the traders did not return to their villages. Today, deterioration is gnawing at the villages and forests are gradually swallowing them up.

Starting point: San Martino, 1380 m.
Destination: Celle di Macra, district of Chiesa, 1270 m.
Length: 18 km.
Grade: Well-marked, distinct trail through a lot of forest. A couple of steep stretches.
Refreshment: In Bassura (tip: gourmet restaurant Lou Sarvanot) and in Palent.
Accommodation: Bassura: 927 m, Locanda Occitana alla Napoleonica, 18 B, HB 50 €, tel. +39 0171/99 92 77, www.locandanapoleonica.it. – **Palent:** 1480 m, Rifugio Alpino, open year-round, 22 B, delicious meals, HB 39 €, Virginia and Matteo Laugero, tel. +39 0171/99 92 34 or +39 347/071 53 27, www.palent.it. – **Celle di Macra/Chiesa:** 1270 m, Posto tappa in the Palazzo Municipale, reservations through Paola Martini (she is also responsible for the Museo Seles), tel. +39 347/138 03 96 or through the community offices, tel. +39 0171/99 91 90. Evening meals in the Locanda Borgata Chiesa, 5 rooms, HB from 42 €, M. Chierici & B. Ferioli, tel. +39 0171/99 91 38 or 342/781 00 78, www.locandaborgatachiesa.it.
Shopping/Services: Bassura: shop, post office. Celle di Macra/Chiesa: shop, post office.
Public transport: Bus stop for the line Cuneo–Dronero–Acceglio: www.benese.it.

Cappella di San Sebastiano.

Tip: Unique frescoes in the Cappella di San Sebastiano (1484), 5 mins. from Celle di Macra/Chiesa on the main road. You can get the key in the shop, »La Butega«.

Roman bridge spanning the Maira River.

From **San Martino inferiore**, walk for a short way along the access road and then turn right. A little later, the P.O. turns off to the left; here, follow the GTA via the *mulattiera* into the valley. Pass an old forge but do not continue to the road, instead (prettier) continue via Arneodi to reach Paschero and then take the Via Bicocca, the ancient mule track, to descend to **Bassura** below.
Now you have the choice to either take the GTA down to the river and, on the opposite side, through the woods to reach the **Cappella La Madonna**, or, to take an alternative, shorter route (this is not drawn on the IGC map but it is well-marked with red waymarkers): walk along the road and down the valley

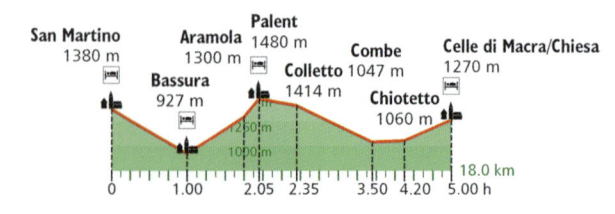

194

until reaching Pessa. Now turn right to descend, cross over the picturesque stone bridge and finally reach the Cappella La Madonna.

A little later, in **Aramola**, you can decide whether to take the somewhat longer route via Palent or to take the P.O. and ascend directly to Colletto. Only two people live year round in **Palent**: Virginia and Matteo Laugero, who run a charming Posto tappa accommodation. Their production of aromatic schnapps and herb cordials have made a name for them and they are happy to invite you to an informative walk through their *genepì* plantation. The only foods that appear on the dining room table here are organic garden vegetables, prepared to delight the palate. The herbal cordial, *genepì*, which is produced from Alpine wormwood (Artemisia genipi), is widely enjoyed throughout the Western Alps. Through the village, descend to the access road and then ascend along the trail to the right. In a wide bend eastwards, cross through the wood to reach **Colletto**, 1414 m. Now continue via Cucchietto, Serremorello, Ciatignano and Sagna to descend to **Combe**, 1047 m. A bit of a thrill along the way is a little excursion via Garino (you simple follow the P.O.), a completely abandoned village. From Combe, continue to the northeast, at first along a stretch of road, then turn right onto the P.O. and afterwards pass through the various hamlets of **Celle di Macra** to reach **Chiesa**.

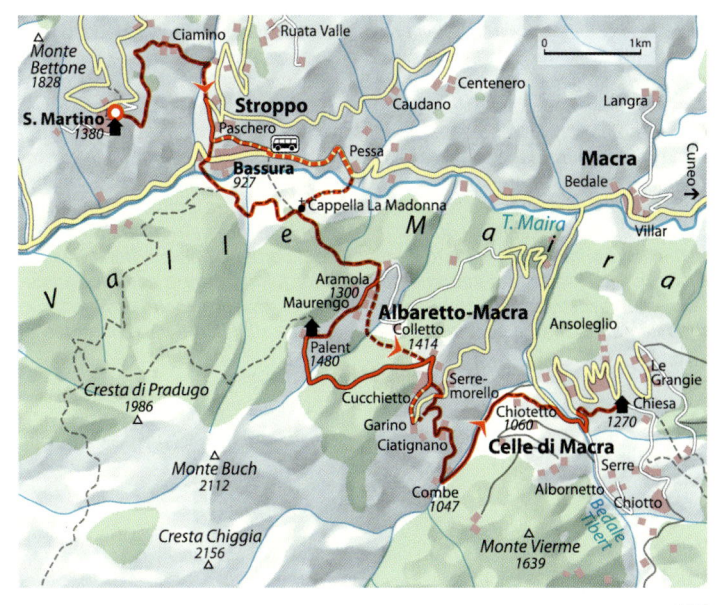

V47 Celle di Macra – Santuario San Magno

5.45 hrs.
↑960 ↓470

The King of Cheeses and a patron saint who watches over animals

The crossing into the Grana Valley leads over long, grassy ridges which open up a splendid view reaching all the way to Monviso. Not infrequently, unfortunately, cloud cover clutches at the ridges and you might have to grope along in the fog. On the other side, in the vast alpine basin at Castelmagno, everything revolves around the milk cow. The Castelmagno is produced here and is celebrated as the »King of Cheeses«.

Thunderstorms are much feared because when cows are driven by the whipping sting of hailstones, they may jump into the abyss, therefore, farmers make a pilgrimage to Saint Magnus. San Magno, born in 699, was a monk in the Swiss city of St.Gallen. Later, he was declared a missionary saint and won great popularity throughout the Alps. For the last six centuries, the Santuario has carried his name; he is the friend of the poor and the patron saint of domestic animals. A grand celebration takes place every year on August 19, the Saint's name day. In a solemn procession, a statue of San Magno is carried around the church and farmers take the opportunity to interact with one another. A chapel has stood in the alpe terrain of Castelmagno since the 15th century. This was erected in 1475 as a donation from Enrico Allamandi, a priest from the Maira Valley. In the 16th century, the chapel was enlarged and in the 18th century, converted to a magnificent baroque church. But it was not until a century later that accommodations for pilgrims were added. Particularly worth seeing are the colourful, life-like frescoes from Pietro da Saluzzo in the Allamandi Chapel, located to the right of the altar in the main church.

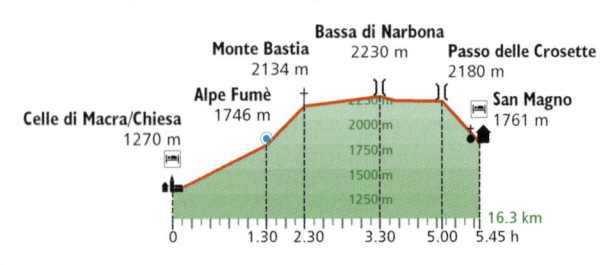

Starting point: Chiesa, 1270 m.
Destination: Sant. San Magno, 1761 m.
Length: 16.3 km.
Grade: Well-marked but sometimes not very distinct paths.
Refreshment: Nothing en route.
Accommodation: Santuario San Magno: Posto tappa in Santuario, 1761 m, beg. July–beg. Sept., 40 B, HB 39 €, tel. +39 0171/98 61 78, www.sanmagno.net. Hotel La Font, just below the Santuario, open almost year-round, 7 DR, 1 suite, HB 49 €, the region's oldest hotel, specialty: meals prepared with Castelmagno, tel. +39 0171/98 63 70, www.castelmagno.is.it.
Shopping: Cheese can be purchased in Chiappi, the village below the Santuario.
Public transport: None available.

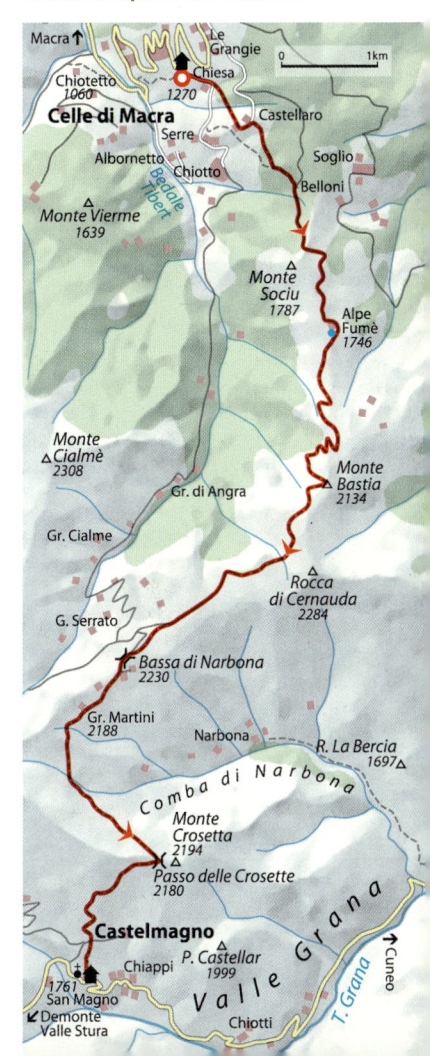

From the **Museum Seles**, take the lovely *mulattiera* up to Castellaro. Above the village, the GTA leaves the P.O. behind by turning right and, after a stretch of wood and meadows, merges with the broad *alpe* trail to reach the **Alpe Fumè**, 1746 m. (Replenish your water bottle here!) A path leads steeply southwards towards a ridge, and reaches it at the **Monte Bastia**, 2134 m. Now follow the ridge, then along the northwest side, reach **Bassa di Narbona**, 2230 m. Further on, at the **Grange Martini**, 2188 m, leave the ridge behind by turning left. The path drops down to a weedy meadowland terrace, then heads south-eastwards, traversing a slope that has been repeatedly damaged by landslips, to reach the **Passo delle Crosette**, 2180 m (and not, as drawn on the IGC map, directly to the Monte Crosetta). Now continue south-westerly through *alpe* terrain (waymarker posts) to the **Santuario San Magno**.

Photo on the next page: the Santuario San Magno; the Allamandi chapel, with 15th-century frescos.

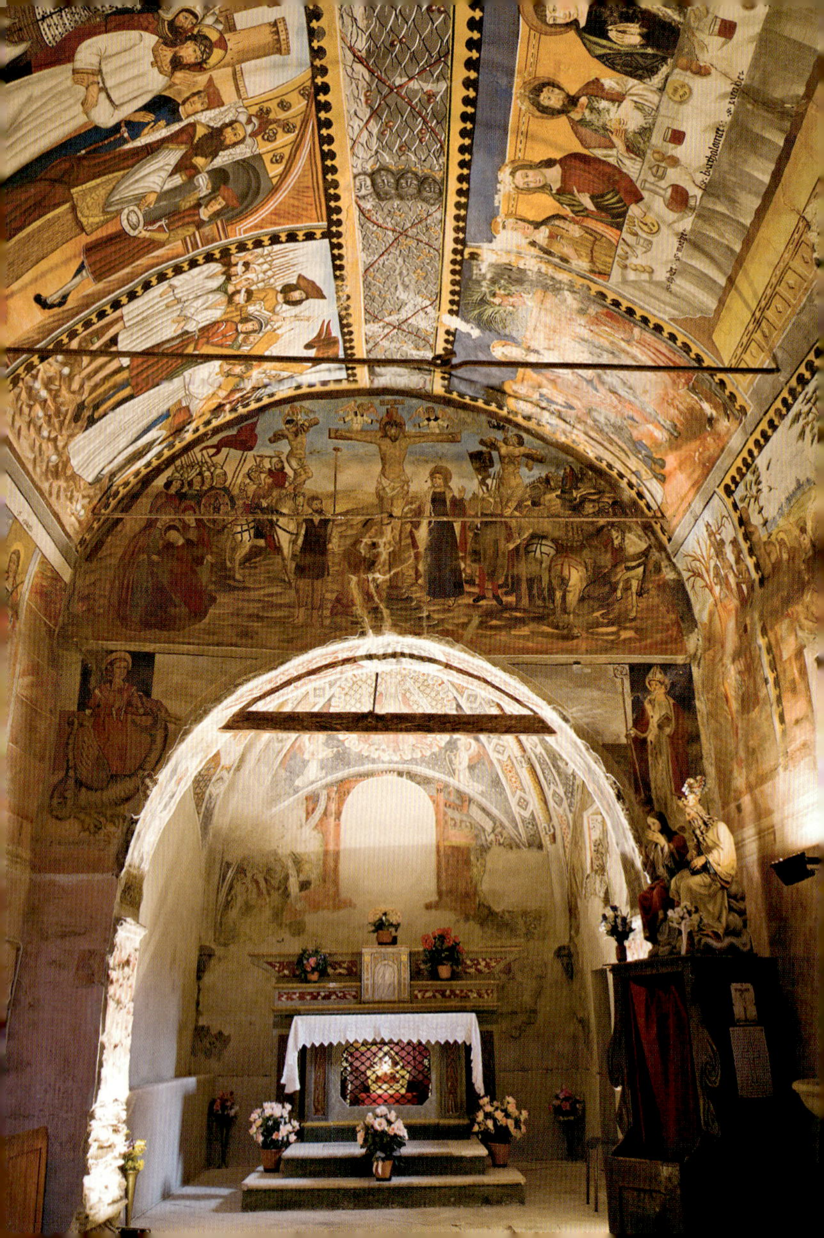

6.00 hrs.
↑720 ↓1300

Santuario San Magno – Sambuco V48

A barren ridge and an unspoiled gorge

Naturally, the confluence of three valleys is strategically important, which is why a vast network of military roads covers the area around the pass crossings between the Maira, Grana and Stura Valleys. Also, fierce partisan resistance held sway here during World War II. The rugged gorge of the Valle della Madonna presents quite a contrast to the open, grass-blanketed but barren mountains of the area.

Starting point: San Magno, 1761 m.
Destination: Sambuco, 1184 m.
Length: 18.5 km.
Grade: Well-marked. During the ascent, a long stretch is along a road.
Refreshment, Shopping/Services and Public transport: See Stage 48.
Accommodation: Also see Stage 48. – **Rifugio Don Franco:** you can pick up the key at the Albergo della Pace in Sambuco.
Alternative: At the Baite Parvo, 1958 m, you could bypass the road. Really reserved for the creatively inclined (!), the trail is marked, but at the beginning somewhat overgrown. The route turns off to the left, crosses over a stream and traverses the eastern slope of the Rocca Parvo to a saddle. In an up-and-down walk along the ridge, reach the Cima Fauniera, 2515 m, and a viewpoint at the Colle dei Morti.

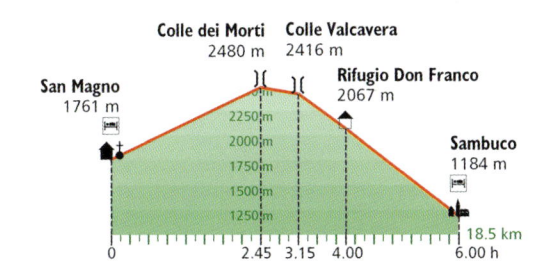

Sambuco.

199

From **San Magno**, the GTA follows the road (somewhat unpleasant stretch when traffic is heavy). You could, of course, try hitchhiking instead. After passing the loop around the Baite Parvo, the GTA short-cuts a couple of bends. On the **Colle dei Morti**, 2480 m, Marco Pantani is captured in stone-hewn action; a photo opportunity for racing bike enthusiasts. From here, a short excursion to the Edelweiss-blanketed Cima Fauniera is also worthwhile. What a panoramic view! Argentera, Monte Matto, Monte Tenibres, the limestone peaks of the Gardetta and the Chambeyron chain, Monviso and much more! After the barren Vallone dei Morti, at the **Colle Valcavera**, 2416 m, leave the tarmac behind. Turn right at first (P 34), then at the next right-hand bend, turn left to descend along the grassy slope. Cross over the *alpe* terrain of Chiaffrera to the **Rifugio Don Franco** (fountain, picnic area). The Valle della Madonna narrows into an exciting gorge; at its end, **Sambuco** is met.

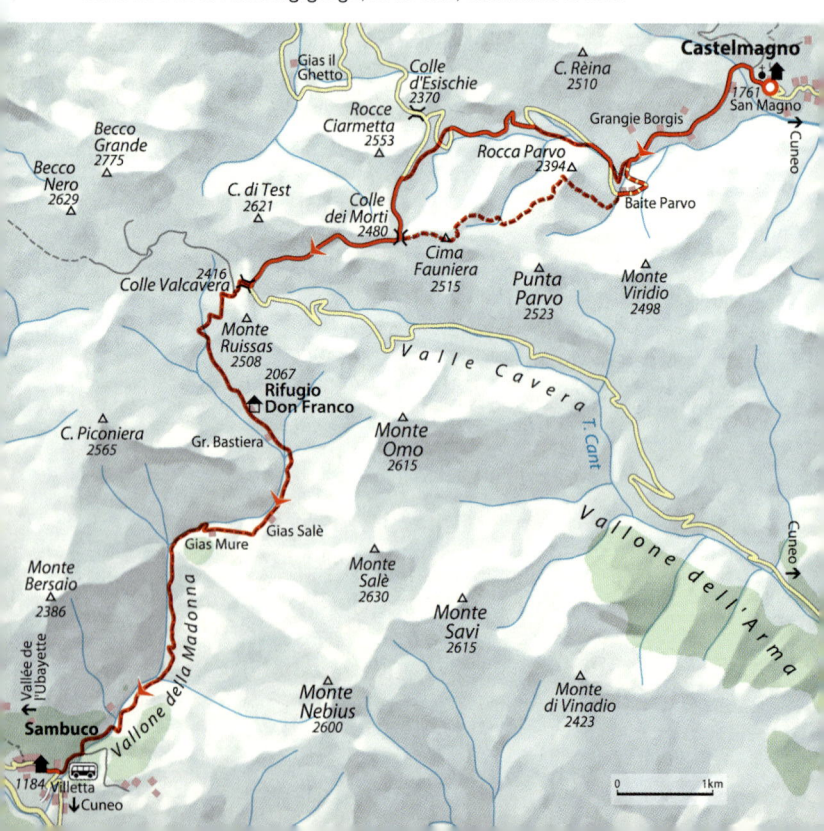

Gias Chiaffrera, Testa di Bandia, Vallone della Madonna.

The Alpine Front: *hardly anywhere else in the Alps is the main ridge so fortified militarily as it is between France and Italy, between Mont Blanc and the Mediterranean. The first fortresses and roads were already established in the 16th century. Disputes and battles surrounding the struggle for power in Europe were centred around a fragmented Italy; especially in the Piedmont where the House of Savoy followed a policy of aggressive politics, ultimately leading to Italy becoming a kingdom. The climax of Italy's historical woes was reached at the hands of the dictator, Mussolini, whose Fascist regime equalled that of the Nazis. The situation became even more torturous after Italy officially broke away from the Second World War in 1943 and the German army occupied the country.*

Especially shocking are the reports written down by Nuto Revelli in »Il disperso di Marburg« (»The Lost Soldier from Marburg«), concerning the so-called »cleansing«. For example, in San Rocco near Cuneo, the Germans, »at the site of the (partisan) attack, shot thirteen innocent civilians dead and laid their poor bodies across the railway tracks so that trains would roll over them and reduce them to shreds«. The worst incident: on 19 September, 1943, the village of Boves was virtually wiped out »in retaliation for the capture of two German soldiers by partisans (...) The murderous acts of the army, the police and the SS not only skyrocketed the number of people who were living underground, but also the number of active partisans. Not until the collapse of the German line of defense in northern Italy in April 1945, was the occupation to meet an end«.

Through the Western Maritime Alps – Smugglers Nest, hot springs and Europe's highest lying monastery

The Western Maritime Alps present an exceptionally rough, rugged and varied relief which discourages the building of villages. Thus, the GTA, and especially the Alternative Stages V48a and V48b, lead through an extremely isolated region which is also a botanist's paradise. There are numerous niches sporting Saxifraga florulenta, a species of flora which grows only in the Maritime Alps (see also pages 218/219); however, if you hope to find them, you must be an expert. Contrariwise, the fire lilies are much more striking when in flower and therefore easier to spot.

At the outset and en route, the spas, Bagni di Vinadio and Terme di Valdieri, provide absolute relaxation.

In between those two, you will find Europe's highest-lying monastery. The Santuario Sant' Anna was a magnet for historical events. Foreign invaders, like the Saracens, used the Colle di Sant' Anna as a crossing, and smugglers and tradesmen used it too, bartering their goods, mostly oil and salt, between Provence and the Piedmont. Later on, military encroachment threw

Sant' Anna di Vinadio, candlelight procession (Stage 51).

Vallone del Valasco, military road to Lago di Valscura (Stage 53).

the region into turmoil with bloody battles. It's true that Sant' Anna di Vinadio is not officially documented until the 11th century, but many indications pinpoint the spot as being used a very long time ago as a prehistoric ritual site. Legend tells of a young girl, Anna Bagnis, who was herding cattle up there in summer. One day, St. Anne appeared to her, standing on a mighty crag, and told her to build a hospice here as a resting place for those using the arduous pack mule hauler's trail to cross the pass. Every year on July 26, St. Anne's name day, there is a grand pilgrimage: a solemn procession leads from the monastery complex to the »*rocher de l'apparition*«, the »rock of the apparition«, to commemorate the Virgin Mary. The church at the monastery is also worth seeing, the walls of which are absolutely plastered with votive tablets and next to the altar, there is a stand full of baby ribbons. St. Anne is the patron saint of pregnant women and protectress of the family, thus the sanctuary is primarily a place of worship and petition for women.

V48a Pontebernardo – Ferriere

3.45 hrs.
↑ 940 ↓ 360

On the trail of the Contrabbandieri

Ferriere (or Ferrere), is the highest-lying settlement in the Stura Valley. Once a lively village, now it is only occupied during the summer. To supplement their income earned in strenuous farming, the villagers also turned to smuggling in order to survive. This »profession« is presented in the Museo del Contrabbandiere (Occitan: Mizoun dal Countrabandier). The atmosphere of this secluded place, especially, serves as a magnet. Take a seat on the shady terrace of the Rifugio Becchi Rossi to enjoy a plate of antipasti and a glass of wine ...

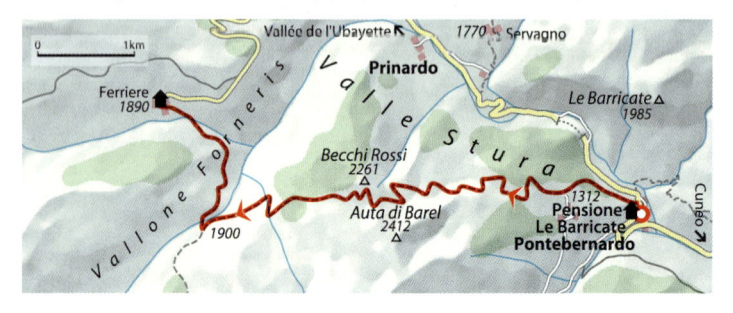

Above **Pontebernardo**, cross over the road and take the footpath westwards to ascend to Murenz, 1567 m. A striking sight, the craggy bastion of the Barricate juts out over the maw of an abyss. Ascend along the military track to the pass, 2244 m, at the **Becchi Rossi** and then continue through the wood, descending into the Forneris Valley. At the stream, the GTA turns off to the right to reach **Ferriere**.

Starting point: In Pontebernardo, 1312 m.
Destination: Ferriere, 1890 m.

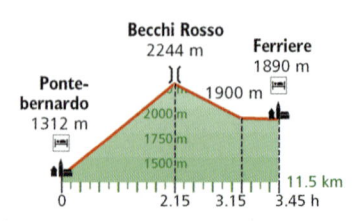

Length: 11.5 km.
Grade: Well-marked.
Refreshment: Nothing en route.
Accommodation: Ferriere: Rifugio Becchi Rossi, 1890 m, June 1–Sept. 30, 22 B, Patrizia and Giorgio Torassa, tel. +39 0171/967 15 or +39 338/ 931 52 88, delicious meals, www.rifugiobecchi-rossi.com. Patrizia and Giorgio also have the key for the Museo del Contrabbandiere.
Shopping/Services: Nothing available.
Public transport: None.

7.00 hrs.
↑1550 ↓1340

Ferriere – Rifugio Migliorero   V48b

Triple Saddle Tour through a narrow fold

Steep up and down walking, but rewarded with many botanical rarities along the way. If you don't have a good eye for spotting, you can take a look around in the botanical garden from Zio John in the Vallone di Pontebernardo. According to insiders, the rare Saxifraga florulenta can even be found growing in the surroundings of the Rifugio Zanotti in Vallone del Piz, and not only in the steep rock faces, where you couldn't go anyway.

Starting point: Ferriere, 1890 m.
Destination: Rifugio Migliorero, 2094 m.
Length: 16.5 km.
Grade: Well-marked paths and military tracks. Steep pass crossings. Slippery scree at the Passo di Rostagno.
Refreshment: Casa per Ferie.
Accommodation: Prati del Vallone: Casa per Ferie »Regina delle Alpi«, 1750 m, Associazione Zio John, mid-June–mid-Sept., 70 B, HB 20 €, tel. +39 333/ 352 23 26, www.ziojohn.com. – The **Rifugio Talarico** and the **Rifugio Zanotti** Zanotti in the neighbouring valley, are both without wardens and services, the keys for both can be picked up in the Casa per Ferie. – **Rifugio Migliorero:** see Stage 49.
Shopping/Services: Nothing available.
Public transport: None.
Note: Three saddles at one go is not every walker's cup of tea. The route could easily be broken up into separate treks.

Pontebernardo.

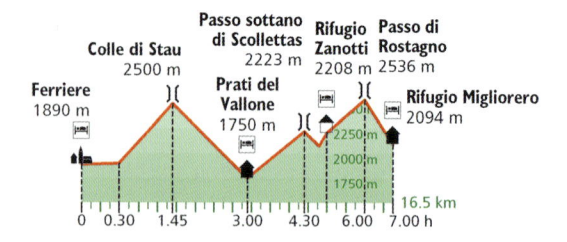

```
                        Passo sottano  Rifugio   Passo di
                        di Scollettas  Zanotti   Rostagno
            Colle di Stau   2223 m    2208 m    2536 m
            2500 m
Ferriere                Prati del              Rifugio Migliorero
1890 m                  Vallone                2094 m
                        1750 m        2250 m
                                      2000 m
                                      1750 m
                                                  16.5 km
   0   0.30    1.45     3.00   4.30   6.00   7.00 h
```

From **Ferriere**, pick up the already familiar trail to return to the stream and, on the other side, turn right onto the trail to the **Colle di Stau**, 2500 m. The entire ridge is criss-crossed by military trails which lead to a variety of ruined fortifications. One of these descends to the southeast and then, at the Gias di Stau, becomes a track road. The GTA short-cuts the bends sometimes. In summer, the meadow-blanketed slopes of the **Prati del Vallone** dazzle with their floral diversity (Asphodel lilies, fire lilies, bluebells and many others).

A former military barracks has been converted into a holiday resort for the spiritual organization, Zio John. You can also visit their botanical alpine garden that the priest, Don Giovanni (everyone called him simply Zio John –

Rifugio Migliorero.

Uncle John), created here in 1979 when he was still alive. The herbs being grown here are also used to make, for example, homemade *genepì* and *Amaro*. On top of that, you can have lunch or spend the night. The route leads eastwards across the meadow to the stream and then, on the opposite side, climbs steeply up through the wood to the *alpe* terrain of the Vallone Scollettas. On the **Passo sottano di Scollettas**, 2223 m, meet up again with military installations and a broad military track, over which you descend a short way into the Vallone del Piz, until the trail turns off to the right to reach the **Rifugio Zanotti**, 2208 m. Cross through the mountain valley behind the huts and then climb steeply to the **Passo di Rostagno**, 2536 m. At your feet, you can see the **Rifugio Migliorero**.

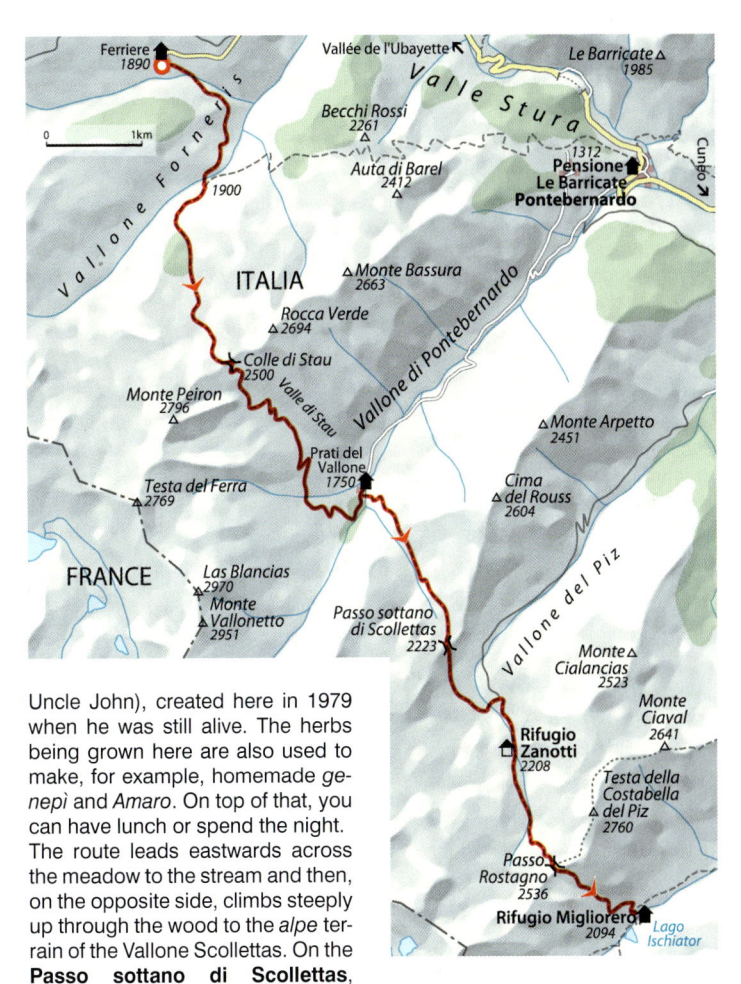

49 Sambuco – Rifugio Migliorero

6.30 hrs.
↑ 1720 ↓ 810

As if a Scottish castle has been dropped into the Alps

The crossing into the neighbouring valley is mostly a steep one, but as soon as you are high above on the meadowland plateau of the Caserma, you will be amazed at the marvellous panoramic view. You can prolong this panorama since there is a ridge trail that does not descend until shortly before reaching the Rifugio Migliorero, but only do this if the sky is perfectly clear and no storms are forecast. Instead, you could descend directly to Bagni di Vinadio or Strepeis, if the weather is not what it should be. Be that as it may, the excursion into the Vallone dell'Ischiator leads to one of the most beautiful mountain huts in the Alps. You feel as if you have landed in Scotland, since the Rifugio Migliorero seems so much like Eilean Donan Castle. Even more so when gossamer wisps of fog rise from the valley and wrap eerily around the castle-like stone structure with a bog tarn at its foot (see photo on page 206).

Caserma.

Starting point: Sambuco, 1184 m.
Destination: Rifugio Migliorero, 2094 m.
Length: 15.1 km.
Grade: Well-marked; a somewhat strenuous ascent; the descent path is steep and somewhat slippery; the climb to the Rifugio is simple.
Refreshment: Nothing en route.
Accommodation: Rifugio Migliorero: CAI, 2094 m, March–mid-Nov., 100 B, AV-HB 37 €, fantastic food, V. & O. Bagnis, tel. +39 0171/958 02 or +39 338/800 94 74.

Shopping/Service: Nothing available.
Public transport: None.
Alternativen: 1. From Colletto Caserma, along the well-marked Sentiero Balcone in up and down walking along the ridge. At the Testa della Costabella del Piz, an exposed, but secured, stretch of descent. No water en route. Sure-footedness & absolute head for heights & perfect weather necessary. 4.30 hrs. to Rif. Migliorero. 2. From the Baita Luca, head directly to Strepeis (see Stage 51); this saves you 2 hrs.

From **Sambuco (1)**, descend in a westerly direction along the access road, cross over the main road and continue along the track to the stream. Past the bridge, the GTA turns off to the left. Climb steeply up through the wood, then even steeper through a blueberry-blanketed slope. Finally, traverse eastwards onto the panoramic high plateau below the Monte Vaccia. Pass the military ruins at **Caserma (2)** and reach the southern edge where the meadowland plateau drops off steeply into the Vallone dell'Ischiator. If you don't take the Sentiero Balcone (Alternative), you must descend here. Only a short way down, the trail passes a spring. On the **Baita Luca (4)**, the steep stretch is over. The country lane to the right leads on the level to the **Ponte del Medico (5)**, where, once again, an ascent through the Vallone dell'Ischiator must be negotiated before reaching the **Rifugio Migliorero (6)**.

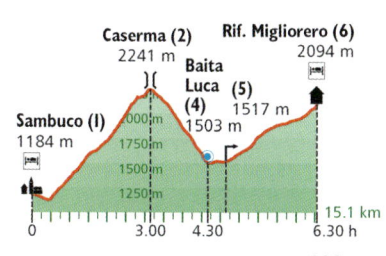

50 | Rifugio Migliorero – Strepeis

4.00 hrs.
↑ 400 ↓ 1220

Hot springs are waiting at the end of this Stage

The steep stretch to the pass doesn't seem to matter when you are presented with such wonderful sights below your feet. It is simply a treat to savour the view of the Rifugio Migliorero from different heights. Further up, at the Passo di Laroussa, the show is turned over to the Argentera, and even the Monviso puts in an appearance. But what a pity that the road to Strepeis is not exactly a walker's delight. The best thing to do is to flag down the first car that comes along (if indeed one comes at all), then you will have more time to spend in the spa.

Starting point: Rifugio Migliorero, 2094 m
Destination: Strepeis, 1281 m.
Length: 10.6 km.
Grade: Well-marked, distinct trail, further up, through boulder fields. Tarmac road starting at San Bernolfo.
Refreshment: Ref. Dahu de Sabarnui.
Accommodation: San Bernolfo: Refugio Dahu de Sabarnui, Beppe Degioanni, 10 B, tel. +39 0171/06 59 51 or 3335/59 95 023, www.rifugiodahuds.com. **Frazione Strepeis:** Albergo Strepeis, 1281 m, 10 mins. away from the spa, 10 DR (HB 49 €) and Posto tappa (14 B, HB 39 €), Margherita Degioanni, tel. +39 0171/958 31. additional accommodation is available in **Bagni di Vinadio**.
Shopping: Shop in Bagni di Vinadio.
Public transport: None.
Information: www.bagnidivinadio.com.
Tip: Terme di Vinadio, bathing area 20 €, 6 p.m–10:30 p.m. 10 €, tel. +39 0171/95 93 95, www.termedivinadio.com.
Alternative: If you choose to head directly to Sant' Anna from the Rifugio Migliorero, you would save yourself the tarmac road starting at Callieri, but the trade-off is a strenuous 8-hour day of walking.

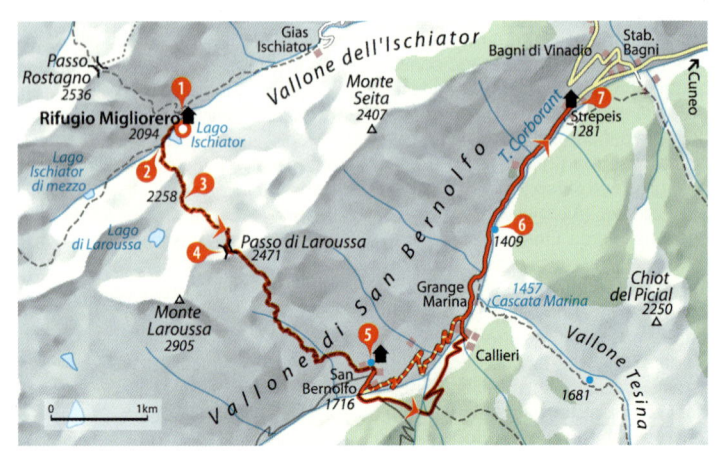

The chapel at San Bernolfo.

From the hut **(1)**, descend to the lakes below and head up the valley, but then immediately turn left onto the trail to reach the **Passo di Laroussa (4)**, 2471 m. From the crest of the pass, you could climb the Monte Laroussa (easy scrambling over rock; 1.30 hrs. for the ascent). A steep descent leads to **San Bernolfo (5)**, once a permanent settlement, but since 1959, only inhabited in the summer. Scientists are still baffled by the log cabin-style buildings which are not typical for this region. It is speculated that Walser were brought here when mining was still being done. The GTA now follows the road, but in the upper section, it can be circumvented. At the car park below San Bernolfo, bear to the right to cross over the stream and, on the opposite side, continue on to **Callieri**. Here, however, do not cross over to the road yet, but continue on a little further and pass the Grange Marina (at this point the trail into the Val Tesina turns off). Along the road, you will finally reach **Strepeis (7)**.

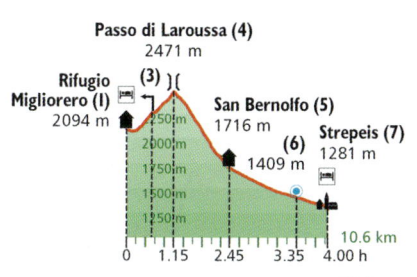

211

51 *Strepeis – Sant' Anna di Vinadio*

5.30 hrs.
↑ 1180 ↓ 430

An enchanted valley and Europe's highest-lying monastery

Only slightly less challenging as the actual GTA route, but scenically far more attractive, is the route through the Tesina Valley, which is why we give this one priority. Rugged, craggy teeth tower up around various high terrains where cobalt-blue lakes are clinging.

Starting point: Strepeis, 1281 m.
Destination: S. Anna di Vinadio, 2035 m.
Length: 11.2 km.
Grade: Well-marked but some stretches are not very distinct. A military trail starting at the Passo Tesina.

Refreshment: Nothing en route.
Accommodation: Santuario Sant' Anna di Vinadio, 2035 m, beg. June–end Sept., rooms HB 42 €, Posto tappa HB 32 €, tel. 39 0171/95 91 25, www.santuariosantanna.it.
Shopping/Services: Nothing available.
Public transport: None.
Alternative: If you wish to remain faithful to the GTA, at Strepeis or before reaching the spa, cross over the stream, take the trail through the Vallone d'Insciauda, then cross over the Passo di Bravaria, 2311 m, and finally reach Sant' Anna, 4.30 hrs.

From **Strepeis (1)**, take the San Bernolfo road up the valley. Turn off to the left, about 45 mins. later, to reach the Grange Marina. Past the bridge, you can also turn left to climb up via the **Cascata Marina (5)**, which is worth seeing; above the waterfall, however, you must keep a close eye on the waymarkers. The trail (P 19) leads along the right bank of the stream. The narrow valley then broadens out into a marvellous scenic backdrop. At the Roccia Leone, the Lion's Rock, the **Capanna di Tesina**, 1947 m, is snuggled up. Past the hut, the P 19 turns off to the left. After a short, steep stretch, reach the next idyllic landscape – a high terrain with a marshland biotope and a lake.

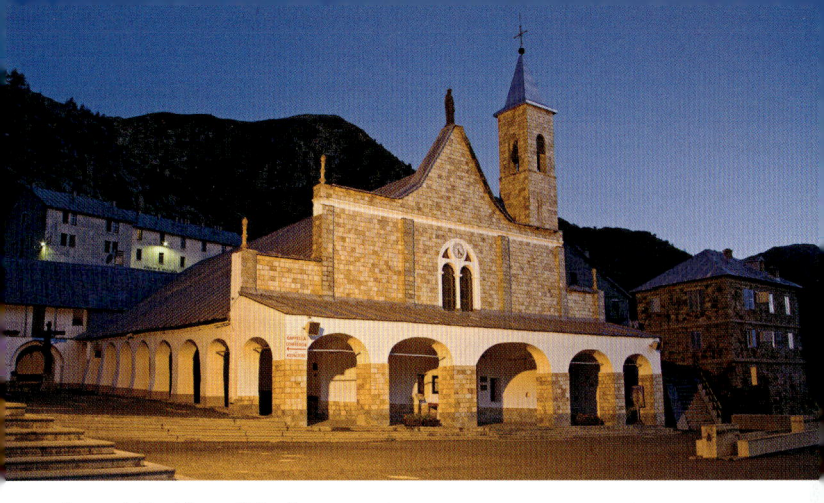

Santuario Sant' Anna di Vinadio.

Weathered Swiss Pines hang over the trail on the way to the **Passo Tesina (9)**, 2400 m. Here, meet up with a military trail which descends to the lakes at Sant' Anna and to the monastery. Finally, pass the holy site of **Sant' Anna (10)**, a solitary blocky boulder with a stairway and a statue of the Madonna, 2066 m. On this spot, the legend has its source (see page 203).

> *For over 40 years, Giorgio Pepino has been the rector of the **Monastery of Sant' Anna** and has distinguished himself through his social commitments. His efforts have brought about the conversion of a number of military barracks into convention centres for young people from all over the world. Every Saturday evening in the summer, a torchlight procession takes place to the statue of the Virgin located below the monastery. Thanks to Don Pepino, a friend of the mountains and a collector of herbs, a genepì is also made and sold here at the monastery.*

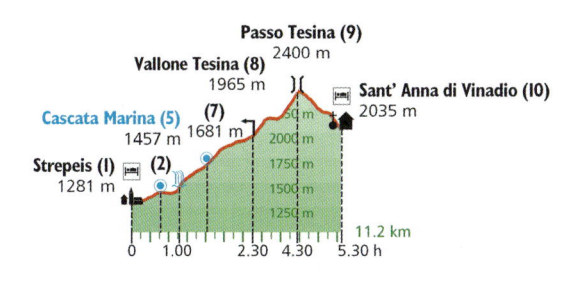

213

52   Sant' Anna di Vinadio – Rifugio Malinvern

5.30 hrs.
↑810 ↓1000

From the ridge marking the border into the Vallone di Rio Freddo

From Sant' Anna, the broad ridge is quickly ascended and then the route continues pleasantly along level military trails. A sea of peaks surrounds us, which also many bicyclists and auto tourists are enjoying on the Colle della Lombarda. The artificial settlement of Isola 2000 tries to remain hidden, but nonetheless, the ski runs, brutally slashed into the landscape, reveal where France is lying. A planned expansion project for the ski area, spreading into Italian territory, was stopped. Thus, only the military trails leave a zigzag pattern in the scenery. An especially beautiful example is the paved trail over the Passo d'Orgials, which, despite the steep, rocky heap of a terrain, allows for a pleasant ascent. On the other side, nature seems at its most pristine and unspoiled, and the Laghi della Valletta are a temptation for a leisurely pause. Only at a second glance do you see that, even here, the military has spun its network of trails.

Starting point: Sant' Anna di Vinadio, 2035 m.
Destination: Rifugio Malinvern, 1839 m.
Length: 14.7 km.
Grade: Excellently marked. Well-laid military trails, some steep stretches.
Refreshment: Nothing en route.
Accommodation: Rifugio Malinvern: 1839 m, CAI, mid-June–mid Sept., at the weekends until mid-Oct., 46 B, HB/AV 39/37 €, Massimo Gemma, tel. +39 0171/95 96 05 or 347/272 51 94.
Shopping/Services: Nothing available.
Public transport: None.
Note: If you wish to abort the trek at this point: by following the red-yellow-marked trail, Lou Viage for the next 4 hrs., via two interesting fortresses, you will eventually reach Vinadio (there's a bus to Cuneo from there).

From the **Santuario (1)**, take the familiar narrow road up the mountain and past the shrine for the Virgin until the military trail forks. Turn left here to reach the Lago del Colle di Sant' Anna, 2156 m. Soon after passing the lake, leave the route (which leads to the Colle di Sant' Anna) behind by turning left onto the military trail that ascends south-eastwards to the Cima Moravacciera, 2407 m. From here, continue pleasantly along the ridge, which acts as a border, while enjoying a view reaching to Monviso and taking in the Tinée in France. From the **Colle della Lombarda (3)**, you can short-cut the road somewhat by crossing northwards through the lake basin. Then another stretch along the road and, at the trail sign, turn right onto the military trail to reach the **Passo d'Orgials (6)**, 2600 m. Zigzags take you up to the twin lakes. Around a bend, the next idyllic upland terrace can be seen with a little tarn perched upon it. At the end of this area, the trail then ascends northwards in order to skirt around the steep juncture where the secondary valley into the Rio Freddo Valley merges. Afterwards, cross through a lovely larch wood to reach the **Rifugio Malinvern (7)**, enthroned upon a little hill, which is separated from the other side of the valley by a deep gorge.

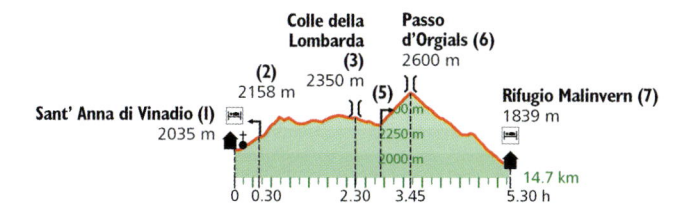

Laghi della Valletta, view from the Passo d'Orgials.

215

53 Rifugio Malinvern – Terme di Valdieri

5.30 hrs.
↑ 780 ↓ 1250

Into the Alpi Marittime nature park – tracking the king's footsteps

Reddish rock, shimmering alpine lakes and the bright green valley of the Vallone di Valasco – here, a royal hunting lodge welcomes you to a nostalgic overnight sojourn. A historical flair has also been preserved in the village, Terme di Valdieri, where you can enjoy complete relaxation in the hot sulphur springs.

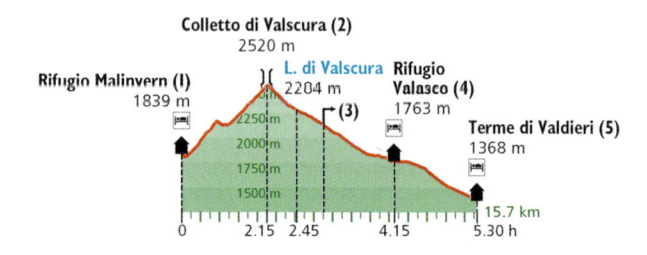

```
                Colletto di Valscura (2)
                     2520 m
                     L. di Valscura   Rifugio
Rifugio Malinvern (1)    2204 m       Valasco (4)
     1839 m                 (3)        1763 m
                                              Terme di Valdieri (5)
                                                  1368 m

                                                        15.7 km
  0        2.15  2.45        4.15         5.30 h
```

Starting point: Rifugio Malinvern, 1839 m.
Destination: Terme di Valdieri, 1368 m.
Length: 15.7 km.
Grade: Well-marked; military trails, designed to ease the steepness.
Refreshment: Rifugio Valasco.
Accommodation: Rifugio Valasco (royal hunting lodge), 1763 m, beg. May–end Sept., 50 B, DR HB 60 €, dormitory HB 40 €, Flavio Poggio, tel. +39 348/323 02 66, www.rifugiovalasco.it. – **Terme di Valdieri:** 1368 m, Albergo Turismo somewhat above the spa, beg. May–end Sept., 12 DR, HB 54/62 €, Roberto Parracone, tel. +39 0171/973 34 or 971 79. Hotel Royal Terme Reali di Valdieri, mid-June–mid-Sept., 100 DR (HB from 88 €, entrance to the spa is included in the price), Posto tappa 15 B, HB 44 €, tel. +39 0171/971 06, www.termedivaldieri.it.
Shopping/Services: A cash dispenser and a post office, no shops until Valdieri, 16 km away.
Public transport: Bus service Mon–Sat 1x daily in the afternoons at 12:00 to Cuneo (1 hr. drive), July/August 2x daily, timetable: www.benese.it. In addition, shuttle bus service between Terme di Valdieri and Entracque, 2x daily, from about end July until end Aug.
Information: Visitor's centre for the Alpi Marittime Nature Park is just opposite the Albergo Turismo, an exhibit, film, info, internet, tel. +39 0171/972 08, www.parcoalpimarittime.it.
Tips: A visit to the spa (9 a.m.–1 p.m., 1:30 p.m.–6 p.m. and 8 p.m.–11 p.m., fee for a half a day 15 €).
To compliment a dip in the thermal waters, a massage would prove quite soothing as well. The Terme di Valdieri is also famous for its sulphurous algae, which is naturally produced on the steps to the pool and then collected for use as a kind of mud wrap. An application makes you look like an alien, but the effects are simply wonderful. These algae are also a part of a line of cosmetics.
Botanical garden (open from mid-June until mid-September, 9:30 a.m.–12:30 p.m. and 2 p.m.–6 p.m., 3 €).

At the **Rifugio Malinvern (1)**, signs are lacking. Take the first path that turns off from the access road to descend to the stream. On the opposite side, you will find the route well-marked. Head south-eastwards in zigzags, onto a knoll above the Lago Malinvern. As if you were standing on a pulpit, you gaze into the »cathedral« of a marvellous valley head. In a short descent, reach the lake and skirt around it to the west. Then the

Terme di Valdieri.

military trail clears a way over the moraine wall of a vanished glacier to ascend to the **Colletto di Valscura (2)**, 2520 m, where you enter the Alpi Marittime Nature Park. Enjoy a sweeping view between Monviso and Argentera. In pleasant zigzags, descend to the **Lago di Valscura inferiore**, 2274 m, a good opportunity for bathing. Cross over the outflow of the lake and continue descending to the left along an artfully-paved track leading into the Valasco mountain valley, where the royal hunting lodge, built in the style of a fort with merlon-crowned towers, catches the eye – the **Rifugio Valasco (4)**. The Reale Casa di Caccia had been heavily damaged by fire and then neglected for many decades before it was finally restored (not necessarily tastefully) and has been used since 2008 as a Rifugio and restaurant which is open to the public. Continue along a broad track road (the bends can be short-cut time and again) to reach **Terme di Valdieri (5)**.

Spellbound by the Argentera Massif – the Alpi Marittime Nature Park

The former royal hunting grounds found here, just like in the case of the Gran Paradiso, have been developed into a nature reserve. Once again, it was King Vittorio Emanuele II who had wielded his royal privilege in 1857. He established a summer residence in Sant' Anna di Vinadio, decreed the construction of hunting lodges and – so that he could enter the mountains on horse-back – created endless miles of pleasant hunting trails which are so much appreciated by today's walkers. His territory extended all the way to the Boréon Valley in France, which belonged to Savoy-Piedmont at the time. Of course, he also enjoyed treatments in the hot sulphur springs and had the facilities expanded to meet the needs of the royal family. Vittorio Emanuele II, not only renowned as an avid hunter, was also known as the *Re Galantuomo*, a beguiling womaniser who, to supplement his marriage with Adelaide of Austria, enjoyed numerous liaisons – the longest of which was with the *Bela Rosin* (Rosa Vercellana), a commoner, who the king even took as his wife before his death. His trysts with the »Lovely Rosa« were spent in one of the »Swiss style« chalets, right next to the stately spa hotel. Recently refurbished, today the chalet would make an excellent accommodation, but unfortunately, no one has stepped forward to lease the property.

»The *dolce far niente* in this quiet alpine valley ...« were words of praise put down (without any female distraction) by the Alpine pioneers, Ludwig Purtscheller and Walter Bodenmann, after they explored peaks here in the summer of 1890. Starting at Terme di Valdieri, they climbed the Monte Matto and the Argentera, but not as the first – that had already been achieved by W.A.B. Coolidge in 1879 with his guides, Christian Almer & Son from Grindelwald.

After the monarchy was abolished in 1946, hunting reserves were established here. In 1979, both the Mercantour National Park, on the French side of the border, as well as the Riserva Naturale Bosco e Laghi Palanfrè (see Stages 57/58), on the Italian side, were created. In 1980, after the Italian state-owned electricity company, Enel, finished the construction of three reservoirs, the Argentera Nature Park was established. In 1995, when the park was fused with the Riserva Naturale, it finally became the Alpi Marittime Nature Park. Since 1987, the two parks have operated in close cooperation. In the meantime, efforts are targeted towards a cross-border International Park and the designation as a UNESCO World Heritage Site.

The narrow alpine folds surrounding the 3297 metre-high Argentera, »Queen of the Maritime Alps«, precludes the settlement of villages. Hard crystalline rock, mostly consisting of gneiss and granite, which lower the permeability of the subsoil, creates a terrain replete with lakes, streams and waterfalls. Only 45 km. from the sea, as the crow flies, glaciers converge here with the

Mediterranean climate to produce conditions for an extraordinary, botanically-rich landscape. It is estimated that 2600 species are to be found in the Maritime Alps, that is, half of all of the plant species in Italy. If you are knowledgeable in botany, you could identify an entire range of endemics (plants that only grow in a certain specific area) in the Maritime Alps. Almost legendary is the Argentera saxifrage (Saxifraga florulenta). An inconspicuous rosette-shaped succulent that can reach an age of over 50 years, but only once in its lifetime produces a flower, a striking pink spike which blossoms just before the plant dies. There is also the Valdieri violet (Viola Valderia), which was discovered here in 1780 by the botanist, Carlo Allioni, and which lends its name to the botanical garden at Terme di Valdieri. The garden is located just behind the visitor centre for the nature park and boasts of some 450 species of plants.

The fauna is plentiful too; hardly anywhere else in the Alps can you come so close to animal life as in the Maritime Alps. Apart from marmots, ermine, Alpine Ptarmigans, mouflon and Golden Eagles, with a little bit of luck, you might even see a Bearded Vulture which, at the end of the 19th century, had completely disappeared from the Alps. Since 1993, twenty-six of these birds of prey were successfully reintroduced into the Maritime Alps. At the beginning of the 90s, wolves have also returned to the Maritime Alps. But indeed, since their territory totals 300 km^2, it is relatively unlikely that you will meet one of these shy animals, which are, by the way, absolutely harmless to walkers. Recently, plans were made by the park administration to bring people in closer contact to the wolf, by establishing an outdoor enclosure near Entracque (see Stage 56).

The eastern side of the Argentera Massif, view from the Rifugio Genova (Stage 54).

54 — Terme di Valdieri – Rifugio Genova-Figari

6.00 hrs.
↑ 1290 ↓ 640

The Argentera is a treasure trove – for stones

Rock walls towering to the heavens, along which the Canalone di Lourousa paints a white line, a truly hair-raisingly steep channel of ice which the Alps pioneers, Coolidge and Purtscheller, chose as the approach route for the first attempt to climb the Argentera ridge. This heap of rock proves to be only barren at first glance; in reality, it is full of true survivalists like the Saxifrage, the ibex or the hut personnel of the Rifugio Morelli-Buzzi. Splashes of colour are also made by the tarns on the other side of the rugged pass, where water power produces expensive electricity.

Starting point: Terme di Valdieri, 1368 m.
Destination: Rifugio Genova, 2020 m.
Length: 16.8 km.
Grade: Well-marked; until the Lago Lagarot, a distinct trail, then stretches crossing scree and boulder fields. A steep descent. At the end, along a dam wall and roads serving the power plant.
Refreshment: Rifugio Morelli-Buzzi.
Accommodation: Rif. Morelli-Buzzi: 2351 m, CAI, June 12–Sept. 12, 54 B, Andrea Cismondi, tel. +39 347/053 14 56 or +39 0171/973 94. – **Rifugio Genova-Figari:** 2020 m, mid-June–mid-Sept., 68 B, HB/AV 46/35 €, Dario Giorsetti, tel. +39 0171/97 81 38, www.rifugiogenova.it.
Shopping/Services: Nothing available.
Public transport: Bus service from Cuneo (Piazza Galimberti) to Terme di Valdieri Mon–Sat 1x daily, 12.00 p.m. July/Aug. 2x daily, 8.10 a.m./2.30 p.m. (timetable: www.benese.it).

Pass the **Hotel Royal (1)** to reach the entrance gate. Descend to the car park, then turn right onto a mule track. Ascend in bends through the wood into the Vallone di Lourousa. Past the Gias Lagarot, the route levels out and passes the **Lago Lagarot**. At the idyllic tarn, you are standing directly below the imposing north face of the Argentera. To the right of the icy thread marking the Canalone di Lourousa, the sheer Corno Stella – the Invincible One – that is, until the day when a count arrived here from Nice: Victor de Cessole, one of the foremost activists in opening up the Maritime Alps and, for three decades, president of the Nice CAI. His first ascent, in August 1903, with Jean Plent and Andrea Ghigo, caused quite a stir. Today, the Corno Stella is criss-crossed by countless rock climb-

Lago Lagarot, view to Canalone di Lourousa.

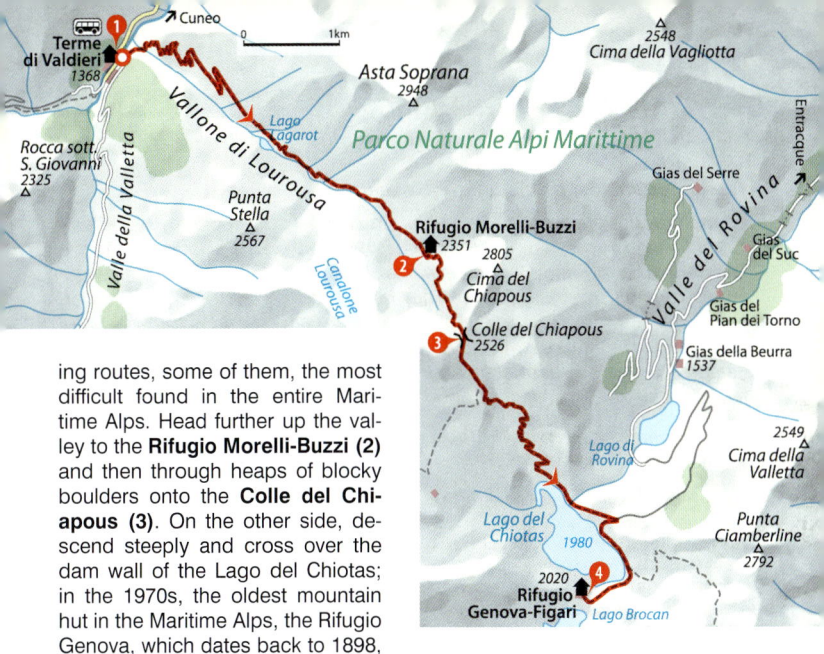

ing routes, some of them, the most difficult found in the entire Maritime Alps. Head further up the valley to the **Rifugio Morelli-Buzzi (2)** and then through heaps of blocky boulders onto the **Colle del Chiapous (3)**. On the other side, descend steeply and cross over the dam wall of the Lago del Chiotas; in the 1970s, the oldest mountain hut in the Maritime Alps, the Rifugio Genova, which dates back to 1898, was submerged in its waters. In 1981, as a replacement, the hydroelectric company gave the CAI a new hut above the lake. From the top of the dam wall, 130 metres high, you get a dizzying view taking in the Lago della Rovina, created by the Enel utility company in 1969 to kick off the production of the hydroelectric plant Entracque which first began operation in 1982 – the largest pumped-storage hydroelectric plant in Europe. For more info: during Stage 56, when passing the Piastra Reservoir, you will find Enel's visitor centre. On the other side of the dam wall, descend along the road to the left. Past a tunnel, turn right onto a trail and in up-and-down walking, heading eastwards around the lake, reach the **Rifugio Genova-Figari (4)**.

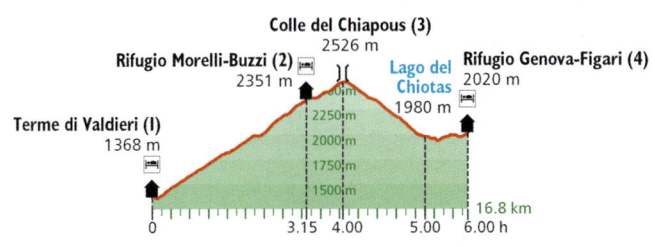

55 Rifugio Genova-Figari – San Giacomo

4.30 hrs.
↑ 490 ↓ 1290

The southernmost glaciers from close up

An entertaining crossing: at the outset, you will be spellbound by the Argentera, followed by the view of Monte Gelàs, where the Alps' southernmost glaciers are probably enduring their final years. A portion of the glacial ice is no longer recognizable as a glacier. They have therefore been named the »Ghiacciai neri«, the black glaciers, since they are covered now with heaps of blocky boulders and glacial till. At the destination for this Stage, you will be attracted by a slow-food locale, and if you still have the energy, you should take a look at the royal hunting lodge nearby.

Starting point: Rif. Genova, 2020 m.
Destination: San Giacomo, 1213 m.
Length: 13.3 km.
Grade: Well-marked, distinct trail. The last kilometers along a rough gravel road.
Refreshment: Rifugio Soria-Ellena (a short detour).
Accommodation: Rif. Soria-Ellena: 1840 m, CAI, mid-June–mid-Sept., May–Oct. at the weekends, 70 B, HB/AV 35/45 €, Mary Bacani, tel. +39 0171/97 83 82, www.rifugiosoriaellena.com. – **Posto tappa di San Giacomo:** 1213 m, nature park hut; evening meal next door in the Baita Monte Gelàs, Easter–late autumn, 22 B, HB 38 €, unique meals, Renzo Gerbino, tel. +39 0171/97 87 04 or +39 333/257 31 29 or +39 333/417 39 12.
Shopping/Services: Nothing available.
Public transport: None.

Lago Brocan with the Rifugio Genova-Figari

From the **Genova hut (1)**, go back a short way along the lake until a trail turns off to the right, heading for the **Colle di Fenestrelle (3)**, 2463 m. At the pass, descend to the valley floor, the **Piano del Praiet (4)**. Once you are there, below the Rifugio Soria-Ellena, meet up with a track road which leads to the left towards San Giacomo. The rough gravel makes walking somewhat unpleasant but, now and again, you can veer off for a stretch.

You are walking along a very important pilgrimage route which leads over the Colle di Finestra to the Madone de Fenestre (the most eminent pilgrimage site in the French Maritime Alps) and which continues as the Way of St. James and leads all the way to Santiago di Compostela.

San Giacomo (6), named after St. James, is a former pilgrim's wayside accommodation. Even Vittorio Emanuele II liked to stay in the central valley of the three Gesso Valleys and no wonder, when you consider the **Casa di Caccia**.

The royal hunting lodge is hidden among centuries-old beech trees at the mouth of the Vallone di Monte Colombo and is most certainly worth seeing (10 mins. from the Posto tappa). Today, the Jesuits use the stately manor as a holiday home for young people. You only need to ask, to be welcomed into the »*Proprietà privata*«.

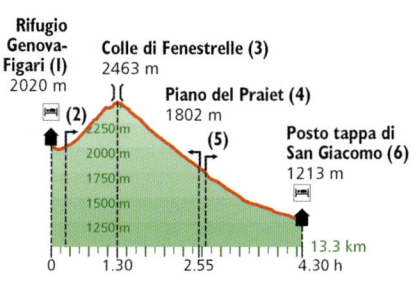

223

56 San Giacomo – Trinità

4.00 hrs.
↑380 ↓500

Where wolves howl

We have allowed ourselves a deviation from the GTA, because we believe a highlight like Entracque should not be left by the wayside, and also, that avoiding a rather unspectacular pass is unlikely to cause any tears. However, a stretch of road is the piper's payment for the excursion to the pretty village at the confluence of the Gesso streams. In summer 2010, the Centro Uomini e Lupi (Man & Wolf) was opened here. With the help of two interactive presentations (in Entracque, next to the tourist office, and in the nearby Wolf Park), visitors will be introduced to a controversial topic in a very gripping way.

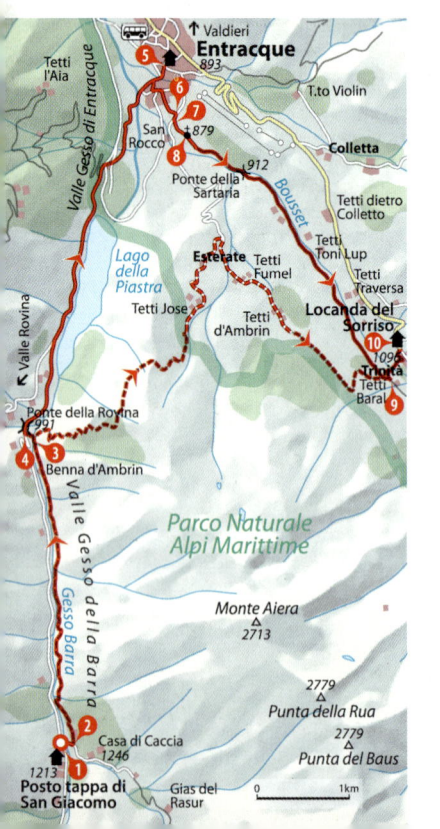

Starting point: San Giacomo, 1213 m.
Destination: Trinità, 1096 m.
Length: 14.2 km.
Grade: Well-marked. Some stretches along a narrow trail along a river. About 2 km. of tarmac, then country lanes.
Refreshment: In Entracque.
Accommodation: Entracque: 893 m, Albergo Pagari, open year-round, 13 R (25 B), HB 42 €, tel. +39 0171/97 80 56. Hotel Miramonti, open year-round, 14 R (25 B), HB from 46 €, tel. +39 0171/97 82 22, www.hotelmiramontientracque.com. Hotel Trois Etoiles, open year-round, 18 R (38 B), HB from 50 €, tel.+39 0171/97 82 83, www.hoteltrois-etoiles.com. – **Trinità:** 1096 m, Locanda del Sorriso, mid-June–end Sept. and at the weekends, 38 B, HB 40 €, Carla and Adelchi de Giovanni, tel. +39 0171/ 97 83 88.
Shopping/Services: Shop, post office, cash dispenser, pharmacy in Entracque.
Public transport: Bus service to Cuneo a number of times daily, timetable: www.benese.it. Shuttle bus July 1– Aug 30, daily and Sundays in Sept. Entracque –Wolf Park–Enel's visitor centre (Piastra reservoir), timetable: www.entracque.org/Servizi/trasporti.aspx.
Information: Centro Visita di Entracque, tel. +39 0171/97 86 16, www.entracque.org.
Tip: Centro Uomini e Lupi: entrance fee 10 €, shows with earphones in D/F/E.

Royal hunting lodge near San Giacomo.

From the **Posto tappa (1)**, descend for some metres down the street, turn right to cross the bridge and then turn left into the campsite. Keeping to the right of the grounds, the trail leads through a wood to reach a stream. Now continue along the bank in up-and-down walking. The stream cuts deeper and deeper into the terrain to become a gorge. Now ignore the **turn-off of the GTA (3)** to the right towards the Colletto del Vailetto, and instead, descend to the **Ponte della Rovina (4)**. On the opposite side of the valley, now follow the road until reaching the fork past the dam wall of the **Lago della Piastra**. The road to the right leads to the dam wall and then to Entracque. Here, you will also find the visitors centre of the Enel Co., at which, you could examine a model of the hydroelectric plant or take part in a guided tour. If

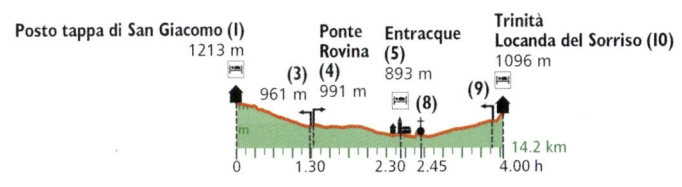

225

Entracque.

you do not wish to follow the road to Entracque, do not turn off at the junction, but instead, wait until a little later when you can turn off onto an access road, from which, further on, you can turn left onto a country lane that takes you to **Entracque (5)** (this route does not appear in the IGC map).
The settlement is perched upon two separate hills. The tourist office is located in the eastern, and backmost, village district. Following the signs for San Giacomo, return to the western village district. Past the church dedicated to St. Antonio (with an interesting parish museum), turn left into the Via Ospedale, then right in the Via Michele Grosso, past the Carabinieri, then reach the **Cappella del Cornaletto (8)** with a fountain. Turn right here, then left onto the Strada Sartaria. At the next trail junction, turn right to cross over the **Ponte della Sartaria**, 912 m, and then continue upstream. As soon as the striking crag, Caire di Porcera, appears to the southeast, you have to keep a good eye out otherwise you may miss the turn-off of the GTA to the left. The GTA follows a country lane to cross the stream and, in a right-hand bend, keep straight on, heading steeply to reach **Trinità (10)**. This tiny hamlet was also once a pilgrim's stop along the Way of St. James.

i ***The mysterious alpine wolf:*** *you can see his tracks, but you can't see him. He is somewhere nearby but invisible. Hunted to extinction in the Alps, he has – since the beginning of the 90s – returned, starting off from the Abruzzi through the Apennines, finally reaching the Alps and then spreading northwards. About 60 wolves are living in the Italian Alps, a somewhat higher number in the French Alps; in Switzerland, only a few solitary animals have penetrated the country, as noted by Francesca Marucco. The biologist serves as the head of the »Progetto Lupo Piemonte«.*

This state-financed wolf project, founded in 1999, is investigating whether it is possible for wolves and humans to coexist, in other words, not only to study the wolf in detail, but also to convince farmers and herdsmen to accept a new awareness of the animals. Not an easy task, since cattle which were once able to graze freely, must now be protected at night behind electric fences.

A special protection is provided by Maremma Sheepdogs, a breed originating in the Abruzzi. These white »teddy bears« are completely integrated into the herd, living right in the midst of a flock of sheep since their day of birth; they even feel like they are sheep. Whether it's a wolf or a walker that comes too near to their charges, in a matter of seconds, the cuddliness has disappeared completely. Because of this, walkers should refrain from the desire to pet these creatures and should keep their distance from the Cani da Pastore when the shepherd is not nearby.

Wolves are not only fantastic climbers and swimmers; they are also powerful long-distance runners. They can roam 100 kilometres in a day with ease; if a quick sprint is called for, they can reach speeds of over 60 kms. an hour. Perfectly camouflaged and equipped with fine-tuned senses, so that they can detect movement in their territory well in advance, observing them in the wild is extremely difficult. But, even without the advantage of direct observation, thanks to scientific means, the wolf's behaviour can be studied. If, for example, a wolf researcher stumbles upon some wolf scat while wandering, he can take the sample to his laboratory and, using genetic engineering, can determine the sex, the wolf pack in question and whether or not the wolf is an alpha male. In addition to using laboratory results, the new Wolf Park strives to make locals, as well as tourists, better acquainted with the wolf: standing at the top of the food chain, the wolf regulates the ecological balance by weeding out weaker animals.

57 Trinità – Palanfrè

5.00 hrs.
↑ 1120 ↓ 840

Above thrilling rock faces

Experience dizzying downward views from the line of rock faces above Trinità. The trail is a tight-rope route above the line, crossing through exposed grassy slopes, followed by a panoramic ridge. From here, you can easily spot the geological differences. The easternmost valley of the three Gesso Valleys divides the dark, hard crystalline rock from the soft limestone and sedimentary rock.

Starting point: Trinità, 1096 m.
Destination: Palanfrè, 1370 m.
Length: 11.3 km.
Grade: Well-marked. Above the tree line, only traces of a narrow path. The traverse of steep grassy slopes demands sure-footedness; dangerous when wet.

Refreshment: Nothing en route.
Accommodation: Palanfrè: Locanda del Parco L'Arbergh, 1379 m, open year-round, 35 B, HB 35/40 €, www.palanfre.it, tel. +39 340/ 697 39 54, Silvana Giordano.
Shopping: Dairy in Palanfrè.
Public transport: None.

From the **Locanda (1)**, turn right onto the narrow street, heading towards Tetti Prer. Soon after, turn right onto a track road, climbing up the mountain, then the GTA turns off to the left onto a path. At a stream gully, the path loops around a steep slope (often damaged by avalanches) over to the other side. Passing through a patch of woods, climb steeply to the grassy roof of the **Caire di Porcera**, 1818 m, with a view of Monviso. A short excursion to the right, leading to the sheer edge, provides knee-shaking downward views. Otherwise, turn left along the ridge to ascend and then a traverse south-east-

Grassy ridge of the Costa di Pianard.

wards through tricky slopes follows. The indistinct traces are partially overgrown with juniper or damaged by landslips, so that every step must be carefully set.

At the **Colle della Garbella (2)**, 2170 m, it gets easy. Head to the right, following the grassy ridge of the Costa di Pianard. Past the highest point, 2190 m, the path descends to the left. In a bend towards the northeast, pass through an alpine basin; the path is also somewhat overgrown here and there. At the Gias Garbella, 1615 m, meet up with a resource road (you can short-cut this from time to time) which leads to **Palanfrè (3)**.

The once lively village (400 inhabitants in its heyday) was deserted completely during the 70s. Only since 2002, a cattle-breeding family lives here year round. Today, you can buy some delicious products in their dairy.

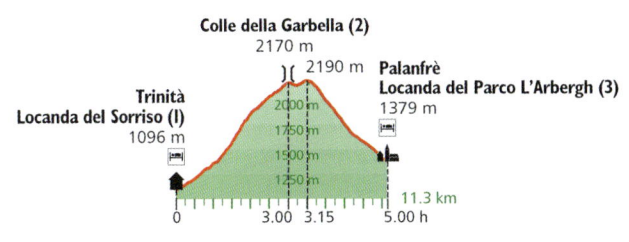

Colle della Garbella (2)
2170 m
2190 m **Palanfrè**
Locanda del Parco L'Arbergh (3)
Trinità 1379 m
Locanda del Sorriso (I)
1096 m

11.3 km
0   3.00 3.15   5.00 h

58 Palanfrè – Limonetto/San Lorenzo

4.30 hrs.
↑ 940 ↓ 810

Through the Bosco e Laghi Palanfrè nature reserve

A century-old beech forest protects Palanfrè from avalanches. Together with the lakes at the valley head, it is the oldest nature reserve in the Italian Maritime Alps. In stark contrast, the ski resort on the northern flank of the Tenda Pass has apartment complexes which seem to press the life out of the archaic Limonetto. An alternative route, waymarked by the owners of the Hotel Arrucador, permits you to skirt around the purpose-built resort settlement. On the way, you can make the acquaintance of the »marmot alpe«.

Starting point: Palanfrè, 1379 m.
Destination: San Lorenzo, 1505 m.
Length: 11.4 km.
Grade: Well-marked. Until reaching the Lago degli Alberghi, a distinct trail. On the final slope, slippery scree; precipitous passages are secured. The continued route is problem-free as long as the terrain is open to grazing livestock. If the grass is high, the waymarkings further below are not always easy to spot.
Refreshment: Nothing en route.
Accommodation: Limonetto: Ristorante L'Ange Blanc, open almost year-round, 8 B, with breakfast 25 €, HP 40–45 €, good food, Stefano & Fabio, tel. +39 0171/92 82 21 – **San Lorenzo:** 1505 m, Hotel Arrucador Relais de Charme, open almost year-round, 3 DR (HB 75 €), one 3-bed-R (HB 68 €), W. Revello & A. Merolt, tel. +39 347/544 14 08 or +39 340/160 26 42, www.arrucador.it, creative rooms, *hammam*, 1st class food; when booked out, Walter & Anja can arrange accommodation in a partner B&B (including transfer).
Shopping/Services: Shop, post office, cash dispenser, pharmacy in Limone (5 km).
Public transport: Bus service to Limone a number of times per day, timetable+Infos: www.limonepiemonte.it

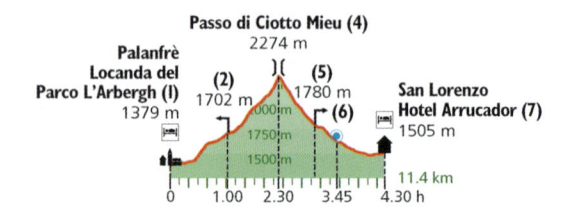

Passo di Ciotto Mieu (4)
2274 m

Palanfrè
Locanda del
Parco L'Arbergh (I)   (2)   (5)
1379 m   1702 m   1780 m   San Lorenzo
                            2000 m   (6)   Hotel Arrucador (7)
                         1750 m   1505 m
                         1500 m
                                              11.4 km
0   1.00   2.30   3.45   4.30 h

230

From **Palanfrè (1)**, head southwards through dense beech forest, then cross over a gully into the *alpe* terrain of the Vallone degli Alberghi (*arbergh* in the local dialect means the »highest pasture in the region«). At a trail junction, about 1 hr. later, turn left to continue to the Lago degli Alberghi, 2038 m, and then the going gets very steep. In the upper section, a cable acts as a guard; at the end, reach the **Passo di Ciotto Mieu (4)**, 2274 m. The descent leads at first north-eastwards through the slope and then in zigzags through mown *alpe* terrain. You must be careful not to miss the **turn-off (5)** for the Stage destination, San Lorenzo, otherwise you could end up in Limonetto. If you meet up with a country lane, you have already gone too far.

During the descent, as soon as you approach the stream, with a small plain below (Pian Madoro), a path turns off to the right (red, triangular markers). The path leads over the stream, passing by »*alpe* caves« carved into the earth (in former times, these were used for cheese storage and as animal pens). Head south-eastwards and then drop to the south to reach the **Gias Boero (6)**, only inhabited during the summer months. From the *alpe* buildings, follow a track road down the valley and then, at a fork, continue by turning right. Just to the left of the trail, you will find the »marmot alpe«, as the locals call the stream bank riddled by the burrows of these animals. If you sit still for a couple of minutes, you will soon be surrounded by these curiosity-stricken »pets«. When the track road forks once again, turn right to the **Hotel Arrucador (7)**, which stands alone at a ski lift, enthroned on a little hill. In winter, high society likes to show off its extravagance by arriving by helicopter from the Côte d'Azur for a little bit of skiing.

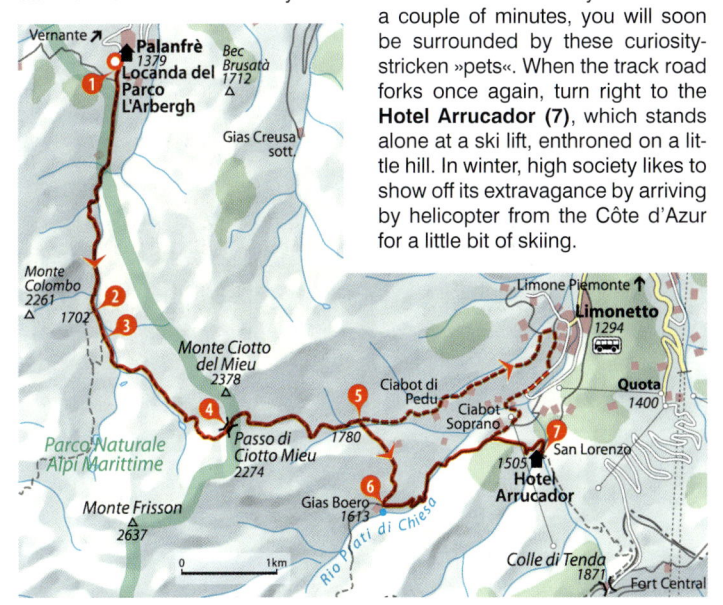

The Ligurian Alps – from the Tenda Pass through the »Piccole Dolomiti« and to the Med

The Tenda Pass, the quickest and most important way from the Côte d'Azur into the Piedmont, was already militarily secured very early in history, and since the reign of Mussolini, the borderline ridge is criss-crossed almost to the Mediterranean with a network of military and *Alpini* trails which make such wonderful panoramic trails today. Thus, it is very easy, for example, to follow the high ridge while enjoying a unique sweeping view where no peak of any significance stands in the way. It is indeed a very special treat to ramble along with a view to the sea. On a clear day, you can even spot Corsica. The Ligurian Alps, which begin at the Tenda Pass, belong marginally to the Limestone Alps. Erosion and water have moulded a fascinating mountain range. Vast, high plateaus, consisting of karst, sinkholes, bizarre rock formations and rugged precipices, are characteristic here and determine the course of the route through the Marguareis Massif. The surface of this terrain hides the most extensive cave system found in Italy – 150 km in total length. After heavy storms or longer periods of rainfall, the underground passages of karst are filled up, causing marvellous waterfalls or streams to spit out in many places. Since 1978, this unique karst landscape, often called the »Piccole Dolomiti«, has been protected as the Alta Valle Pesio e Tanaro nature park; in 2011, it was renamed Parco del Marguareis. In actuality, the GTA ends in Viozene in the Tanaro Valley (or you could say it »begins« there, since Italian and British walkers usually trek the route in the opposite direction). This would be an ending at Nowhere since there is hardly any real connection to a public transport network here. The Med presents a much nobler final destination and thus it has been the custom of German-speaking walkers to finish the trek from the Ligurian borderline ridge all the way to the beach at Ventimiglia. Starting at the Monte Saccarello, the route follows the Alta Via dei Monti Liguri (AVML). One of the many highlights along this stretch is the *Alpini* path, chipped into a rock face, which runs boldly through the flanks of the Monte Pietravecchia and the Monte Toraggio. The two mountains also occupy a special niche for the botanist; in May or June, the sunny side of the Monte Toraggio is blanketed with peonies. Since 2007, the area is a protected nature reserve – the Parco Naturale delle Alpi Liguri. The transformation from Alpine to Mediterranean occurs with snap abruptness on the penultimate day.

Parco del Marguareis (Stage 59, Alternative 2).

59 | Limonetto/San Lorenzo – Rifugio Garelli

8.00 hrs.
↑1450 ↓990

Military ramble between the Med and the Monte Rosa

From the Tenda Pass, on a clear day, you can actually see the Mediterranean and the Monte Rosa at the same time. One fortress after the other are lined up along here. You will pass by two of the six mountain fortresses, among them, Fort Pepin, which is the best preserved due to its remote location. Although the military tracks here are also very popular with motorized excursionists, the walker can always resort to the ridge trails. At the Colla Piana, you will be immersed in a unique karst landscape, and after circling the Conca delle Carsene, climb up below the northern sheer faces of the Margareis to reach the most striking hut to be found in the nature park that shares its name.

Starting point: Limonetto, 1294 m, alternatively San Lorenzo, 1505 m.
Destination: Rifugio Garelli, 1965 m.
Length: 23.1 km.
Grade: Well-marked, mostly military trails. This is the GTA's Crowning Stage.

An early start is essential. No water available en route (except at the Gias dell'Ortica)! Be absolutely sure to take along an extra water bottle.
Refreshment: Nothing en route.
Accommodation: Rifugio Garelli: 1965 m,

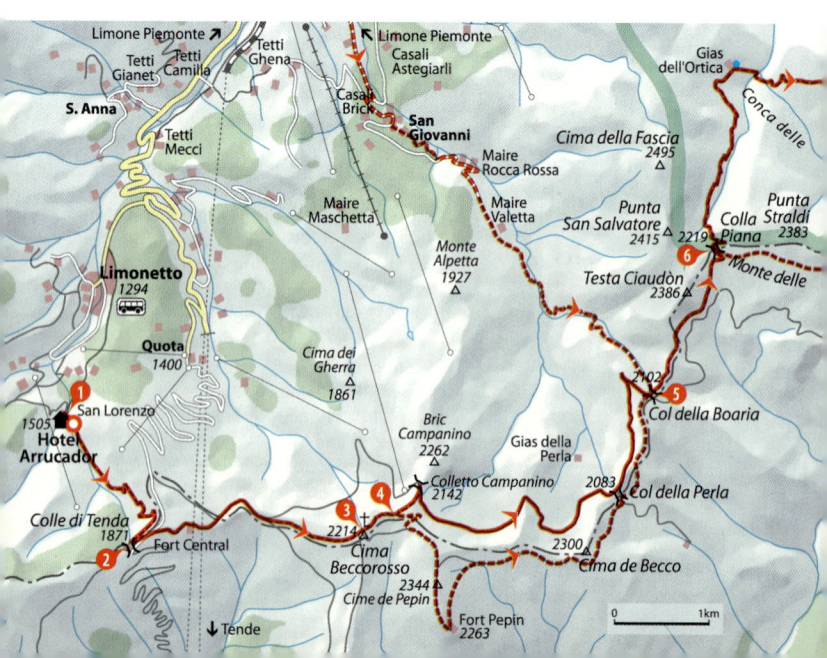

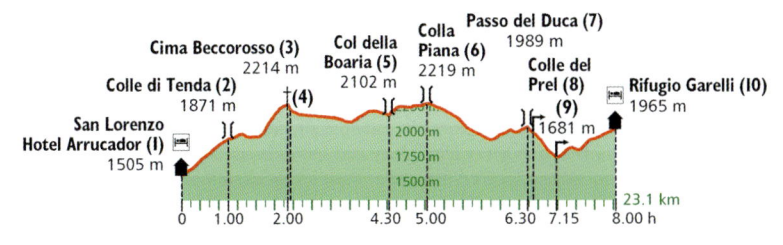

CAI, mid-June–mid-Sept., 90 B, AV-HB 33 €, delicious meals, own greenhouse, Guido Colombo, tel. +39 0171/ 73 80 78 or 339/770 99 37. – **Rifugio Alpino Don Barbera:** 2079 m, nature park hut, mid-June–mid-Sept., 50 B, HB 43 €, Osvaldo Castagna, tel. +39 0174/ 177 10 00 or 333/270 03 14, www.rifugiodonbarbera.it. – **Rifugio San Remo:** 2078 m, to pick up the keys, see Stage 62. – **Verdeggia:** 1090 m, Albergo il Poggio, open year-round, 12 R, tel. +39 0184/941 89 or +39 333/465 12 50.

Shopping/Services: Nothing available.
Public transport: Limonetto see Stage 58.
Alternatives: 1. Starting from Limone Piemonte: this long Stage can be cut by 1 hr. if, from Limone, you ascend directly to the Col della Boaria, or if you take a taxi to the Tenda Pass.

2. From the Colla Piana, you can reach the Rifugio Alpino Don Barbera in 1.45 hrs. On the next day either via Carnino to reach Upega (4 hrs.) or along a ridge directly to Monte Saccarello or the Rifugio San Remo, 6 hrs. (refer also to the maps for Stages 60–62).

3. You could also spend the night in Verdeggia (south of Monte Saccarello).

From the **Hotel Arrucador (1)**, head eastwards, cross over a stream gully and reach the ancient Roman road. Below the Fort Central, the »Strada Romana« merges into a broad military track; turn right to follow it for a few minutes to the **Colle di Tenda (2)**, 1871 m. The historical pass road is winding down the southern flank in 46 hair-pin bends, a bicyclist's dream or nightmare, also for the pack mule trader of times gone by, who was transporting heavy loads of salt and other goods along the most important »Via del Sale«, back and forth between the Piedmont and Provence.

235

> ℹ️ At the **Fort Central**, you are standing above the oldest road tunnel in the Alps, which was drilled through the ridge in 1882 and has greatly facilitated the border traffic between Italy and France. A total of six mountain forts defend the **Tenda Pass**, but, these never had to undergo a test for their effectiveness. Built by the Italians at the end of the 19th century, the forts are situated on territory belonging to France since 1947. Although in 1860, Italy had surrendered all of the area beyond the Alps' central ridge to France, the upper Roya Valley, as well as a section of the Maritime Alps, were kept. In 1947, the border was set along the central ridge.

At the fork in the road for Fort Tabourde, leave the military track behind and take up the path following the crest of the ridge. At the saddle **(4)** past the cross, which marks the summit of the **Cima Beccorosso (3)**, 2214 m, you can choose between the longer route to the right via Fort Pepin or the descent to the left to reach the military track, saving you some metres of climbing until reaching the Col della Boaria (this is not pleasant to walk due to the rough chipping surface).

At the **Col della Boaria (5)**, 2102 m, the route follows the military road which was built under Napoleon and leads to the **Colla Piana (6)**, 2219 m, where

Tenda-Pass, Fort Central.

Col della Boaria with the Argentera Massif, view from Colle dei Signori.

the Capanna Morgantini is located (only accessible to speleologists). Just past the point of crossing, an especially beautiful stretch of the original road construction can be seen. While passing through the Conca delle Carsene (*Cars* = karst), a fascinating piece of karst topography follows.

Head north to the **Gias dell'Ortica**, 1855 m (m (spring). Traverse above the *alpe*, then at a fork, turn right through a depression and head eastwards to reach the **Passo del Duca (7)**, 1989 m. From the **Colle del Prel (8)**, 1930 m, somewhat below, turn right into the Vallone del Marguareis. You can save yourself some metres of climbing when you continue along the traces of a path that you can clearly see a little lower down. From the Laghetto del Marguareis, 1928 m, head northwards through the slope to reach the **Rifugio Garelli (10)**. The architectural style of the hut mirrors the surrounding mountains and has won a prize for its exemplary furnishings. The little meadowland plateau, Pian del Lupo (Plain of the Wolf), in the foreground, is delightful during the mountain springtime, boasting an abundance of orchids and the rare yellow Checkered Daffodil. Taking in the northern rock faces of the Marguareis, the view also sweeps over the Po Valley plain to fix on a mighty section of the alpine ridge. On a clear day, you can spot Gran Paradiso, Monte Rosa and the Matterhorn.

60 — Rifugio Garelli – Upega

7.00 hrs.
↑970 ↓1640

Where witches dance – ridge walking on karst

Although the GTA skirts around the Cima Pian Ballaur and the Cima delle Saline, when the weather is fine, a walking excursion along these high ridges is a real gem. The route offers a peek into a craggy kingdom, brimming with mystical legend; this is reflected in the names of places along the way: Cima delle Masche (Witch's Peak), Rocca di Maraquaia (from the local dialect, »il Magu«, The Wizard), Cima Pian Ballaur (the summit where witches dance). In Viozene in the Tanaro Valley, the official GTA finally ends.

Crossing over the Saline.

Starting point: Rif. Garelli, 1965 m.
Destination: Upega, 1297 m.
Length: 17.5 km.
Grade: Well-marked. Do not attempt the crossing at Saline during foggy weather because the trail is barely discernible. A steep stretch during the descent demands sure-footedness and an excellent head for heights. The only water source is at the Rifugio Carlo Bossi; be absolutely sure to take enough water with you. The GTA route is somewhat easier.
Refreshment: Nothing en route.
Accommodation: Upega: 1297 m, Rifugio La Porta del Sole, beg. June–end Sept., 24 B, HB 40 €, delicious meals, Costantini family, tel. +39 0174/39 02 15 (maybe closed in 2013; alternative: B&B Il Larice, tel. +39/0174/390189, www.bblarice.it). – **Rifugio Mondovi:** 1761 m, CAI, mid-June until mid-September, June/October, at the weekends, 61 B, Mariolino Canavese, tel. +39 0174/655 55, www.rifugiomondovi.com. – **Rifugio Mongioie:** 1520 m, CAI, March 1–Sept. 30, 50 B, HB/AV 31/37 €, Giovanna & Silvano Odasso, tel. +39 0174/39 01 96.
Shopping/Services: Nothing available.
Public transport: Bus service only in mid-summer Upega – Ormea, info for the timetable: Comunità Montana Alta Val Tanaro, tel. +39 0174/80 67 21.
Information: Tourist office in Ormea, tel. +39 0174/30 21 57, www.ormea.eu.
Alternatives: 1. The GTA skirts northwards around the ridge via the Rifugio Mondovi, 2.30 hrs., and then crosses over into the Tanaro Valley via the Passo di Saline, 2 hrs.
2. If you want to keep on the GTA to reach the official terminus in Viozene, do not descend all the way to Carnino, but instead, continue eastwards via the Colla di Carnino to the Rifugio Mongioie, 1.45 hrs.

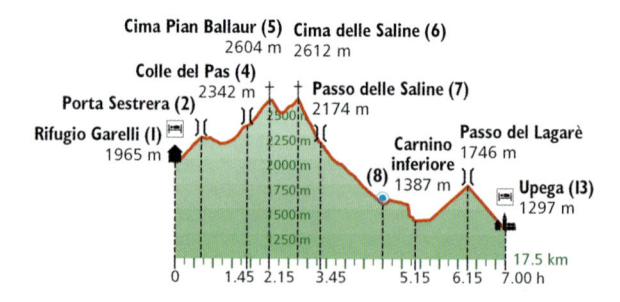

```
Cima Pian Ballaur (5)  Cima delle Saline (6)
      2604 m          2612 m
   Colle del Pas (4)
Porta Sestrera (2)   2342 m     Passo delle Saline (7)
                                2174 m
Rifugio Garelli (1)                          Passo del Lagarè
                                   Carnino   1746 m
  1965 m                          inferiore
                                 (8) 1387 m         Upega (13)
                                                    1297 m

                                                       17.5 km
 0    1.45 2.15   3.45         5.15  6.15  7.00 h
```

From the **Rifugio Garelli (1)**, head eastwards onto the **Porta Sestrera (2)**, 2225 m. After a short descent, turn right onto the path forking to the right **(3)**. This traverses south-eastwards to reach the Lago Rataira (*rataira* is the word for »bat« in the local dialect) and then leads steeply onto the **Colle del Pas (4)**. The Piaggia Bella, »the beautiful plain«, lies at your feet and is notable for its large sinkhole, an important entranceway to the system of caves beneath the Marguareis Massif, Italy's largest and deepest. The underground labyrinth of the Piaggia Bella sports a length of 54 km. with 14 entranceways, the labyrinth of La Bassa, in the neighbouring Vallone dei Maestri, measures 23 km., although speleologists have still been unable to find the connection which surely exists. The water flowing from the Marguareis uses these passages and only appears again to the light of day in the gorge Gola delle Fascette. From the pass, turn left along the ridge to climb to the summit of the **Cima Pian Ballaur (5)**, 2604 m. The path skirts southwards around the sheer eastern precipice. Crossing through lush meadowland with Edelweiss, climb onto the saddle and, on the other side, onto the **Cima delle Saline (6)**, 2612 m. The descent is located only a little southwards from the cross which marks the summit, along a craggy outcrop (be careful, slippery scree), then the route gets easier as it crosses a ridge of scree onto the **Passo delle Saline (7)**, 2174 m. Here, you meet up again with the GTA. An important route for transporting salt crossed over at this point; this is mirrored in the place names. From the pass, descend southwards. Before the valley narrows towards the Gola delle Saline, meet up with a memorial cross. Past the gorge, the trail continues above the Rifugio Carlo Bossi (closed to the public). Past a **fountain (8)**, reaches a trail junction. To the left, the GTA continues on to the Rifugio Mongioie, but we bear right to reach **Carnino inferiore**, 1387 m (since its conversion into holiday homes, the village is inhabited once again, at least in summer) and to Carnino superiore, 1397 m, where the path to **Passo del Lagarè**, 1746 m, turns off southwards, and leads to **Upega (13)**.

Rifugio Garelli.

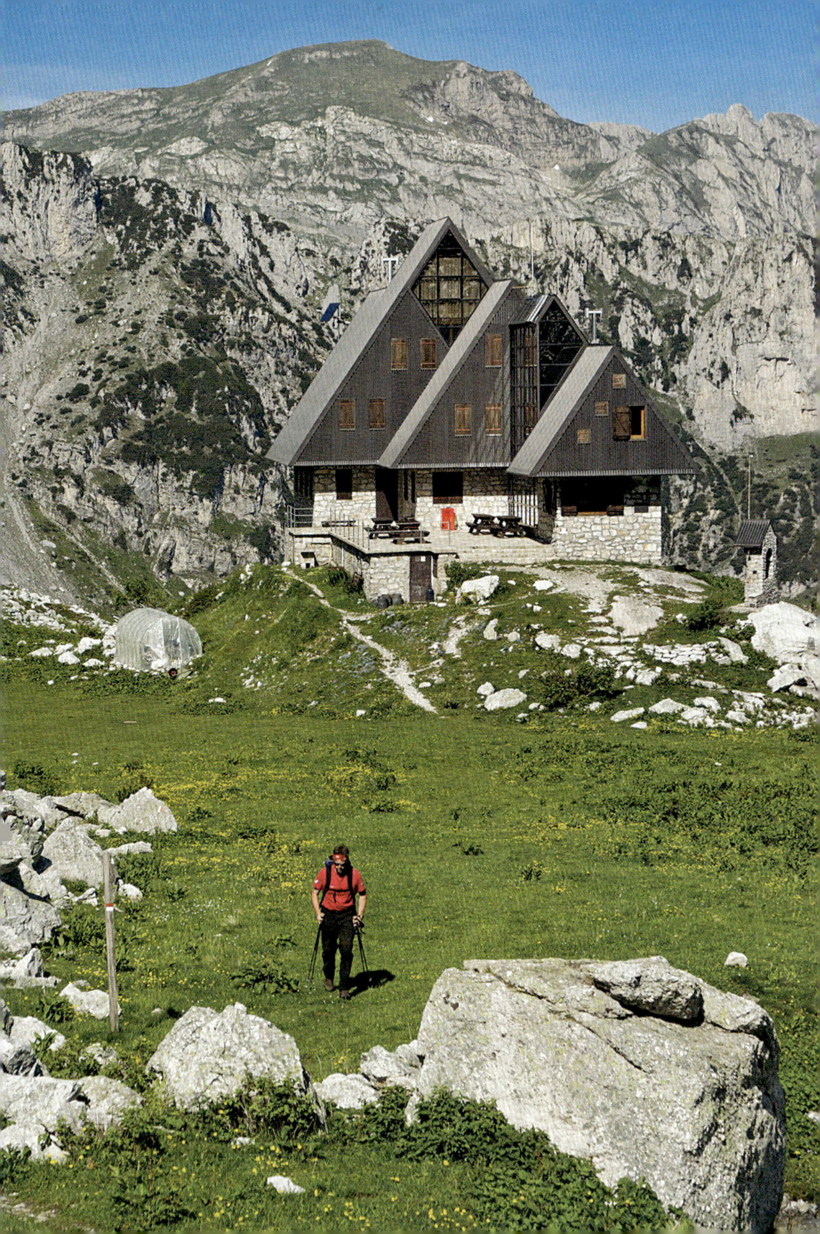

61 Upega – Monesi di Triora

2.30 hrs.
↑490 ↓410

An historic Alpine region, torn apart by borders

The villages of Carnino, Upega and Piaggia in the uppermost Tanaro Valley, form the community of Briga Alta. The name refers to the region settled by the Brigascans; combined with the Roya Valley around La Brigue (now belonging to France) and the Verdeggia region (which is now Ligurian), as well as with Viozene (today, Ormea), this was once a single community. Up until 1947, the upper Roya Valley, on the other side of the Tenda Pass, and Monte Saccarollo both belonged to Italy. The border and community shifts have torn apart the Brigascan's alpe terrain and the mountain people have lost their source of livelihood. The last shepherd gave up in 1979. Carnino has been abandoned, Upega counts only four inhabitants living there year round. The local dialect would have completely died out long ago if it wasn't for the efforts of two organizations, »A Vaštéra« and »Il Nido d'Aquila«, who keep a close watch on their cultural heritage, providing, for example, a Brigan dictionary and two regularly published newspapers in the Brigan language.

Starting point: Upega, 1297 m.
Destination: Monesi di Triora, 1376 m.
Length: 9.6 km.
Grade: Not marked until after crossing the 2nd stream (red dots), but nevertheless a distinct trail and an easy Stage.
Refreshment: Nothing en route.
Accommodation: Monesi di Triora: Albergo La Vecchia Partenza in the newer section of the settlement, 1376 m, open almost year-round, DR and 4-bed room (20 B), HB 50 €, delicious meals, Monica Arnaldi, tel. +39 0183/32 65 74, www.lavecchiapartenza.it.
Shpping: Shop in Piaggia as well as in Monesi di Triora.
Public transport: None.
Tip: More on the Brigascans at www.vastera.it; www.patrimoine-labrigue.org.

From **Upega (1)**, take the main road to cross over the stream, then turn left through the camping area. The track road soon becomes a path following the stream. At a trail junction, turn left (turning right would return

Upega.

you to the road). Cross over two streams. The trail is very distinct due to mountain-bike tracks. At the **Colletta Salse (3)**, 1627 m, meet up with the road to Monesi, but soon, at the crest of the pass, turn off to the right onto the forestry road leading to Margheria Binda. Enjoying views over the wooded hills that stretch all the way to the sea, and later of the Marguareis Massif, continue on the level. Shortly before reaching the *alpe* huts at the **Margheria Binda (4)**, turn left onto the path signed for »Valcona soprana«. At the point where this merges into a broader trail, head right to continue at the same height, passing through woods to reach a panoramic ridge. Piaggia and Monesi lie at your feet; the one village is in the Piedmont, the other in Liguria, geographically, only separated by a river, but indeed, worlds apart due to bureaucracy. The locals complain that while the province of Cuneo turns some of its attention to its mountainous area, the province of Imperia only focuses on the coast.

From **Piaggia (6)**, take the upper street to the unattractive apartment complex of **Monesi (7)**, where the accommodation is located. The ski station appears quite slipshod, but the good food served at the Albergo La Vecchia Partenza more than compensates for this.

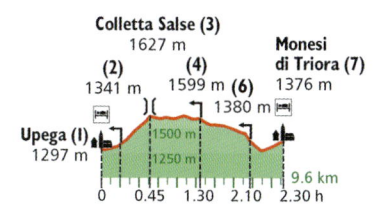

62 Monesi di Triora – Colla Melosa

7.00 hrs.
↑ 1350 ↓ 1180

A holy mountain, but not a perfect world

In Monesi, it was already clear to see that the northern side of the Monte Saccarello serves as ski resort. Military roads scar the mountain flanks as well. The mighty Redentore on the summit much prefers to gaze towards the sea – a beautiful image conjuring up an ideal world. At the same time, the villages of the hinterland are falling into ruin while the coast is full to bursting. En route, these unique villages, only found in the south, clinging to the ridges like castles, catch the eye again and again. In Italy, the French phrase, »Nid d'Aigle« (Eagle's Nest), has taken hold. In France itself, they are known as »Villages perchés«.

Starting point: Monesi, 1376 m.
Destination: Colle Melosa, 1545.
Length: 23.3 km.
Grade: Well-marked; mostly pleasant military tracks. No water available en route! It is best to take along an extra bottle of water with you.
Refreshment: Nothing en route.
Accommodation: Rifugio San Remo: 2078 m, CAI, self-catering hut, you can pick up the keys in the shop at Tiziana (tel. +39 333/259 47 21) in Piaggia or in the restaurant in Monesi di Triora, 14 €/AV 8,50 €, deposit 25 €. You will get your deposit back by presenting a receipt after you return the keys at the Rifugio Allavena, 30 B, kitchen, oven. For larger parties, you can pre-arrange meals: tel. +39 0184/55 91 56, www.caisanremo.it. – **Colla Melosa:** 1545 m, Rifugio Franco Allavena, CAI, open year-round, 70 B, AV-HB 32 €, Alfredo Bruzzone, tel. +39 0184/24 11 55. More comfort and better food is right next door in the Rifugio Colle Melosa, May–end Sept., and at the weekends, 7 DR, HB 60/70 €, Lura Lai & Pierangelo Borfiga, tel. +39 0184/24 10 32 or +39 335/823 56 78, www.collemelosa.it.
Shopping: Only in Piaggia.
Public transport: None.

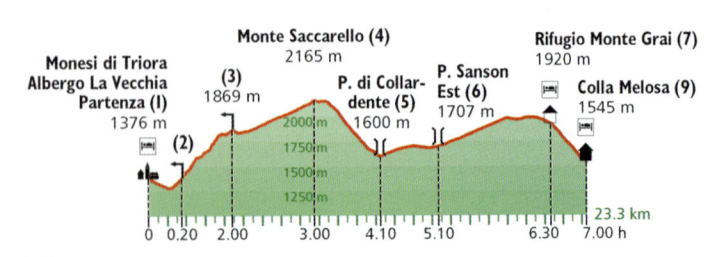

244

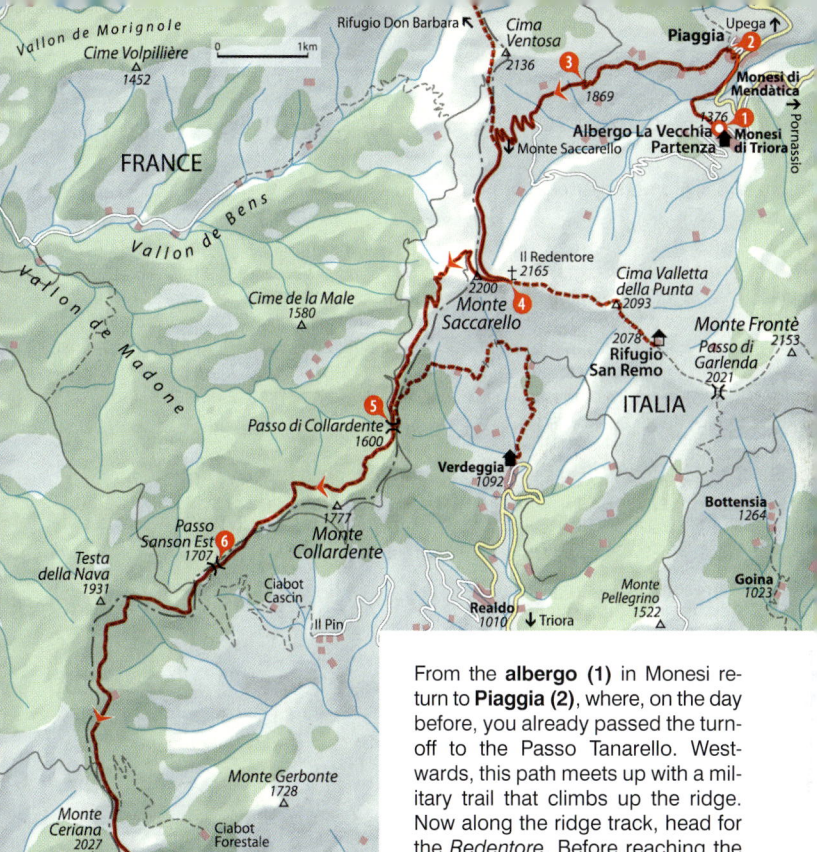

From the **albergo (1)** in Monesi return to **Piaggia (2)**, where, on the day before, you already passed the turn-off to the Passo Tanarello. Westwards, this path meets up with a military trail that climbs up the ridge. Now along the ridge track, head for the *Redentore*. Before reaching the summit of the Monte **Saccarello**, (excursion to the **Redentore** in 10 mins.), meet up with the Alta Via dei Monti Liguri, which turns off to the right **(4)** and leads the rest of the way to the Med. This descends through the western flank of the mountain into woodland, where the borderline ridge becomes broad and gentle. Changing from wood to meadow and back again, the pleasant military tracks lead to the **Rifugio Monte Grai (7)**, 1920 m (self-catering hut, the key can be picked up in the Rif. Allavena). Here, turn left to descend to the **Colla Melosa (9)**.

245

63 *Colla Melosa – Gola di Gouta*

5.30 hrs.
↑ 550 ↓ 890

Bold Alpini mountain paths

Once again, the borderline ridge rears up with two striking limestone peaks. Paths have been hewn out of the sheer rock faces of Monte Pietravecchia and Monte Toraggio. Extremes merge here in the botanical sense as well; lavender, Edelweiss, peonies, golden chain – depending on the season, lovely scents and colourful flowers embellish the trail's edge. Two possibilities are presented here: the Alta Via, through the western sides of the two mountains, or the Sentiero degli Alpini, through the eastern sides. It is also interesting to combine the two: first, take the spectacular leg along the eastern side, then, via the Gola dell'Incisa, change over to the western side.

Starting point: Colla Melosa, 1545 m.
Destination: Rifugio Passo Gouta, 1213 m.
Length: 17 km.
Grade: Well-marked; it's true that the Alpini path leads through exposed terrain, but it is very broad and easy to walk.
Refreshment: Nothing en route.
Accommodation: Rifugio Passo Gouta, privately-owned, 21 B, HB 60 €, tel. +39 329/493 99 78, maybe new management. If closed: from the accommodation at the Colla Melosa, reserve an overnight stay in the B&B Casa di Giacomo (4 R; communal kitchen; no evening meal, 35 €/pers. + 30 € transfer fee; tel. +39 339/613 25 42). *Patron*, Dario, will pick you up from Passo Gouta.
Shopping/Services: Nothing available.
Public transport: None.

Sentiero degli Alpini.

From the **Colla Melosa (1)**, ascend along the gravel road for about 1 km. At the Fontana Italia, in a right-hand bend, the Sentiero degli Alpini turns off to the left. This crosses over a gully then after a short stretch through a wood, meets the rugged eastern wall of the Monte Pietravecchia. In easy up-and-down walking, the path, sometimes hewn into the rock, leads through dizzying sheer rock faces. At the notch between Monte Pietravecchia and Monte Toraggio, a couple of steep zigzags wind up to a fork in the trail where you must decide between the eastern and the western side of Monte Toraggio. Both high mountain trails are sensational: the route through the eastern side is shorter and there are fewer metres of height to negotiate. The western route, on the other hand, opens up an unobstructed view over the Roya Valley and all the way to the peaks of the Mercantour National Park. This route leads from the **Gola dell'Incisa (5)**, 1685 m, to the Passo di Fonte Dragurina, 1810 m, and then, after a steep descent, meets up again with the eastern route. The trail continues to the **Col Corbeau** (or Corvo) **(9)**, lying to the west. Soon after, the path broadens into a track road. Pass by the **Rifugio Muratone (10)**, 1174 m (without warden or services), to reach the **Passo Muratone (11)**, 1158 m. In another ascent, reach the fork at **Scarassan (12)** and continue to the left through a wood to the **Rifugio Passo Gouta (13)**.

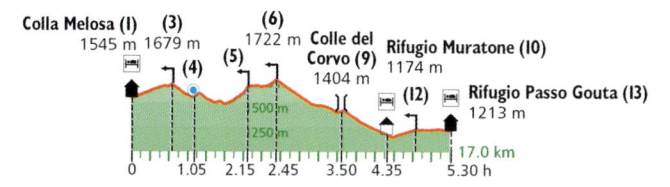

247

64 Gola di Gouta – Rifugio Alta Via

4.30 hrs.
↑180 ↓860

The sea is already outrageously near

You still feel like you are walking in the Black Forest and then suddenly, the atmosphere changes. You actually get your first whiff of southern climes; your surroundings become sparser, brittle, sultry. Now a broad military track sets the direction; you could almost reach out to touch the sea, but the ridge seems to never end.

Starting point: Rifugio Passo Gouta, 1213 m.
Destination: Rifugio Alta Via, 528 m.
Length: 17.6 km.
Grade: Well-marked, mostly military tracks. An easy walk. The Rifugio Alta Via does not appear on the IGC map (but in the Kompass map Nr. 640).
Refreshment: Nothing en route.
Accommodation: Azienda Agrituristica Rifugio Alta Via: 528 m, beg. April–beg. Nov., 9 B and tents as well, HB 45 €, Silvano, tel. +39 0184/20 67 54 or 347/114 81 74.
Shopping: Nothing available
Public transport: None.
Alternative: About 2 hrs. longer, the main route of the AVML crosses over the borderline ridge. Until reaching the Colle Scarassan, you have to backtrack a stretch. Below the Colla Sgora, both routes merge once again.

From the **Rifugio (1)**, turn right to follow the narrow road northwards, crossing over the knob and through the wood to reach a clearing. Now, turn left to con-

View from the Rifugio Passo Gouta to the Mediterranean.

tinue along a rough gravel-surfaced military track that soon becomes very panoramic, more or less keeping to the same level of height. At the **Colla Sgora**, the AVML drops down from above.

Not until the sign, »Bassa d'Abellio«, appears do we leave the AVML-marked track behind; after all, the rough gravel surface has become more and more unpleasant as time goes by, and anyway, the Sentiero Balcone presents a shorter route. Unfortunately, it is poorly marked. Below the **Bassa d'Abellio (2)** it meets up again with the track. At the **Passo del Cane (4)**, 596 m, 596 m, the AVML wants to continue via Monte Erisetta, which would mean a detour away from the Stage's destination. So, your best bet is to continue along the track until reaching the **Rifugio Alta Via (6)**.

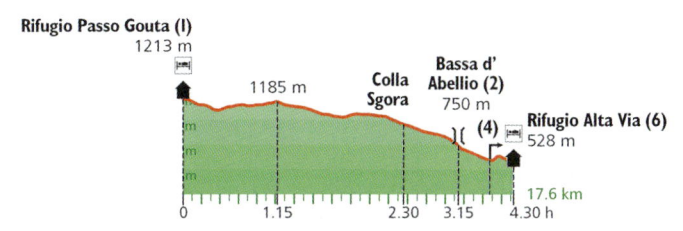

65 Rifugio Alta Via – Ventimiglia

4.00 hrs.
↑240 ↓770

The garden of the South

Now you have arrived in the South. Thorny macchia blankets the slopes, interspersed with vineyards and plots of olive, fig and cypress trees. The downward view into the valley also reveals the nearness of the coast – a maze of roads, greenhouses and storehouses. However, almost to the very end, the route remains a solitary one. An exclusive residential area, tropical gardens and swimming pools are sealed off from the outside world. But now you find yourself standing directly above the Med and Ventimiglia. What a sight!

Starting point: Rif. Alta Via, 528 m.
Destination: Ventimiglia, 0 m.
Length: 13.1 km.
Grade: Well-marked, sometimes narrow paths, some stretches along roads. Easy.
Refreshment: Nothing en route.
Accommodation: Ventimiglia: The B&B La Terrazza, in the the historic centre, has the most flair; only 3 DR à 80 €, Claudio Capuccio, tel. +39 347/260 89 08, www.laterrazzadeipelargoni.it. Another B&B, only a few minutes away on foot, with 1 DR, one 3-bed room (35/40 €), just above the Pizzeria Porta Nizza, Fortunato Zoccali, tel. +39 0184/23 84 37. Hotel Sole Mare directly at the beach, 27 DR (à 120 €), Milvia Albenga, tel. +39 0184/35 18 54, www.hotelsolemare.it. Next door and at the same price, Sea Gull, tel. +39 0184/35 17 26, www.seagullhotel.it. Unfortunately, both hotels are plagued by construction noise, since a new harbor is being built right in front of them. The Hotel Giuseppe directly at the

Ventimiglia and its palm tree planted gardens. What a lovely ending.

Rifugio Alta Via (I)   (4)   Madonna
528 m   529 m   delle Neve (6)
                              358 m   Ventimiglia (7)
                                              0 m
                                                        3.1 km
0   0.30   2.00   4.00 h

railway station has lovely rooms but is somewhat noisy, only a couple of minutes away from the beach, tel. +39 0184/ 35 79 69, www.hotel-giuseppe.com.

Shopping/Services: Ventimiglia: shops, a large market every Friday, cash dispenser, post office, doctor, pharmacy.

Public transport: The railway line via Genoa in the regional north is quicker and shorter but nowhere near as lovely as the one for the Tenda railway line which runs along a spectacular stretch through the Roya Valley to Cuneo.

From the **Rifugio (1)**, turn left to follow the street until a track road leads to the right onto the crest of the ridge (AVML waymarkers). Now continue on the western side of the Cima Tramontina (transmission tower). At **La Colla**, 450 m, cross over the road and continue southwards in up-and-down walking through an arid terrain. To the east, enjoy a lovely view of Dolceacqua with its famous arched bridge. At the **Madonna della Neve (6)**, meet up with a fork in the trail. The AVML turns off to the right. If the path is overgrown, you can turn left along the road to skirt around this stretch. After negotiating the **Monte della Fontane** (military ruins), a short ascent follows, leading south-eastwards to an exclusive residential area. You can see the skyscrapers of Monte Carlo. At the end, traverse an arid slope to reach **Ventimiglia (7)**.

Index

A
Alagna 82, 86
Alpe Arcella 135
Alpe Baranca 76, 78
Alpe Bettelmatt 40
Alpe Brüc 78
Alpe Camino 67
Alpe Cavanis 113
Alpe Cheggio 58, 60
Alpe Chiaromonte 106
Alpe Costa Rossa 135
Alpe Crosenna 161
Alpe della Colma 60, 62
Alpe del Lago 66, 68
Alpe della Preia 59
Alpe del Vecchio 73
Alpe Devero 34, 42, 44
Alpe di Colla 115
Alpe di Cruina 36
Alpe Druer 99
Alpe Maccagno 87
Alpe Pra 111
Alpe Praghetta 115
Alpe Rocco 113
Alpe Stafel 38
Alpe Teste Inferiore 59
Alpe Toglie 144, 146
Alpe Trasinera Bella 80
Alpe Veglia 44, 47
Alpe Vorco 83
Alpe Waira 55
Alpi Marittime nature park 216, 218
Alta Valle Antrona nature park 51, 58
Alta Valsesia nature park 64
Alta Via dei Monti Liguri 233
Antronapiana 61
Aosta valley 84
Aramola 195
Argentera 218, 220, 222

B
Baceno 42
Bagni di Vinadio 202, 210
Baita Luca 209
Balboutet 152

Balme 122, 126, 129
Balsiglia 154
Bassa d'Abellio 249
Bassa di Narbona 197
Bassura 193
Becchi Rossi 204
Belvedere 77
Bergerie Assietta 153
Bessans 122
Biella 85
Biolloco 84
Bivacco Alpe Pian Lago 69
Bivacco Bertoglio 174
Biv. Blessent Redentore 114
Bivacco Ettore Conti 42
Bivacco Gino Gandolfo 129
Bivacco Marigonda 56
Bivacco Orsiera 147
Bobbio Pellice 161
Bocchetta delle Oche 111
Bocchetta di Campello 73
Bocchetta di Gattascosa 55
Bord 53
Bosco dell'Alevè 169, 175
Bosco e Laghi Palanfrè nature reserve 230
Bric Rond 161
Briga Alta 242
Brigascans 242

C
Campello Monti 64, 68, 70, 72
Campo 59
Campo Base 180, 183
Canavese 84, 85, 97, 102
Capanna Corno Gries 36, 38
Capanna Renata 95
Cap. Sociale Ravetto 134, 137
Cappella del Cornaletto 226
Cappella di Santa Maria Maddalena 92
Cappelle 120
Cappia 107
Carcoforo 78, 80
Carnino 239, 242
Casa di Caccia 223
Cascata del Pis 156

Cascata Marina 212
Caserma 209
Castello 177
Cateri 117
Celle di Macra 193, 196
Centro Culturale Borgata 179, 191
Centro Uomini e Lupi 224
Ceresole Reale 103, 118, 124
Chialvetta 183, 186
Chiappera 183
Chiazale 176, 180, 190
Chiesa (Bellino) 176, 179, 190
Chiesa (Rimella) 72, 76
Chisone Valley 140
Cima Beccorosso 236
Cima delle Saline 238
Cima Fauniera 199
Cima Pian Ballaur 238
Col della Boaria 236
Colla Melosa 244, 246
Colla Piana 236
Colla Sgora 249
Colle Baranca 78
Colle Barant 165
Colle Bettone 192
Colle Bicocca 190
Colle Ciarbonet 185
Colle Costa Fiorita 131
Colle Crest 113
Colle Croce di Ferro 134
Colle Cucco 96
Colle d'Egua 79
Colle dei Morti 200
Colle dei Viso 172
Colle del Chiapous 221
Colle della Crocetta 125
Colle della Garbella 229
Colle della Gianna 167
Colle della Lace 99
Colle dell'Albergian 156
Colle della Lombarda 215
Colle della Mologna Grande 89
Colle dell'Assietta 153
Colle dell'Orsiera 148
Colle dell'Usciolo 69

252

Colle del Mud 83
Colle del Pas 240
Colle del Prel 237
Colle del Termo 80
Colle d'Enchiausa 183
Colle di Bellino 182
Colle di Fenestrelle 223
Colle di Pian Spergiurati 108
Colle di Serrevecchio 159
Colle di Stau 206
Colle di Trione 128
Colle Giulian 163
Colle Lazoney 89
Colle San Giovanni 192
Colletta Salse 243
Colletto 195
Colletto Battagliola 177
Colletto di Gran Guglia 161
Colletto di Valscura 217
Colletto Galmont 159
Colle Valcavera 200
Combe 195
Conca dei 13 laghi 160
Cornetti 127, 131
Crampiolo 42
Crissolo 166
Cuneo 178

D
Desate 92
Devero-Veglia nature park 34
Didiero 154, 158
Domodossola 50, 56
Dora Baltea 102

E
Ecomuseo della Pastorizia 188
Ecomuseo delle Guide Alpine di Balme 127
Elva-Serre 191
Entracque 219, 224

F
Fenestrelle 149
Ferriere 204, 205
Fondo 106, 110
Forno 70
Fort Central 236
Fort Pepin 236

G
Ghigo di Prali 158, 160
Gias Boero 231
Gola dell'Incisa 247
Gola di Gouta 246, 248
Gondo 47, 52
Gondo Gorge 50
Gran Bosco di Salbertrand nature park 150
Grand Escarton 176
Grange Collet 182
Grange Espeireà 177
Grangia Vottero 135, 137
Gran Paradiso National Park 102, 112, 114, 116, 119
Gries Pass 36, 38

I
Il Trucco 134, 138
Isola 44
Ivrea 85

L
La Foresteria di Massello 154
Lago Chiaretto 172
Lago del Laux 147, 154
Lago di Devero 43
Lago Vannino 41
Lanzo valleys 122
La Res 77
La Serra Morenica 108
Laux 156
Le Capanne 104, 106
Lepontine Alps 34
Ligurian Alps 232
Limonetto 230, 234
Locasca 61

M
Maddalena 177
Maira source 184
Maira Valley 178
Malzat 161
Margone 133
Marguareis 233
Masonaje 113
Meana di Susa 142, 144
Molini di Calasca 62, 66
Monesi di Triora 242, 244
Montagne Seu 150, 153
Monte Bastia 197
Monte Camino 95
Monte Estelletta 185
Monte Ghincia Pastour 171
Monte Pietravecchia 246
Monte Rosa 84
Monte Saccarello 245
Monte Toraggio 246
Monviso 166, 168, 170
Morgone 129
Museo di Pels 190
Museo di Seles 193

N
Noasca 118
Nufenen Pass 36

O
Occitania 140
Oropa 85, 94, 97
Oropa-Sport 95, 97
Orsiera Rocciavrè nature park 146

P
Palanfrè 228, 230
Palent 193
Parco del Marguareis 233
Parco Naturale delle Alpi Liguri 233
Passo dei Gialit 49
Passo del Cane 249
Passo del Duca 237
Passo della Gardetta 187
Passo del Lagarè 240
Passo della Preia 59
Passo delle Crosette 197
Passo delle Possette 47
Passo delle Saline 240
Passo del Maccagno 89
Passo di Campo 58
Passo di Ciotto Mieu 231
Passo di Larussa 211
Passo di Rocca Brancia 187
Passo di Rostagno 207
Passo di Valtendra 45
Passo d'Orgials 215
Passo Gallarino 174
Passo Muratone 247
Passo Nefelgiù 41
Passo Paschiet 131
Passo San Chiaffredo 175
Passo sottano di Scollettas 207
Passo Tesina 213
Peccia 88
Pedemonte 83
Perabella 117

Piaggia 242, 244
Pialpetta 124, 126
Piamprato 110, 112
Pian della Regina 166
Pian del Re 171
Pian Melzè 166, 170
Pian Meyer 175
Piano del Praiet 223
Piccole Dolomiti 232
Piedicavallo 91
Piedimulera 63
Pietrabruna 139
Pontebernardo 186, 188, 204
Pontechianale 174
Ponte della Rovina 225
Pontegrande 62
Porta Sestrera 240
Po source 169, 170
Po Valley 140, 168
Prà del Cres 120
Prati del Vallone 205, 206
Pratorotondo 183
Punta Cerisira 161
Puy 148

Q
Quincinetto 100, 104

R
Rifugio Alevè 176
Rifugio Alpe Laghetto 56, 58
Rifugio Alpetto 169, 170, 173
Rifugio Alpino Don Barbera 235
Rifugio Alta Via 248, 250
Rifugio Arlaud 150, 152
Rifugio Bagnour 173, 176
Rif. Barbara Lowrie 164, 166
Rifugio Boffalora 78
Rifugio Cà d'Asti 137
Rifugio Chiaromonte 106
Rifugio Città di Busto 38
Rifugio Coda 97
Rifugio dei Walser 73
Rifugio Ferioli 82
Rifugio Gardetta 186
Rifugio Garelli 234, 238
Rifugio Gattascosa 54, 56
Rifugio Genova-Figari 220, 222
Rifugio Jervis 164
Rifugio Lago Verde 161
Rifugio La Riposa 137

Rif. Madonna della Neve 91
Rifugio Malinvern 214, 216
Rifugio Margaroli 38, 42
Rifugio Melezè 180
Rif. Migliorero 205, 208, 210
Rifugio Mondovì 239
Rifugio Mongioie 239
Rifugio Monte Grai 245
Rifugio Morelli-Buzzi 220
Rifugio Muratone 247
Rif. Passo Gouta 246, 248
Rif. Quintino Sella 169, 171
Rifugio Rivetti 87, 90
Rifugio Roncaccio 70
Rifugio San Bernardo 56
Rifugio San Remo 235, 244
Rifugio Savoia 97
Rifugio Soria-Ellena 222
Rifugio Talarico 205
Rifugio Valasco 216
Rifugio Vulpot 129, 132, 134
Rifugio Zanotti 205
Rima 80, 82
Rimella 72, 76
Riva Valdobbia 86
Rocca Senghi 180
Rocciamelone 123, 134, 136
Rodoretto 158
Ronco 112
Rosazza 91

S
Salbertrand 150
Sambuco 179, 188, 199, 208
San Bernolfo 211
San Giacomo 222, 224
San Lorenzo 114, 116, 230, 234
San Martino 179, 190, 193
San Pietro 61
Santa Maria 105
Santa Maria di Fobello 77
Sant' Anna (Bellino) 180
Sant' Anna di Vinadio 203, 212, 214
Sant' Antonio di Val Vogna 86, 87
Santuario San Giovanni 90, 94

Sant. San Magno 196, 199
Saretto 181
Scatta d'Orogna 44
Scatta Minoia 42
Scopriminiera 158
Sengie 101
Simplon 50
Strepeis 209, 210, 212
Stura Valley 178
Succinto 109
Susa 138, 142
Susa Valley 123, 140

T
Talosio 112, 114
Tenda Pass 230, 232
Terme di Valdieri 202, 216, 220
Testa dell'Assietta 153
Toce 34
Trasquera 47
Traversella 107
Trinità 224, 228
Trovinasse 97, 100
Tschawiner See (lake) 55

U
Upega 238, 242
Usseaux 146, 152, 154
Usseglio 129, 132

V
Val Anzasca 50
Valdieri 216
Val Formazza 38
Valle dell'Orco 120
Valprato 112
Valsesia 84
Val Vogna 87
Varaita Valley 168, 178
Varzo 44, 47
Ventimiglia 250
Verdeggia 235
Villanova 160, 164
Villaretto 129
Viozene 233
Viviere 185, 186

W
Waldensians 140
Walser trails 34

Z
Zwischbergen 52, 54